WITHDRAWN

Popular Music and Youth Culture: Music, Identity and Place
Cultures of Popular Music
Guitar Cultures (edited with K. Dawe)
Researching Youth (edited with M. Cieslik and S. Miles)

After Subculture

Critical Studies in Contemporary Youth Culture

edited by

Andy Bennett and Keith Kahn-Harris

palgrave
macmillan

First published 2004 by
PALGRAVE MACMILLAN
Houndmills, Basingstoke, Hampshire RG21 6XS and
175 Fifth Avenue, New York, N.Y. 10010
Companies and representatives throughout the world

PALGRAVE MACMILLAN is the global academic imprint of the Palgrave
Macmillan division of St. Martin's Press, LLC and of Palgrave Macmillan Ltd.
Macmillan® is a registered trademark in the United States, United Kingdom
and other countries. Palgrave is a registered trademark in the European
Union and other countries.

ISBN 978–0–333–97711–8 hardback
ISBN 978–0–333–97712–5 paperback

This book is printed on paper suitable for recycling and made from fully
managed and sustained forest sources. Logging, pulping and manufacturing
processes are expected to conform to the environmental regulations of the
country of origin.

A catalogue record for this book is available from the British Library.

Library of Congress Cataloging-in-Publication Data
After subculture : critical studies in contemporary youth culture / edited
    by Andy Bennett and Keith Kahn-Harris.
       p.   cm.
    Includes bibliographical references and index.
    ISBN 0–333–97711–4 (cloth) — ISBN 0–333–97712–2 (pbk.)
    1. Youth. 2. Subculture. I. Bennett, Andy, 1963– II. Kahn-Harris,
    Keith, 1971–
    HQ796.A3358 2004
    305.235—dc22   2003068745

Printed by the MPG Books Group in the UK

Contents

List of Figures

Notes on the Contributors

Andy Bennett is Lecturer in Sociology at the University of Surrey. Prior to studying for his PhD at Durham University he spent two years in Germany working as a music teacher with the Frankfurt Rockmobil project. He has published articles on aspects of youth culture, popular music and local identity in a number of journals including *Sociology, Sociological Review, Media Culture and Society* and *Popular Music*. He is author of *Popular Music and Youth Culture: Music, Identity and Place* (2000) and *Cultures of Popular Music* (2001), and co-editor of *Guitar Cultures* (2001). Andy is Chair of the UK and Ireland branch of the International Association for the Study of Popular Music (IASPM) and co-convenor of the British Sociological Association Youth Study Group.

Gerry Bloustien is a Senior Lecturer and programme director in Communication, Culture and Media at the University of South Australia. She has published internationally on youth and popular culture, her recent work on Buffy stemming from her own fandom and her ongoing fascination with the role of fantasy and play in everyday life. She is the editor of *Musical Visions*, a lively collection of contemporary debates about Australian popular music from Indigenous and non-Indigenous practitioners and academics, and *Envisioning Ethnography*, a special edition of *Social Analysis* on the complexity of visual ethnographic methods. Her *Girl Making* (2003) is across-cultural ethnography on the processes of growing up female.

Ben Carrington teaches Sociology and Cultural Studies at the University of Brighton.

David Chaney is Emeritus Professor of Sociology at the University of Durham. His main field of interest throughout his career has been contemporary cultural history. He is author of *Cultural Change and Everyday Life* (2002) and of many articles on the changing cultural forms of later modernity.

Simon Frith is Professor of Film and Media at the University of Stirling, Scotland. He is author of *Sound Effects* (1981), *Performing Rites* (1996) and editor (with Will Straw and John Street) of the *Cambridge Companion to Pop* *and Rock* (2001). When he was young he wrote on the sociology of youth (and was even a contributor to *Resistance Through Rituals*, 1976).

Keith Kahn-Harris received his doctorate from Goldsmiths College on the global Extreme Metal music scene. He has been a Fellow at the Mandel School for Advanced Educational Leadership, Jerusalem and a visiting scholar at the Monash University Australian Centre for Jewish Civilization, Melbourne. He currently works as an independent research consultant, specializing in the field of Jewish communal and educational development, and as an associate lecturer with The Open University.

Paul Hodkinson is Lecturer in Sociology at the University of Surrey. His research interests concern the relationships between media, commerce and collective forms of identity. Such issues are explored via a comprehensive reworking of the notion of subculture in his book, *Goth: Identity, Style and Subculture* (2002), a publication which gave rise to national media reviews and interviews. He has also published various additional papers and chapters based on his extensive PhD research of the goth scene. Paul is newsletter editor for IASPM UK and Ireland, and in 2003 was co-organizer of an international conference on 'Scenes, Subcultures and Tribes'.

Sian Lincoln has recently completed her PhD thesis entitled 'Private Space and Teenage Culture: Age "Zones" and Identity', in the Department of Sociology at Manchester Metropolitan University. Her research interests lie in contemporary youth culture, post-subculturalism, new media technologies, and cultural and spatial geography.

Peter J. Martin is Dean of Undergraduate Studies in the Faculty of Social Sciences and Law at the University of Manchester, and is a former Head of the Department of Sociology at Manchester, where he has taught since the 1970s. He graduated with MA(Hons) in Sociology at the University of Edinburgh, and received MA(Econ) and PhD degrees from the University of Manchester. Current research interests include the normative organization of jazz improvization, interactional analysis, and the effects of automobility on contemporary culture. Among his publications are *Sounds and Society: Themes in the Sociology of Music* (1995), various articles on the sociology of music, and (with J. A. Hughes and W. W. Sharrock) *Understanding Classical Sociology* (2nd edn, 2003) and *Understanding Modern Sociology* (2003). He is a long-standing member of the Musicians Union, as well as Associate Editor of *Jazz UK*.

Hilary Pilkington is Professor of Sociology and Russian Studies, and Director of the Centre for Russian and East European Studies, at the University of Birmingham, where she teaches modules on youth, culture and society, and on contemporary Russian society and culture. She has been working on youth issues in Russia for over a decade and is currently engaged in research into the cultural contexts of young people's drug use in provincial, urban Russia. She has published widely on Russian youth, including: *Russia's Youth and Its Culture: A Nation's Constructors and Constructed* (1994); (as editor) *Gender, Generation and Identity in Contemporary Russia* (1996); and (with Elena Omel'chenko, Moya Flynn, Uliana Bliudina and Elena Starkova) *Looking West? Cultural Globalization and Russian Youth Cultures* (2002).

Geoff Stahl completed his PhD at McGill University in Montreal. He is currently pursuing post-doctoral work at Humboldt University in Berlin. His interests include scenes, subcultures and the relationship between music-making and place-images. His publications include articles in *Public* and *Perfect Beat*, and he has co-edited an anthology, *Night and the City: The Nocturnal Side of City Life* (2004).

Paul Sweetman is a Lecturer in Sociology at the University of Southampton. He has published articles and chapters on contemporary body modification, fashion and the body in subcultural studies, and his research interests as a whole centre around issues of the body, identity, fashion and consumption. He is currently working on two books: *Fashion and Social Theory* and *Picturing the Social Landscape* (co-edited with Caroline Knowles).

Brian Wilson is Assistant Professor in the School of Human Kinetics at the University of British Columbia in Vancouver, Canada. His research interests include youth culture, media constructions of race and gender, audience studies, social movements, and the sociology of sport and leisure generally. His published work appears in such journals as the *Canadian Journal of Sociology*, the *Canadian Journal of Communication*, the *Sociology of Sport Journal*, the *International Review for the Sociology of Sport*, and the *Journal of Sport and Social Issues*. Brian is currently leading a project funded by the Social Sciences and Humanities Research Council of Canada, entitled: 'Connected Youth: A Study of Youth-Driven Social Movements, Globalization and Community in the Age of the Internet'.

Acknowledgements

The original idea for this book came from a day seminar held by the British Sociological Association Youth Study Group at the University of Surrey in September 1999. We are grateful to those who attended and contributed to the seminar. We would also like to express our thanks to Catherine Gray and Kate Wallis, our editors at Palgrave Macmillan, for having belief in this project, and for giving us highly constructive advice throughout the various stages of work involved in the production of the book. Thank you too to the individual chapter authors for their input, and for their efficient and professional working practice.

Finally, we owe a special debt of gratitude to the Birmingham Centre for Contemporary Cultural Studies, whose ground-breaking work on youth culture has inspired successive generations of youth researchers throughout the world.

ANDY BENNETT
KEITH KAHN-HARRIS

Introduction

ANDY BENNETT AND KEITH KAHN-HARRIS

The concept of subculture has dominated the study of youth, style, music and leisure in the related fields of sociology and cultural studies since the mid-1970s, when the Birmingham Centre for Contemporary Cultural Studies (CCCS) published its seminal account of post-Second World War British working-class youth, *Resistance Through Rituals* (Hall and Jefferson, 1976). Drawing on the cultural Marxism of Gramsci (1971) and Althusser (1971), the CCCS interpreted post-war youth subcultures, such as the Teddy boys, mods and skinheads, as pockets of working-class resistance to the dominant hegemonic institutions of British society. Representing as it did the first attempt to provide a systematic social theory of music and style-driven youth cultures, *Resistance Through Rituals* quickly became a key text both in youth research and in the teaching of youth culture as an academic subject. The study, together with the post-Centre work of theorists such as Paul Willis (1978), Dick Hebdige (1979) and Angela McRobbie (1980), remains highly influential in contemporary academic research and teaching on the subject of youth culture.

The present book represents an attempt to reassess critically the value of sub-cultural theory as an analytical model in the study of youth. Some may question the need for a text which takes as its central focus the critique of *subculture*, such critiques being by now relatively commonplace in sociology and cultural studies (see, for example, McRobbie, 1980; Clarke, 1981; Brake, 1985; Cohen, 1987; Redhead, 1990; Harris, 1992). Moreover, such is the rarity of positive uses of the CCCS conception of subculture in research since the 1970s and early 1980s, it might be thought that there is little need to provide 'yet another' critique of the concept at all. But it is precisely the continuing ubiquity of critical approaches to the CCCS' conception of subculture that is problematic, not to say curious.

One possible reason for this continued ubiquity of the concept of subculture is that it remains a centrally defining concept in post-CCCS work on youth, style and music, but a concept used in an increasingly arbitrary fashion. As Bennett (1999a) observes, subculture 'has arguably become little more than a convenient 'catch-all' term for any aspect of social life in which young people, style and music intersect' (p. 599). However, despite subculture's widespread use, and despite its existence as a theorized concept long before the CCCS,

1

criticisms of subculture centre almost exclusively around the work of the CCCS. The 'debate' over subculture has therefore remained locked within the parameters of a rather narrow critical discourse. Thus there is a need to go beyond a critical evaluation of the CCCS's work, and present a sustained evaluation of the concept of 'subculture' itself.

The need for such an evaluation is made more urgent by the shifting cultural terrain of youth itself. While arguably always far less tightly bound into style-specific groupings than the CCCS maintained, the increasing proliferation of youth styles since the 1980s (see Polhemus, 1997), combined with increased opportunities for 'style mixing' (McRobbie, 1994), has led to the growing fragmentation of youth culture. In his study of British punk rock during the late 1970s, Hebdige (1979) made the then controversial claim that: 'Punk reproduced the entire sartorial history of post-war working-class youth cultures in "cut up" form, combining elements which had originally belonged to completely different epochs' (p. 26). The brioleurist qualities that Hebdige identified in punk are now far more widely pronounced in the stylistic innovations of youth. This view is supported by Muggleton (2000), who describes the '1980s and 1990s [as] decades of subcultural fragmentation and proliferation, with a glut of revivals, hybrids and transformations, and the co-existence of myriad styles at any one point in time' (p. 47). In such a complex cultural terrain, the question of subculture's applicability, with all its connotations of cultural and spatial coherence, becomes ever more pressing.

There are three principle aims to this collection. First, to take stock of the various ways in which subculture has been applied in CCCS and post-CCCS research. Second, to consider whether or not there is still theoretical and empirical justification for the application of subculture in a world increasingly characterized by cultural fragmentation (Chaney, 2002a). Third, to consider how flexible the term is, and how far it can be reapplied and reappropriated in new ways – and, conversely, how far the CCCS' use of the term might have for ever predetermined its connotations. In this Introduction, however, we must first revisit briefly the subcultural theory of the CCCS and examine some of the key issues raised in the critical debate that followed the publication of the key CCCS' writings on subculture. This is followed by a summary of the ways in which the chapters in this book progress the subculture debate and reassess the value of subculture as an analytical concept in contemporary youth research.

The Origins of Subcultural Theory

As historical research on youth illustrates, down the centuries there have been gangs and groupings of young people possessing those characteristics which, in more recent times, have been referred to as 'subcultural' sensibilities. A case in point here is Pearson's (1994) account of the London 'apprentices' of the seventeenth and eighteenth centuries who (according to Pearson), 'were thought of as a separate order or subculture ... Various attempts were made to regularize the conduct of apprentices, banning them from participation in football games, playing music, or drinking in taverns' (p. 1166; see also Pearson, 1983, pp. 190–4). A similar scenario is described by Roberts in relation to the Northern Scuttlers, a nineteenth-century gang based in the neighbouring cities of Manchester and Salford in north-west England. As Roberts (1971) explains, the Scuttler 'had his own style of dress – the union shirt, bell-bottomed trousers, the heavy leather belt, pricked out in fancy designs with the large steel buckle and the thick, iron-shod clogs' (p. 123). A non-British comparison is provided by German youth theorist, Detlev Peukert, in his study of the 'Wilden Cliquen' ('wild crowds') of 1920s Germany. As Peukert (1983) notes, in addition to stylistically distinctive clothing, these youth groups also wore 'coloured bracelets, earrings and tattoos' (p. 67).

Precisely when the term 'subculture' was first used as a means to describe such visually and behaviourally distinctive sensibilities of youth is unclear. Tolson (1997) argues that, while not referring to 'subculture' as such, the foundations of subcultural theory can be seen in the writing of Henry Mayhew, the nineteenth-century philanthropist whose research on poverty in London contributed to a new public awareness of the nature and origins of poverty in industrial urban settings. Mayhew's work, however, is not youth-specific, and his allusions to 'subculture' suggest a complex network of deviant practices utilized by 'the poor' as a means of survival in the course of their everyday lives.

It is this broader understanding of 'subculture' that underpins its initial appearance in mainstream sociological work during the early twentieth century, when it became a key conceptual framework for the famous urban sociology of the Chicago School. Challenging the then dominant psychological interpretations of deviance by theorists such as Cesare Lombroso, which suggested the existence of a 'criminal personality' (see Sapsford, 1981), the Chicago School theorists argued that deviance, when studied in its socio-cultural context, could be shown to be a normal response 'determined by cultural norms, and not a symptom of psychological deficiency' (Frith, 1984, p. 40).

Chicago School theorists put forward a range of models to explain how deviant subcultures served to 'normalize' forms of deviant behaviour. Becker (1963) argued that deviant behaviour is the product of *labelling*; that 'social groups create deviance by making the rules whose infraction constitutes deviance and by applying those rules to particular persons and labelling them as outsiders' (p. 9). Delinquent subcultures, according to Becker, become locked into a process of 'deviance amplification' in which the initial negative responses of the dominant society result in such subcultures committing further acts of deviance, which in turn reinforces the stigmatization conferred upon them. Merton (1957) introduced the concept of 'means and goals' in a model that sought to explain deviance as a solution for groups lacking socially prescribed 'means' to obtain material and cultural rewards. According to Merton, deviant subcultures are deviant only inasmuch as they produce deviant means to acquire commonly-targeted social goals. Finally, Matza and Sykes (1961) contested the notion that 'deviant' subcultures will in each case resort to some form of anti-social behaviour. Instead, they argued, many such groupings are *legitimate* subcultures whose system of *subterranean* values, while deviant in that they offer non-conformist routes to pleasure and excitement, do not challenge or disrupt the dominant society as such.

Subcultural Theory and the CCCS

The Chicago School's conceptualization of subculture as a means of under-standing deviance in a socially situated context provided a key tenet for subculture's use as a theoretical framework by the CCCS. Prior to the publication of the CCCS' work, British youth research had retained a strong focus on issues of community and locality which, in many ways, mirrored the Chicago School's work in a British context. For example, Mays' (1954) study of juvenile delinquency in Liverpool argued that such delinquency was part of a local *tradition* as young males received and put into practice the deviant norms that were a part of everyday life in many underprivileged neighbourhoods of Liverpool. A similar view is presented in Patrick's (1973) research on Glasgow gangs during the 1960s. According the Patrick, the long-standing tradition of gang culture in certain parts of the city was underpinned by a historical cycle of socio-economic hardship. This emphasis on locality and community is carried on to some extent in early CCCS work: for example, Cohen's (1972) study 'Subcultural Conflict and Working Class Community'. Drawing on research conducted with young people on new housing estates in East London, Cohen argued that the collective stylistic responses of the former were linked with what Cohen termed the 'magical recovery of com-munity' – that is, the attempt to revive a sense of community following the break-up of traditional working-class communities as a result of urban redevelopment during the 1950s, and the relocation of families to 'new towns' and modern housing estates.

With the publication of *Resistance Through Rituals* in 1976, however, the emphasis shifted away from issues of locality and community towards a macro perspective on class in which youth subcultures were interrelated as spectacular indicators of the ongoing class struggle in British society. Using the original Chicago School premise that subcultures provide the key to an understanding of deviance as normal behaviour in the face of particular social circumstances, the CCCS reworked this model of subcultural deviance as a means of interpreting the stylistic responses of working-class youth in post-war Britain which, it was argued, represented a series of collective reactions to structural changes taking place in British post-war society.

The post-war period was characterized by increasing economic affluence in Britain and the USA. In Britain especially, the temporary absence from the world market of major exporters such as Germany, France, Japan and Italy meant that the nation enjoyed an unprecedented rate of economic growth. Output rose by some 35 per cent between 1951 and 1961, while real average earnings increased by approximately 2.7 per cent a year (Leys, 1983, pp. 60–1). Consequently, consumerism, once a luxury reserved for the wealthier classes, 'began to develop among all but the very poorest groups' (Bocock, 1993, p. 21).

According to some commentators, notably Zweig (1961), the post-war consumer boom acted to erode traditional class distinctions as the affluent working class effectively bought into the lifestyle of the middle classes. Post-war youth style was also regarded as an aspect of this process, facilitating young people's assimilation into a unified teenage consumer culture (Abrams, 1959). The CCCS contested this interpretation of post-war youth. It was claimed by the Centre that the emergent style-based youth cultures, while indeed indicative of newly acquired spending habits, symbolized at a deeper level that class divisions were still very much a feature of post-war British society. The increased spending power of working-class youth, it was argued, may have raised their profile as consumers but did nothing to alter their life chances in real terms:

> There is no 'subcultural solution' to working-class youth unemployment, educational disadvantage, compulsory miseducation, dead-end jobs, the routinisation and specialisation of labour, low pay and the loss of skills. Subcultural strategies cannot match, meet or answer the structuring dimensions emerging in this period for the class as a whole. (Clarke *et al.*, 1976, p. 47)

The concept of youth resistance employed by the CCCS is adapted from the work of Gramsci (1971), who argued that class relations in late capitalist societies centred around an ongoing 'hegemonic' struggle. According to Gramsci, as capitalism progresses, the power of the bourgeoisie can no longer be assured through domination but has to be won by consent. This involves a shift from economic to ideological (that is, hegemonic) control. However, the very nature of hegemonic power means that it can be subjected to challenges from the subordinate classes. Relating Gramsci's model to post-war British working-class youth, the CCCS maintained that the process of creating subcultural solutions to material problems involved simultaneously the winning of *space* – 'cultural space in the neighbourhood and institutions, real time for leisure and recreation, actual room on the street corner' (Clarke *et al.*, 1976, p. 45). The negotiation of space for the collective expression of subcultural identities, it was argued, constituted a challenge to authority that formed part of the 'theatre of struggle' which, according to Gramsci, characterized class relations in late modern society (ibid., p. 44).

Specific examples of subcultural 'strategies' of resistance are examined in a series of case studies. John Clarke's (1976) essay on skinhead culture develops Phil Cohen's (1972) work in arguing that the skinhead style represents 'an attempt to re-create through the 'mob' the traditional working class community as a substitution for the real decline of the latter' (Clarke, 1976, p. 99). Jefferson's examination of the Teddy boy style argues that the latter reflected the 'Teds' ' "all-dressed-up-and-nowhere-to-go" experience of Saturday evening' (1976, p. 48). The relative affluence of the Teddy boys allowed them to 'buy into' a middle-class image – the Edwardian suit revived by Savile Row tailors in 1950 and originally intended for a middle-class market. Jefferson argues that the Teddy boys' 'dress represented a symbolic way of expressing and negotiating with their symbolic reality; of giving cultural meaning to their social plight' (ibid., p. 86). Similarly, Hebdige claims that the mod style was a reaction to the mundane predictability of the working week, and that a mod attempted to compensate for this 'by exercising complete domination over his private estate – his appearance and choice of leisure pursuits' (1976, p. 91).

Ultimately though, for all the symbolic creativity represented by post-war subcultures, resistance does not and cannot alter the fundamentally class-based order of society. Subcultures 'solve', but in an imaginary way, problems which at the concrete material level remain unresolved, (Clarke *et al.*, 1976, pp. 47–8). Moreover, according to Hebdige (1979), the resistant qualities of any given subcultural style is ultimately compromised because of its incorporation and commodification by the fashion industry. The CCCS thus offered a bitter-sweet analysis of subculture, one that celebrated its achievements at the same time as noting its inevitable limitations.

Criticisms of the CCCS

Although highly influential in youth cultural studies, the CCCS' model of subcultural resistance has been criticized on a number of grounds. McRobbie and Garber (1976) highlight the CCCS's failure to provide accounts of girls' involvement in subcultures. Although perhaps a male-dominated phenomenon, it is argued, subcultures were by no means exclusively male.[1] Reluctance among male sociologists to engage with the sphere of family and domestic relations, it is suggested, also played its part in ensuring the absence of girls from the subcultural worlds depicted by the CCCS. Thus, as McRobbie (1980) observes, 'while the sociologies of deviance and youth were blooming in the early seventies the sociology of the family was everybody's least favourite option' (p. 68). According to McRobbie and Garber, however, the domestic sphere of the family home provided a resource for vibrant forms of subcultural activity among teenage girls. In their study 'Girls and Subcultures' (1976), McRobbie and Garber identify a strong 'Teeny Bopper' culture among pre-teenage girls. The Teeny Bopper culture centred around the creative use of domestic space by teenage girls – the decorating of bedroom walls with posters of pop idols, and the use of the sitting room to play records, read teen magazines and watch TV programmes such as 'Top of the Pops'. According to McRobbie and Garber (1976), Teeny Bopper culture 'can be viewed as a meaningful reaction against the selective and authoritarian structures which control girls lives' (p. 220).

A further problem identified with the CCCS' work on youth is its unqualified equation of post-war patterns of youth consumerism with notions of working-class resistance. As Muggleton (2000) notes, such a premise rests on the essentialist notion that members of subcultures were indeed exclusively, or even predominantly, working-class, this being theoretical conjecture rather than proven fact. Moreover, even if we are to accept that post-war youth consumerism was driven initially by working-class youth, it is still difficult to accept the CCCS's argument that consumer goods were used uniformly in strategies of resistance. As Bennett (1999a) observes:

> Such a contention rests on the rather tentative notion that, having gained an element of freedom to pick and choose between an increasing range of consumer items, working-class youth were somehow driven back to the fact of class as a way of articulating their attachment to such commodities. It could rather be argued that post-war consumerism offered young people the opportunity to break away from their traditional class-based identities, the increased spending power of the young facilitating and encouraging experimentation with new, self-constructed forms of identity. (p. 602)

The view that post-war style offered young people an opportunity to construct new identities not bound by tradition or habit (Featherstone, 1991a) but rather by a newly experienced consumer reflexivity is also supported by Chambers

(1985), who suggests that: 'In contrast to the anonymous drudgery of the working week, selected consumer objects provide the possibility of moving beyond the colourless walls of routine into the bright environs of an imaginary state' (p. 17). Similarly, Miles (1995), in considering the CCCS's equation of consumption with resistance, argues that such an approach 'concentrate[s] on symbolic aspects of sub-cultural consumption at the expense of the actual *meanings* that young consumers have for the goods that they consume' (p. 35). Finally, Frith (1983) suggests that:

> The problem is to reconcile adolescence and subculture. Most working-class teenagers pass through groups, change identities, play their leisure roles for fun; other differences between them – sex, occupation, family – are much more significant than distinctions of style. For every youth 'stylist' committed to a cult as a full-time creative task, there are hundreds of working-class kids who grow up in a loose membership of several groups and run with a variety of gangs. There's a distinction here between a vanguard and a mass, between uses of leisure *within* subcultures. (pp. 219–20)

The issue of young people playing their 'subcultural' roles for 'fun' is never really considered by the CCCS. Similarly, the issue of passing through one's youth without ever being a committed stylist, or belonging to a group or gang, is given only a cursory mention in *Resistance Through Rituals*. Indeed, it is significant in this respect that a second edited volume on youth culture, Mungham and Pearson's *Working Class Youth Culture*, also published in 1976, has received far less attention despite its more sustained focus on the mundane practices of 'ordinary' young people. In relation to this point, Murdock and McCron, two of the contributors to Mungham and Pearson's volume, argue that the formulation of 'class' upon which the CCCS subcultural theory is based may, in itself, be a rather oversimplistic model that glosses over significant variations in class sensibilities. Thus, they argue, the CCCS model:

> tends to draw too tight a relation between class location and sub-cultural style and to underestimate the range of alternative responses. The problem is not only to explain why styles such as the mods or the skinheads developed within a particular class strata at the times and in the forms they did, but also to explain why adolescents in essentially the same basic class location adopted other modes of negotiation and resolution (Murdock and McCron, 1976, p. 25).

An equally important criticism of the CCCS's work is its failure to consider local variations in youth's responses to music and style. As Waters (1981) notes, 'geographical specificity is a factor in subcultural studies that cannot be overlooked [and consequently] works need to tone down their stress on the universality of subcultures, and make a concerted effort to focus on ... regional subcultures' (p. 32). Related to this is the problem that the subcultural theory developed by the CCCS is an essentially British concept, formulated with a view to studying a specific section of British youth – white, working-class males – at a particular point in post-Second World War British history. As such, it is very difficult to transpose the CCCS's subcultural theory to other national contexts. This point is illustrated effectively by Brake (1985), in relation to the Canadian youth cultural experience:

> If there is a tradition of resistance in Canadian youth culture, it is at an individualistic rather than a collective level. The vast size of the country acts against any distinct yet common themes ... Further, at a more banal level, the long and severe winter which covers most of Canada localises youth cultures to the cities, and even there public spaces tend to be shopping malls, which do little to generate collective gatherings and are easy to control. (p. 145)

A similar example is offered by Pilkington in considering the disjuncture between Hebdige's (1979) reading of UK punk's subversion of consumerist lifestyles and the articulation of the punk style in Russian cities. Thus, as Pilkington (1994) explains, 'there can ... be no social base for a movement subverting consumerist lifestyles in a society where a safety pin or a dustbin bag is an article of deficit, not abundance' (p. 228).

Further problems arise in attempting to apply the CCCS's work to other national academic environments whose scholars do not share the structuralist concerns of the CCCS theorists. Reflecting on the limitations of the CCCS work from a Scandinavian perspective, Fornäs (1995) notes how:

> Stronger ties with continental hermeneutics, psychoanalysis and critical theory hindered the total dominance of structuralism, thereby also avoiding the fetishism and reification of subcultural styles which characterized parts of the British 1970s tradition. (p. 6)

The specificity of CCCS subcultural theory to a British academic context is further evidenced by youth culture research in the USA, which has remained far more sensitive to issues of race, culture and locality as factors that cut across, or at the very least problematize, structuralist explanations of youth. Thus, for example, Rose's (1994a, 1994b) work on hip-hop culture in the USA, despite mapping the rise of hip-hop in relation to broadly similar socio-economic conditions to those identified by Cohen (1972) in his work on white, British, working-class youth style-based youth groups twenty years earlier, resists using the term 'subculture' and instead identifies hip-hop as an extension of those issues and tensions felt by all members of ghetto communities in the USA. Thus, observes Rose (1994a):

> Identity in hip hop is deeply rooted in the specific, the local experience and one's attachment to and status in a local group or alternative family. [Hip-hop] crews are new kinds of families forged with intercultural bonds which, like the social formation of gangs, provide insulation and support in a complex and unyielding environment and may, in fact, contribute to the community-building networks which serve as a basis for new social movements. (p. 78)

This acknowledgement of the role of style, music and other popular cultural resources in 'creating' rather than merely confirming 'communities', has led US researchers to reject the concept of subculture and to seek alternative theoretical frameworks. Thus Lewis (1992) has suggested that music and style-based youth groupings are better understood as 'taste cultures'. Relating this to popular music, a primary resource around which contemporary youth cultures are constructed, but conspicuously absent in CCCS work (see Laing, 1985), Lewis argues that musical taste 'dramatically cuts across standard indicators such as social class, age, and education in creating groupings with common musical expectations and symbolic definitions' (p. 141).

A further problem associated with the CCCS is its failure to acknowledge the role of the media in the creation of subcultures and subcultural identities. According to Thornton, rather than emerging as fully-formed, grass-roots expressions of youth solidarity, subcultures are the product of youth's dynamic and highly reflexive relationship with the mass media. The mass media are responsible, argues Thornton (1995), for providing youth with many of the visual and ideological resources they incorporate into collective subcultural identities: ' "subcultures" do not germinate from a seed and grow by force of their own energy into mysterious "movements" only to be belatedly digested by the media. Rather, the media and other cultural industries are there and effective right from the start' (p. 117).

A final drawback with the CCCS's subcultural approach is the very limited definition of 'youth' that it suggests. By focusing on youth as an age category (that is, sixteen to twenty-one), the CCCS failed to appreciate the symbolic value of style and other popular cultural resources for transforming youth into an ideological category, a state of mind rather than a particular stage in life. This quality of 'youth' has become more noticeable in recent years as subsequent generations of 'youth' have reached adulthood yet refused to 'grow up', using music, style and various forms of memorabilia as a means of retaining a sense of 'youthfulness' even as they approach middle age (Ross, 1994; Calcutt, 1998; Bennett, 2001). Thus, for example, as Ross (1994) observes:

> an entire parental generation [is] caught up in the fantasy that they are themselves still youthful, or at least more culturally radical, in ways once equated with youth, than the youth of today...It is not just Mick Jagger and Tina Turner who imagine themselves to be eighteen years old and steppin' out; a significant mass of baby boomers partially act out this belief in their daily lives. (p. 8)

Post-subcultural Theory

The problems identified with subcultural theory, combined with the apparently increasing fragmentation of youth style since the 1980s, has given rise to an emerging analytical approach to the study of youth culture which can loosely be termed 'post-subcultural' theory. Introduced by Redhead (1990) and developed by Muggleton (1997, 2000), this approach argues that the structurally grounded concept of subculture, if always problematic, has become increasingly redundant in relation to contemporary youth culture which, according to Polhemus, 'reside[s] in a sort of streetstyle themepark' (1997, p. 149). Underlying the move towards post-subcultural analysis is an argument that subcultural divisions have broken down as the relationship between style, musical taste and identity has become progressively weaker and articulated more fluidly. This alleged breakdown of subcultural divisions was first noted by Redhead in his study of the early British rave scene. According to Redhead, rave was 'notorious for mixing all kinds of styles on the same dance floor and attracting a range of previously opposed subcultures' (1993a, pp. 3–4). During the early 1990s, Redhead and a group of researchers based at the Manchester Institute for Popular Culture (MIPC) used the developing dance music scene as a means of applying a postmodern critique of the CCCS work. Thus, it was argued, the combined effects of post-industrialization and the increasing amounts of unstructured free time available to young people had given rise to a new 'clubbing culture' which dissolved structural divisions such as class, race and gender as the dance floor crowd became collectively immersed in the club experience (see Redhead, 1993b).

The increasing centrality of retro-culture is another factor that many post-subcultural writers believe has led to the new sensibilities of style exhibited by contemporary youth. Thus, according to Polhemus (1997):

> We now inhabit a Supermarket of Style where, like tins of soup lined up on endless shelves, we can choose between more than fifty different styletribes. Jumbling

geography as well as history, British punk circa 1976 sits on the shelf next to 1950s American Beatnik or late Jamaican Ragga (p. 150).

Polhemus goes on to note how this has resulted in the assembling of individual styles from the many different images and looks available: 'In the end, in the mix, the possibilities are unlimited: an Armani suit worn with back-to-front baseball cap and "old school" trainers, a "Perfecto" black leather jacket worn with tartan flares, a Hippy caftan worn with rubber leggings, DMs and a Chanel handbag' (ibid.). A more balanced view of post-subcultural youth's relationship to style is offered by Muggleton, who argues that, although notions of style and identity are certainly not as rigidly composed as was argued in CCCS and post-CCCS work, nor are they as arbitrary in design as supposed in the post-modern-tinged writing of Pohlhemus *et al.* Certainly there is scope for innovation and style-mixing, claims Muggleton, but even among post-subcultural youth conventions apply. Thus, he observes:

> Stylistic change... is best understood in transformative terms, as a gradual, partial and evolutionary process, not as sudden shifts in whole identities, as some postmodern commentators would have it... Appearance is not free-floating, available to be put on and cast off as a mere whim. To engage in such acts would be seen as evidence of one's superficiality and inauthenticity, for style is viewed as an expression of one's inner self (Muggleton, 2000, p. 103).

Other theorists whose work has been associated with the post-subcultural approach have focused on the increasing fluidity of youth cultural member-ships and attempted to provide analytical frameworks to account for this while still acknowledging the collective dimensions of youth cultural groupings. Bennett (1999a; 2000) examines this issue using Maffesoli's concept of *tribus* or neo-tribes. Underpinning Maffesoli's use of this concept is a concern to illustrate the increasingly fluid and unstable nature of social relations in con-temporary society. According to Maffesoli (1996), the tribe is 'without the rigidity of the forms of organization with which we are familiar, it refers more to a certain ambience, a state of mind, and is preferably to be expressed through lifestyles that favour appearance and form' (p. 98). Bennett applies Maffesoli's ideas to contemporary dance-music culture. According to Bennett, the dance-club setting, through its provision of a space for expressions of 'togetherness' based on articulations of fun, relaxation and pleasure, can be seen as one of many forms of temporal engagement through which such neo-tribal associations are formed.

The concept of neo-tribalism is also used in Malbon's work on contempor-ary dance-music culture. Malbon makes effective use of neo-tribal imagery together with Maffesoli's (1996) attendant notion of 'sociality' as a means of underscoring the 'tactile...forms of communality' which characterize the contemporary club crowd (Malbon, 1999, p. 26). However, Malbon is critical of Maffesoli's failure to empirically situate his work, which, it is argued, renders Maffesoli's analysis insensitive to hardened discourses of stylistic convention and cultural 'competence' which may persist even as collective associations became more multiple, fluid and transitory. Thus, observes Malbon:

> although provocative and useful in evoking some contemporary forms of temporary community and the sociality through which such belongings are established, Maffesoli's 'neo-tribes' thesis fails to evoke the demanding practical and stylistic requirements and competencies that many of these communities demand, and through which many of them are constituted (1999, p. 26).

Reimer (1995) and Miles (2000) favour the term 'lifestyle' (originally introduced by Weber (1978[1919]) and adopted in recent work on culture and identity by theorists such as Featherstone (1991a,b) and Chaney (1996a)) over 'subculture' as a more accurate theoretical model through which to address and interpret the shifting identity politics and stylistic associations of contemporary youth. The concept of lifestyle focuses on the issue of consumer creativity, acknowledging the ways in which commodities function as cultural resources (Fiske, 1989) whose meanings are generated at the level of the everyday through the inscription of collective meanings. Similarly, lifestyle attributes the reflexivity which informs individual consumer creativity to a desire on the part of individuals to take an active part in the making and remaking of their image and identity. In the case of youth, this may lead to ongoing shifts in musical and stylistic taste, thus giving rise to more temporal forms of youth cultural affiliation than those depicted in the subcultural work of the CCCS and post-CCCS theorists.

An alternative term to lifestyle and neo-tribe that is being used increasingly in research on youth and music, is 'scene', a term that is also extensively used in the everyday discourse of young music followers and stylists. There are two poles around which uses of the term cohere (Irwin, 1997). One is to signify some kind of loose sense of the theatricality of social situations as in 'making a scene' (Goffman, 1956). The other is to signify some kind of much more located and 'subcultural' space. It is the latter sense that has been drawn on for many years by researchers as a descriptor for local sites of cultural, particularly musical cultural, production and consumption (see, for example, Becker, 1957; Newton, 1961; Gaines, 1990; Kruse, 1993; Bennett and Peterson, forthcoming 2004). In recent years, researchers have made a more concerted effort to theorize the term more rigorously, and Will Straw's work has been particularly influential here. According to Straw, 'scenes' 'actualize a particular state of relations between various populations and social groups, as these coalesce around specific coalitions of musical style' (Straw, 1991, p. 379). Straw argues that scenes may be both local and trans-local phenomena, a cultural space that may orientate as much around stylistic and/or musicalized association as face-to-face contact in a venue, club or other urban setting. Straw's article has sparked a plurality of sophisticated uses of scene in recent years. Drawing on Straw's work, Harris (2000) uses scene to highlight the interconnectedness of production and consumption within musical contexts that are both global and local. In contrast, Shank (1994) uses the term to highlight the affective, bodily aspect of local contexts of music-making in a way that is reminiscent of the concept of neo-tribe. The use of scene is not, however, confined to musical practice. In a special issue of the Canadian journal *Public*, edited by Janine Marchessault and Will Straw (2001), the various contributors have used the term as a way of creating 'a framework that encompasses the material specificities of global place building and urban experience' (p. 5). Straw argues in the same issue (ibid., pp. 245–57) that scene remains a productive term through a flexible and anti-essentialist quality that allows it to encompass an exceptionally wide range of cultural practices.

The Continued Significance of Subcultural Debates

At stake in the subcultural and post-subcultural debates is more than the substantive question of how best to approach contemporary youth culture. One of the reasons why the debate surrounding subculture is important is that it has provided a crucial space within which wider debates in social and cultural theory have been played out. Pre-CCCS, uses of subculture drew on contemporary symbolic interactionist and functionalist theory. The CCCS itself provided a sustained attempt at applying Gramscian Marxist analysis and, particularly in Hebdige's (1979) work, exemplified an important attempt to synthesize these approaches with structuralism and post-structuralism. Post-subcultural debates have, in their various ways, taken seriously contemporary critiques of 'essentialism' and the concomitant emphasis on fragmented and contradictory practices and identities.

Standing over these various theoretical and methodological exertions is a question that will not go away: how to define the 'space' within which youth cultural activity occurs. In other words, 'where' does youth cultural activity take place? CCCS approaches and their antecedents stress the visibility of subculture as an identifiable space (identifiable externally and, in perhaps different ways, to their members) – a space that can be 'seen' and analysed. Post-subcultural approaches are less sure about the identifiably of a specific site of youth cultural activity. Such is the fluidity and fragmentation of youth culture that there are only barely identifiable and transitory spaces to whose vagueness terms such as a lifestyle, neo-tribe and scene provide an appropriately opaque and ambiguously spatial response.

Perhaps one reason why subculture persists as a point of critique and of inspiration is that its identifiability and coherence provide an effective point of departure for contemporary research. It may be hard to identify quite where youth cultural activity is located and just what lifestyle and neo-tribes connote, but in subculture there is at least an identifiable, knowable and researchable space that provides a point of departure in examining what contemporary cultural activity 'is not'. In approaching the questions set out at the beginning of this chapter, the various contributors to this book continue a tradition of engaging critically with crucial theoretical and empirical issues in contemporary youth culture research. In struggling with subculture, they also struggle with how to situate and identify the manifold sites of youth cultural activity.

The first two chapters in the book comprise a theoretical re-reading of subculture and contemporary culture more broadly defined. Such a re-reading is important, both in terms of mapping the theoretical territory on which subcultural theory was established and considering why, in the light of more recent formulations of culture and identity, subculture is now seen to be a flawed conceptual model. In Chapter 1, Peter Martin suggests that a key problem with subcultural theory is its insistence on presenting subcultures as 'given' – that is, as self-sustained social entities. Missing from this analysis, argues Martin, is any attempt to consider the role played by social actors themselves in the construction of 'subcultural' identities. Martin then goes on to consider how subculture, together with other forms of social categorization, might be more productively considered as a reflexively used form of representation. In Chapter 2, David Chaney considers how the increasing fragmentation of culture in contemporary society renders the concept of subculture problematic. According to Chaney, the central tenet of subcultural theory's project – the demonstration of subcultural groups' self-effected distance from dominant cultural ideologies – has become essentially redundant in social settings characterized increasingly by cultural pluralism.

The second part of the book builds on the foundational work of the first part in its elaboration and empirical illustration of the theoretical issues respectively considered by Martin and Chaney. This begins with Geoff Stahl's study of local music-making practices in Montreal. According to Stahl, the relatively narrow range of class-based stylistic responses described under the banner of 'subculture' are inadequate as a framework for exploring the diverse range of collective activities and practices that characterise those involved in music-making in Montreal. Drawing on the work of theorists such as Straw (1991) and Blum (2001) Stahl goes on to argue that such activities and practices are more productively examined and understood using the concept of 'scene'. In the following chapter, Ben Carrington and Brian Wilson consider the impact of contemporary dance-music forms, such as house and techno, on youth cultural formations and the way these have been theorized by sociologists and cultural theorists. They go on to argue that, in conceptualizing dance-music cultures as fluid, neo-tribal social groupings, current research overlooks the extent to which issues of class, gender and race continue to inform the contemporary dance music scene. On a broader level, they argue, the application of such theoretical perspectives has the effect of 'depoliticizing' youth culture.

In Chapter 5, Paul Sweetman offers an alternative, but equally critical, account of the neo-tribal perspective and its application to contemporary youth. Sweetman argues that, while the fluidity and temporality associated by Maffesoli (1996) with the neo-tribal condition holds some value for our understanding of contemporary youth culture, at the same time it functions to essentialize a pluralistic array of youth cultural sensibilities and practices, many of which continue to centre around more permanent forms of collective identity and togetherness akin to the concept of subculture. Sweetman explores this contention using the example of the tattooed body which, he suggests, functions as a more permanent marker of difference and alternative, 'subcultural' allegiance, thus problematizing the notion of fluidity and temporality inherent in neo-tribe theory.

In Chapter 6, Sian Lincoln revisits and revises the concept of 'bedroom culture', first used by Angela McRobbie during the 1970s in her work on the subcultural practices of teenage girls. In addition to noting the changes that have taken place with the realm of teenage girls' bedroom culture since the 1970s, a product of both the increased freedom enjoyed by teenage girls and the advent of new technologies, notably the mobile phone, Lincoln argues that McRobbie's original concept of bedroom culture as informed by a common set of gender-coded products (notably dedicated 'teeny' magazines and posters of 'teen idols') has been replaced by a more individualistic and reflexive approach to the organization of the bedroom space.

Keith Kahn-Harris, in Chapter 7, reconsiders the importance of the 'spectacular' in youth culture in the light of his research on the global Extreme Metal music scene. He shows how, while Extreme Metal scene members produce spectacular, transgressive practice, the obscurity of the scene is such that the CCCS subcultural model of spectacle – exposure – moral panic – incorporation is not valid in this case. Furthermore, the scene's practices are orientated towards a comfortable, unspectacular everydayness that can at times overwhelm the pleasures of spectacular transgression that draw members into the scene in the first place. Kahn-Harris shows how the sometimes unsuccessful desire to balance the spectacular and the unspectacular, the everyday and the transgressive within the scene represents a response to the dangers of spectacular resistance that the subcultures studied by the CCCS experienced.

The focus of the book extends beyond the cultural practices of Western youth cultures in Chapter 8, where Hilary Pilkington demonstrates the inadequacies of both subcultural and post-subcultural theory for studying the experiences of youth in the Russian Federation. As Pilkington illustrates, while Western subcultural studies have been orientated routinely around the symbolic transformation of consumer goods and their incorporation into patterns of style-based resistance, such work has little relevance in the Russian context, where access to consumer goods is only now, at the start of the twenty-first century, becoming a reality for many young people. Similarly, argues Pilkington, while post-subcultural studies of Western youth speak of reflexive 'lifestyle' projects as overtaking issues of tradition and class in the framing of identities, in the Russian context youth cultural affiliation continues to orientate much more firmly around the perceived commonalties engendered by class, tradition and shared local experiences.

Paul Hodkinson's study of goths in Chapter 9 presents an insight into a youth cultural group which, although well-established since the mid-1980s, has largely been overlooked in academic research. In many ways, the permanence and easily identifiable nature of the goth 'image' harks back to other visually demarcated youth cultures, such as 'punk', from which the goth style took some of its initial inspiration. Indeed, central to Hodkinson's study is the argument that, while the oft-cited 'pick and mix' quality of contemporary youth style may work for a number of youth cultural contexts, this is not the case for the goth scene, which continues to display some of the more 'traditional' notions of stylistic unity and cohesion that have consistently been associated with the notion of subculture.

In Chapter 10, Gerry Bloustien focuses on the cult of fandom for the TV series 'Buffy the Vampire Slayer', as this manifests itself at dedicated 'Buffy Nights' held in a city-centre pub in Adelaide, Australia. As Bloustien notes, although style-based subcultural groups and fan groups for horror, science fiction and other forms of TV drama exhibit many similar properties, notably in issues of group loyalty and collective identification, the practice of style has taken precedence over the practice of fandom because of the latter's more mundane, everyday connotations. Bloustien then goes on to consider the systematized cultural work involved in the organization of the 'Buffy Nights' around which her study focuses, and how individual fans' descriptions of the meaning and significance of Buffy for them can be seen within a collective context of fan-culture. Bloustien concludes by arguing for a broadening of subcultural theory to embrace the more mundane, everyday contexts in which such practices of fandom are collectively enacted.

In the last chapter, Andy Bennett considers the implications of the Internet for our understanding and use of subculture in the study of youth. As Bennett points out, if the original subcultural theory, and the critical studies which followed, were centred around the face-to-face interactions of youth and its appropriation of physical spaces, the Internet offers new avenues for collective youth cultural practice which transcend both space and time. Bennett then goes on to consider to what extent youth's appropriation and use of the Internet can be said to be giving rise to new forms of subcultural activity, whose collective practices centre not around common visual appearance or shared local experience, but take shape in the virtual spaces of the Internet.

Finally, in his Afterword, Simon Frith offers a critical assessment of the book's contribution to the subcultural debate, based on his personal experience as a youth researcher working at the time of the CCCS. As Frith observes, because of the socio-historical specificity of its subcultural analysis, and root-edness in the burgeoning Cultural Studies project of the early 1970s, the CCCS work is inherently difficult to critique and evaluate from the perspective of the present day. Nevertheless, Frith shows how the practice of 'revisiting' the CCCS, a practice exemplified in this book, is a valuable one. Frith demon-strates how the chapters in the book offer insights into the continuities and developments in thinking and writing about youth between the time of the CCCS and now, together with the benefits of broadening the lens of youth research in a way that acknowledges both the spectacular and the mundane, the global and the local, the young and the 'post-young' as co-existing aspects of the ongoing everyday practices that constitute the increasingly complex arena of 'youth culture'.

Note

1   Indeed, Stan Cohen goes as far as to call into question the male-centred nature of some subcultural groups. Thus, in *Folk Devils and Moral Panics*, his study of mods and rockers, Cohen contends that 'in many ways Mod was a more female than male phenomenon' (1987, p. 186).

PART 1
THEORETICAL READINGS

CHAPTER 1

Culture, Subculture and Social Organization

PETER J. MARTIN

As the Introduction to this book illustrates, the concept of subculture retains a central significance in the theoretical and empirical study of youth. Missing from much of the subcultural literature, and those studies that have offered critiques of subculture, however, is an examination of the links between subculture, and 'post-subcultural' models, and broader theoretical developments in sociology. This aim of this chapter is to illustrate and contextualize such links. In particular, I shall suggest that the current reconsideration of the concept of subculture is a manifestation of a more general movement, in which the collective concepts established by the early pioneers of modern sociological thought have been reconsidered in the light of both theoretical critique and empirical results. The issues raised were already evident in the divergence between the early programmatic formulations of the sociological agenda produced by Emile Durkheim and Max Weber. For Durkheim, society was a reality greater than the sum of its parts, and it was this reality, which could be described in terms of 'social facts' – external to individuals, and exerting constraints on them – that formed the core subject-matter of sociology. By contrast, as we shall see, Weber began from an opposite starting point – the idea that the acting individual is the fundamental sociological reality. Subsequent debates about these contrasting approaches largely revolve around the now-familiar opposition between the concepts of social 'structure' and of human 'agency', and of the distinction between 'macro' and 'micro' approaches to sociological analysis.

In what follows, however, I wish to reject the (somewhat evasive) notion that such terms are simply 'two sides of the same coin', or alternative approaches to the conceptualization of social order. Fundamental to Weber's 'social action' perspective is the claim that 'structural' concepts – like 'society', 'culture' or 'subculture', do not describe real entities at all, but are useful, indeed essential, ways in which the social order may be conceptualized. However, to regard such 'structural' concepts as though they referred to real things entails the logical error of reification – treating an idea or a concept as if it were a real, tangible, object. So it will be argued that the use of 'collective' concepts in sociology has brought with it a progressive realization of their inadequacies, and a gradually emerging consensus around the idea that social life must be understood as enacted by real individuals in real situations.

This theme can be exemplified by considering the ways in which the concept of subculture has been used. From a Durkheimian 'structural' perspective, the culture of a society appears as a more-or-less integrated totality, within which individuals or groups may 'deviate' through inadequate 'socialization' or lack of integration. In Thrasher's now-classic study of 'The Gang' (1927), 'delinquent' gangs of young men were found to be concentrated in the deprived slum areas of Chicago – districts in which educational and employment opportunities were very limited. Later, Robert Merton (1938), developed a theoretical model which aimed to show how deviant subcultures could be generated by these structural features of society. In America, Merton argued, the goals of occupational success and material prosperity were held up to everyone. But the achievement of these by legitimate means was not open to all equally, and in fact is differentially structured: whole groups of people are disadvantaged systematically by such factors as poverty, lack of education, or racial discrimination. Within these groups, then, there is a definite pressure to adopt deviant means in order to obtain material rewards, or to maintain one's self-esteem – for example, by criminal or 'anti-social' behaviour which rejects conventional values and standards. Thus 'deviant' subcultures may be explained as a result of tensions within the overall social structure (Sharrock *et al.*, 2003, p. 179).

This sort of explanation of the origins of subcultures has been highly influential, and not just among 'structural-functional' theorists such as Merton. It is still used today, for example, to account for differences in the crime rates among various social groups. But for interactionist sociologists it was not a satisfactory explanation of subcultures. First, the structural approach is unable to explain why most people in, for example, deprived or ethnic minority groups, are not deviants or criminals. Second, and of great importance in the present context, interactionists rejected the premise that society was a 'structured' totality. Instead, like Weber, they saw society not as a real entity, but as the outcome of a perpetual process of conflict and negotiation among individuals and the groups they form. Thus, for interactionists, the laws of a society do not represent (as Durkheim had supposed), its 'core' values; they are, rather, the outcome of a struggle among different groups, with different amounts of power, to have their own values and beliefs legitimated as official (Sharrock *et al.*, 2003, p. 180). Thus symbolic interactionists have always assumed that modern urban societies are multicultural, in the sense that they are made up of a wide variety of groups with different lifestyles and values. Moreover, a good deal of interactionist research has been concerned with the ways in which the collective patterns of social activity that are often called subcultures may be seen to emerge in a wide variety of social settings.

Moreover, from an interactionist point of view, 'subcultures' are not homogeneous groups with clearly bounded memberships (as they are sometimes taken to be), but are to be understood as useful ways of *representing* processes of collaborative social action, and characterizing the activities of identified groups. To avoid misunderstanding, it should be said immediately that this approach does *not* entail a neglect of such macro-sociological phenomena as power, social structure, or patterns of inequality. It does, however, propose that such phenomena must be understood as the *outcomes* of the activities of real people in real situations, *and the ways in which these are represented.*

Culture, Subculture and the Sociological Discourse

It is widely accepted that the origins of modern sociological thought lay in the emerging critique of the individualism which was fundamental to Enlightenment thought (Hughes *et al.*, 2003, pp. 7–10). For René Descartes, the thinking individual was the irreducible source of human knowledge, and for Thomas Hobbes the 'social contract' was the result of competitive individuals agreeing to political regulation by the sovereign in the interests of all. Perhaps most famously, economists, in the footsteps of Adam Smith, developed the concept of 'economic man', a model of human beings that took them to be calculating individuals who, if given the chance, would act rationally in pursuit of their interests.

In reaction to this way of thinking, certain early modern thinkers developed distinctively sociological ideas as they sought to demonstrate the inadequacies of individualistic ideas as the basis for an understanding of human societies. In the eighteenth century, the thinkers of the 'Scottish Enlightenment' developed the idea that: 'Individuals we certainly are and rational we certainly are but an individualistic rationalism is inadequate as a *social* theory' (Berry, 1997, pp. 47–8). In France, Montesquieu's argument that the laws of a society reflect its underlying pattern of organization influenced Comte's view of societies as organic wholes, and Durkheim's later conception of 'social facts' which were collective properties of societies (Hughes *et al.*, 2003, pp. 155ff). Many other examples could be given – such as Karl Marx's idea that the real 'historical actors' were social classes rather than individuals.

What is of primary interest here, however, is the formation of a sociological discourse around a set of concepts denoting various kinds of collectivities: most generally society itself, conceived as an entity with describable properties, but also such familiar terms as social structures and systems, nations and states, communities, institutions, families, classes, formal and informal organizations, groups, professions, tribes, gangs and so on. It is within this discourse, moreover, that sociological concepts of culture, and later subculture, acquired their distinctive connotations; sociologists speak routinely of the 'culture' of a collectivity as the more-or-less coherent set of norms, values and beliefs shared (at least to some extent) by its members, and have frequently used the concept of 'subculture' to refer to ideas held by identifiable groups within these collectivities – which are distinctly different from those generally shared by members, or which may oppose them. Thus, as we have seen, Thrasher (1927) discussed the ways in which the particular social environment of young men in some parts of Chicago effectively segregated them from mainstream society, leading to the emergence of gangs whose values and behaviour patterns were in direct contrast to those sanctioned by the authorities.

Later work in the Chicago tradition of situated ethnography did much to elucidate the links between the social location of groups and the nature of the 'subcultures' which developed. A good deal of this work echoed Thrasher's study, relating the emergence of oppositional and dissenting youth subcultures to the social circumstances of young people, particularly men. Similarly, symbolic interactionists have investigated ways in which distinct 'occupational cultures' develop on the basis of the social location and particular problems of people in specific occupations, developing particular 'perspectives' that lead them to interpret their social worlds in particular ways, and which in turn may have a decisive effect on their own identities. More generally, interactionist analyses have explored the basic (if sometimes implicit) hypothesis that the 'perspectives' people develop, or in other words the *content* of subcultural belief systems, are a consequence of their location in social space and their experience of it. The implications of this working hypothesis, however, raise some awkward issues for the conventional notions of culture and subculture mentioned above. Because, if people's ideas and values, perhaps even their sense of identity, are dependent on their experience of different social contexts – class, community, occupation, religion, ethnicity and so on – it follows that there will be considerable heterogeneity in the 'culture' of a modern (or post-modern) society. If so, it may not make much analytic sense to speak of a society's culture as being more-or-less homogeneous or integrated. Even if people speak the same language, for example, they may desire or value quite different things, and possibly even fight each other to achieve them. While Durkheim spoke of the need for members of societies to be sufficiently attached to the *conscience collective*, Weber's view of the social order is based on the idea that conflict, competition and the struggle for advantage are ubiquitous, even when overt conflict and physical violence are absent (Welser, 1978, pp. 38–40).

This picture of societies as pluralistic, and of norms, values and beliefs as being contested, also emerges from research in the interactionist tradition. For example, in contrast to the Durkheimian idea of laws and social rules as in some way expressing the conscience collective of the whole society, Lemert (1972) analysed the process through which, in modern America, laws were enacted as a consequence of the struggle among various interested groups, all pursuing their own points of view. Moreover, such laws will almost invariably bear the imprint of compromizes reached in the political process: when incompatible values are involved, 'laws and rules represent no group's values nor values of any portion of a society. Instead they are artifacts of compromize between the values of mutually opposed, but very strongly organized, associations' (ibid., p. 57). So the work of Lemert, and later Becker, on 'deviant' subcultures led them to focus not on the qualities of their members or their activities, but on the essentially political process (because it involves the exercise of power) through which such subcultures are constituted, identified, stigmatized, marginalized or 'dealt with' by authorities in various ways (Becker, 1963). Clearly, the interactionists' critique of the notion of a homogeneous culture also suggests the inadequacies of regarding subcultures as deviating in some way from an orthodox or mainstream culture. From this point of view, the social order is not to be conceived of as an integrated system but rather as the outcome, at any particular time, of a perpetual struggle for advantage among individuals and groups. Some have many resources, both material and symbolic, others have very few; some occupy positions of power and authority, while others may challenge or resist them. In this sense, any group or association whose members subscribe to an identifiable set of ideas could be described as a 'subculture', whether they be members of political parties, churches, trade unions, tenants' action groups, armies, New Age travellers, heavy metal fans, professionals, football supporters, and so on.

Such groupings *could* be described as subcultures, then, but would there be any analytic value in doing so? If the concept of a 'culture' at the level of a whole society is inherently problematic, so is the related concept of subculture: it may therefore be more useful to regard organized patterns of social life as a perpetual process of competition, conflict, negotiation and so on, in which people pursue their interests in the light of a whole range of possible values and beliefs (see, for example, Strauss, 1978). A further implication should be mentioned at this point, and one that suggests itself as soon as we refer to collective concepts such as 'political parties', 'churches' or 'heavy metal fans'. Quite simply, while it is useful, in fact indispensable, to use these terms for the purposes of communication, neither political parties nor churches, nor any other such grouping, is a unified entity in which all the members share the same ideas and motivations. On the contrary, these sorts of groupings are themselves the sites of conflicts, disputes, negotiations and so on concerning all sorts of practical and ideological matters. Political parties, for example, are notoriously divided into factions arguing over policies and strategies, while church members and their priests argue over matters of doctrine – and it is doubtful if there is *any* identifiable social group that constitutes a collectivity such as 'heavy metal fans'. And so on.

Two points of some significance for the present argument emerge from this: first, that for the purposes of sociological analysis the sorts of collective concepts listed above (and all the other possible ones) are useful not as definitions of identifiable groups but rather as *symbolic representations* of fluid, sometimes even amorphous, sets of social relations. Second, as interactionists have always insisted, regardless of how orderly, formalized or routine such sets of social relations are – as, for example, in armies or bureaucracies – they must always be *enacted* by real people in interaction with others. This may well be a simple, common-sense point – yet its implications have often been forgotten by sociologists who, in rightly emphasizing the distinctively social aspects of human life, have sometimes wrongly assumed the reality of collectivities, or ascribed causal powers to them. With this in mind, it is worth recalling the passages in which Weber sought to provide a basic conceptual framework for sociological analysis.

Weber and the 'Concepts of Collective Entities'

In contrast to Durkheim's focus on collectivities, Weber's outline of 'empirical sociology' was based on the premise that: 'Action in the sense of subjectively understandable orientation of behaviour exists only as the behaviour of one or more *individual* human beings' (Weber, 1978, p. 13, emphasis in original). This short sentence conveys two of the most fundamental themes of Weber's sociology. The context is his contention that the specific subject-matter of sociology is social action; here he repeats, first, the idea that action is social 'insofar as its subjective meaning takes account of the behaviour of others and is thereby oriented in its course' (ibid., p. 4). Weber is seeking to distinguish social action from analyses of the human individual, as, for example, 'a collection of cells', or as a series of 'bio-chemical reactions'. Such analyses may be very useful, but they are not sociology, since they are not concerned with 'the subjective meaning-complex of action' (ibid., p. 13). Despite Weber's somewhat misleading use of the term 'subjective', he is concerned to describe social action so as to emphasize its collaborative, interactional nature: the ways in which the individual 'takes account of the behaviour of others' by interpreting situations (that is, giving them meaning), and formulating courses of action in the light of these interpretations.

It is evident that, in these respects, Weber's perspective is consistent with that developed by G. H. Mead (Blumer, 1969) and others who influenced symbolic interactionist thought. However, it is the second of Weber's themes that is of particular relevance at present. This is the idea that actions can only be carried out by 'one or more *individual* human beings'. Again, Weber wishes to separate the sociological from other perspectives, and thus to establish its distinctiveness as a rigorous mode of analysis. It may be useful (for example, for legal reasons) to treat collectivities such as 'states, associations, business corporations and foundations' as if they were individual persons. Indeed, for entirely practical reasons we often find it necessary to do so, as when we say things like: 'I had a phone call from the hospital' or 'Why don't we go to McDonald's?' Weber's point is that such expressions are to be understood as instances of conceptual shorthand, useful – in fact indispensable – in everyday activities, but quite unsatisfactory for the purposes of sociological analysis:

> for the subjective interpretation of action in sociological work these collectivities must be treated as *solely* the resultants and modes of organization of the particular acts of individual persons, since these alone can be treated as agents in a course of subjectively understandable action. (Weber, 1978, p. 13)

Weber makes three further points about the relationship between sociological work and 'collective concepts' (ibid.). First, that the use of such terms is often necessary 'in order to obtain an intelligible terminology' (ibid., p. 14). Again though, Weber takes the opportunity to re-emphasize his fundamental theme: 'for sociological purposes there is no such thing as a collective personality which "acts". When reference is made in a sociological context to a state, a nation, a corporation, a family or an army corps, or to similar collectivities, what is meant is, on the contrary, *only* a certain kind of development of actual or possible social actions of individual persons' (ibid.).

Second, while collectivities in this sense are not 'real' sociological groups, it is 'fundamentally important' to recognize that collective concepts are, nevertheless, used by people *as if* they referred to real entities and, what is more, entities which possess 'normative authority'. Here Weber uses the example of the 'state', which exists sociologically as 'a complex of social interaction of individual persons', but which is treated by citizens as if 'it' had normative authority, so that 'its acts and laws are valid in the legal sense'. Thus, an understanding of the meaning and use of collective concepts is essential if the sociologist is to reach an understanding of individuals' actions. 'Actors,' says Weber, 'in part orient their action to them [collective concepts], and in this role such ideas have a powerful, often a decisive, causal influence on the course of action of real individuals' (ibid.).

Third, Weber wishes to emphasize the contrast between his perspective and that of those who attempt to analyse society as an 'organic' whole 'within which the individual acts' (ibid.). This view of society as a whole with identifiable component parts may be useful, says Weber, as a preliminary orientation to an investigation. However, as suggested above, 'if its cognitive value is overestimated and its concepts illegitimately "reified", it can be highly dangerous' (ibid., p. 15). Moreover, for Weber, to treat societies as real entities or organic wholes (as in a 'functional' explanation) involves not only the logical error of reification but also involves the analyst in imposing meanings on activities or patterns of social action, independently of the meanings the actions may have for the people carrying them out. This external determination of the 'meaning' of actions is clearly incompatible with Weber's insistence that the elucidation of actors' 'subjective' meanings is at the heart of sociological explanation, which can and must go beyond what is possible in the natural sciences – that is, to achieve a 'subjective understanding of the action...of individuals' (ibid.).

The Deconstruction of Collective Concepts

The argument of this chapter is that the collective concepts which came to constitute the orthodox discourse of sociology have increasingly been revealed as empirically and theoretically problematic, and that efforts to reformulate them are consistent with a focus on the processes of *symbolic representation* and the *enactment* of social relations. Thus the present reconsideration of the concept of subculture may be understood as part of a developing critique; so, before considering the concept itself, it may be useful to note some examples of this more general process.

The nation-state

The problems raised by accepting the concept of 'society' as an entity or an organic whole have already been mentioned. The related idea of the 'nation' has also been taken as the basic unit for sociological analysis (and often as identical with 'society'). This usage, however, has been questioned, particularly since Anderson's (1983) argument in *Imagined Communities* that the essence of nationhood consists in the way in which 'the state' is 'imagined': 'In fact all communities larger than primordial villages of face-to-face contact (and perhaps even these) are imagined' (ibid., p. 15). The implication of Anderson's discussion is to cast doubt on the analytic value of such concepts as 'nation', 'people', 'state', and so on, and to redirect our attention to processes of representation and the practices of real people.

Social class

Marx's idea of the bourgeoisie and the proletariat as the two great opposed classes in capitalist societies has been enormously influential. Even among non-Marxist sociologists, the *concept* has generally been taken for granted: Giddens (1981), for example, declared that 'there are only, in a given society, a limited number of social classes (p. 105). Since then, however, the concept has been seen as far more problematic – How are classes to be defined? Where do the 'middle classes' fit in? How can classes be reconciled with other forms of inequality, such as gender or race? Thus the (inevitable) failure of socio-logists to agree on how many classes there are, or what their 'boundaries' are, should remind us that the concept does not refer to an observable entity. Socio-logists studying the 'class structure' are not simply describing reality in an objective way – rather, they are engaged in an active process of definition based on their own beliefs and theoretical commitments (Martin, 1987, pp. 68–9). In this context, therefore, the idea of class is one way in which researchers have tried to represent social inequality – but other ways could be effective for other purposes.

The concept of organization

Influenced by functionalism and systems theory, much work in the sociology of organizations treated them as more-or-less integrated 'systems'. Against this background, Bittner argued that this mode of conceptualizing organiza-tions was not scientifically neutral, but a particular representation of the social relationships involved. Such 'rational' models expressed the perspective of the 'managerial technician', and should not be 'treated as having some sort of privileged position for understanding [the organization's] meaning' (Bittner, 1974, p. 76). In short, the concept of the 'formal organization' reflects the rationality of those who seek to control it, as against others (for example, employees or customers) who may have alternative 'rationalities'. Moreover, even the most tightly regulated organization has to be enacted by those involved in it.

The family

Similarly, it has been argued that 'the family' is not an irreducible unit, but a way or representing kinship relations. For sociological purposes, Morgan (1996) argues, the term should be used as an adjective rather than a noun: the family 'is not a thing but a way of looking at, and describing, practices which might also be described in a variety of other ways' (p. 199). Once again, the implication is to focus our attention on processes of representation and enactment.

Other examples of the 'deconstruction' of collective concepts in sociology could be given; for the present, however, the point is that the problems that such concepts have produced for both empirical and theoretical work have generally led to reformulations which emphasize the themes of *symbolic representation*, and the *enactment* of social life.

Rethinking 'Subculture'

Enough has been said, I hope, to establish the main contention of this chapter – that the reconsideration of the concept of subculture may usefully be seen in the context of a more general, developing critique of the collective concepts that at one time were considered foundational for sociological analysis. Moreover, it is clear that an alternative approach, emphasizing processes of collaborative interaction and the formation of identities within these, was well developed in the work of interactionist sociologists. This perspective was particularly influential in the 1960s and early 1970s, yet was largely eclipsed in the following two decades by work at the Centre for Contemporary Cultural Studies at the University of Birmingham. Researchers at the CCCS were influenced by structuralist ideas and by the notion of subcultures as symbolic systems; the effect, as Atkinson and Housley have argued, was to redirect attention away from real-time, observable social interaction and towards a concern with theory – for example, in the analysis of 'discourse' (Atkinson and Housley, 2003, pp. 75–6). While much important work was produced at the CCCS, it may be argued from a sociological point of view that this general approach inherited the theoretical problems of earlier structural perspectives, particularly in regarding subcultures as clearly defined groups whose members' activities were organized around a distinct set of values and beliefs.

However, it is evident that, even in its earliest formulations, the idea of sub-cultures as bounded social groups has been problematic. Becker (1963), for example, in one of the most influential discussions – of musicians as a 'deviant' subculture – at certain points indicates some of the ways in which the musicians were linked to the wider 'square' society (one, for example, 'definitely identified himself with the Jewish community') (p. 99). It has been widely recognized, too, that the successive 'youth subcultures' that have been studied – Teddy boys, mods, rockers, hippies, punks, and so on – have in fact only attracted a minority of their appropriate age-groups (see, for example, Murdock and McCron, 1976); what is more, researchers have long been familiar with the phenomenon of the subculture members whose participation does not involve the adoption of an all-encompassing lifestyle, but is more like a leisure-time activity, pursued at weekends, and on holidays and special occasions such as music festivals. More recently, too, it has been pointed out that the supposedly 'counter-cultural' values of the late 1960s did not extend to challenging the institutionalized patriarchy of the wider society: as Whiteley (1998), among others, has shown, the position of women within the 'counter-culture' was clearly subordinate (p. 167), and in this respect the 'alternative' culture did not so much threaten established values as reproduce them.

Despite these and other indications that 'subcultures' were in fact fluid, porous, amorphous and transitory, there has been a tendency to treat them as identifiable, more-or-less coherent social groups. Willis (1978), for example, has argued for an understanding of the relationship between particular youth groups and the cultural artefacts and practices they adopt in terms of a struc-tural 'homology' 'concerned with how far, in their structure and content, particular items parallel and reflect the structure, style, typical concerns, attitudes and feelings of the social group' (p. 191). Thus Willis sought to understand the links between the values of the groups he studied (bike boys and hippies) and their preferred music (rock 'n' roll and progressive rock, respectively). Middleton's (1990) view, however, is that, in doing so, Willis runs the risk of reifying both the social groups and the music, and exaggerating the homogeneity and the coherence of both: in short 'the connection between music and sub-culture is drawn much too tightly; the "purity" of both subcultures is a fiction, their opposition to dominant culture exaggerated' (p. 161). The fundamental problem, Middleton argues, arises from Willis's 'uncompromising drive to homology', which leads to 'a relative neglect of the subcultures' relationships with their parent cultures, with the dominant culture and with other youth cultures, and the stress on internal coherence leads to circularity of argument' (ibid.). As I have argued elsewhere, such attempts to establish systematic cor-respondences or structural 'homologies' between cultural values and practices, on the one hand, and underlying patterns of social organization, on the other, are likely to exhibit all the failings of 'structural' sociology more generally, with its toolkit of collective concepts and its presupposition that social groups can be defined unambiguously as entities (Martin, 1995, p. 162).

It would be quite wrong, however, to associate Willis only with the idea of homology. For one thing, there is less emphasis on the idea in his later work, although it has not disappeared entirely (Willis, 1990, p. 154). Moreover, significantly in the context of the present argument, he has always sought to emphasize the active part played by individuals in the creation of their own symbolic worlds within the cultural parameters of their social location. Indeed, Willis's ethnographically-based accounts of the processes of 'symbolic creativity' (ibid., pp. 1ff) among young people have done much to reorient our understanding of 'subcultural' meanings and practices – away from the idea that such meanings and practices are reflections of the fundamental structure of a social group, and towards a realization that it is through such symbolic representations and activities that the sense of 'group-ness' or of 'belonging' is actively constituted (see also Bennett, 2000 and Frith, 1996). Among the strengths of Willis's perspective is his focus on 'grounded aesthetics' – the processes, rooted in the everyday experiences of individuals, through which they collaborate to create significant symbolic 'worlds' – worlds that can provide a sense of identity and belonging, the affirmation of values and meanings, above all a cultural space that offers both relief, and temporary release, from mundane pressures. In contrast to critics of 'mass' culture, Willis also shows also how such worlds can be created through the active appropriation and specific uses of mass-produced consumer commodities. Indeed, the range of potential symbolic resources for the construction of what he terms the 'common culture' of young people is enormous – television and videos, computer games, magazines, fashion and clothing styles, music, sport, pubs and clubs, and so on. It is important too to note the crucial role of the mass media in these processes – not simply through the imposition of passive conformity, but in providing a vast range of symbolic representations, which may be defined in positive or negative ways, and appropriated accordingly. In this context it is useful to recall Thornton's account of the ways in which the mainstream mass media not only provided young people with criteria for the evaluation of 'authenticity' and the accumulation of 'subcultural capital' (or otherwise), but also played an active role in the constitution of subcultural 'groups' themselves (Thornton, 1995, p. 132).

The concept of 'subcultures' as identifiable, coherent social groups, then, is no longer analytically central to the work of Willis, or other recent researchers in the field of contemporary culture. On the contrary, as I have argued in relation to other collective concepts, what may be seen emerging is a reformulation of the concept in terms of general processes of (a) symbolic representation, and (b) enactment:

(a) The concept of 'subculture' itself may be understood as a symbolic repre-
     sentation of certain sets of social relationships and practices, which
     emphasizes some aspects at the expense of others. The term itself has
     been used by researchers in this way, and the designation of certain
     'groups' – especially if these are portrayed as being threatening or harmful –
     is a frequent and often consequential tactic of the mass media. Moreover,
     the identification of such groups may be an important, if more diffuse,
     way in which individuals can experience a sense of inclusion or exclusion,
     and a corresponding sense of identity. Analytically, the implication is to
     focus attention on *the modalities of the symbolic representation of the social
     world* rather than on efforts to identify and define actual groups of
     people, and then to ascribe to them values and practices that are held to
     be characteristic.

(b) In turn, it must be recognized that processes of representation occur in and
     through the actual practices of individuals and groups in real social set-
     tings, in a relationship of mutual influence. The experience of a sense of
     identity or belonging, for example, is to be understood as arising through
     an active collaborative process in which individuals participate with others
     in creating and sustaining a sense of self and others, and engaging in
     certain sorts of activities, which may often have a ritual character (Collins,
     1981), and which confirm and sustain significant meanings held in common.
     The active participation in such social 'worlds' – however transitory, informal
     and apparently mundane they may seem – is not, of course, limited to the
     activities that have been represented as deviant or subcultural; indeed, as
     Finnegan (1989) has argued, such involvements, of all kinds, are funda-
     mental to participation in social life more generally (p. 329).

The sort of reformulation suggested here is consistent with a discernible movement in the sociological analysis of culture away from attempts to 'decode' or
'decipher' texts or cultural objects for their presumed inherent 'meaning', and
towards a concern with the ways in which they are *used* by real people in real
situations (Becker, 1989; Martin, 2000). In directing analytical attention
towards the ways in which social activities and relationships are represented, this
brings into focus both the interactional 'work' done by people as they constitute their social worlds, *and* the similar processes of representation involved in
researchers' or media portrayals of particular 'groups'. Such a perspective is also
consistent with an understanding of social groups and communities, as neither
being tied to a particular geographical location nor in fact identifiable as sets of
'members': this view, it may be suggested, is particularly appropriate to a period
in which such relationships, and cultural knowledge generally, are increasingly
acquired and experienced through the electronic media rather than face-to-face

contact, and in which technological and social conditions can facilitate the emergence of what Willis has called 'proto-communities' (1990, pp. 141ff).

Conclusion

The aim of this chapter has been to view the current debate about the concept of subculture in the context of a much longer-term movement in sociological thought, in which the collective concepts developed by early theorists have been reformulated in ways that recognize the processes through which people actively constitute their social worlds. I have suggested that this movement was anticipated in, and owes much to, the work of Max Weber, and that it is apparent in efforts to reformulate concepts such as state, class, formal organization and family. Other examples could be given – what emerges from all of them, though, is a recognition of the analytical importance of processes of symbolic representation, and of social life as enacted.

It may be added that the argument presented here is also consistent with the work of those who have detected in recent years a significant move away from the theoretical presuppositions and research preoccupations of 'structural' sociology, and towards 'interpretive' or 'interactional' approaches. Fine and Kleinman (1979), for example, drew attention to 'the general assumption that subcultures are homogeneous, closed social entities' and the need to formulate an alternative approach based on interactionist premises (p. 6). Fine (1993) has argued subsequently that since the 1960s many of the basic ideas of interactionist thought have been absorbed into mainstream sociology, while Maines (2001) suggests that this process has been both important and largely imperceptible – as he puts it, 'sociologists over the years have learned a way of talking about themselves and their discipline in a way that has compartmentalized interactionist work and relegated it to the margins of scholarly consideration while simultaneously and unknowingly becoming more interactionist in their work' (p. xv). Collins (1981) has also argued that progress in sociological work depends on the adoption of a programme of theoretical and empirical translation, which 'reveals the empirical realities of social structures as patterns of repetitive micro-interaction'. Such chains of micro-encounters generate the central features of social organization – authority, property and group membership – by creating and recreating "mythical" cultural symbols and emotional energies' (p. 985). More recently, Jenkins (2002) has also drawn attention to 'the general and long-standing sociological misconception which has always overstated, indeed fundamentally misunderstood, the solidity and boundedness of collectivities' (p. 59), and argued for a conception of sociology founded on the basic reality of the 'human world' (ibid., pp. 63ff).

These authors, and others, share a recognition that the situated interactions of real people are the fundamental social reality. A primary sociological focus on this, however, does *not* entail a neglect of power relations, social structures and other apparently 'macro' phenomena. On the contrary, the implication is that such phenomena must be understood as arising from, and being sustained through, collaborative interaction. So it is important, finally, to emphasize that, while individuals may thus be seen to 'make' their identities, and their 'worlds', this does not mean that they have the ability to define meanings or construct selves just as they please. On the contrary, it is precisely in the engagement between individual subjectivities and the 'objective facticities' of the social world (Berger and Luckmann, 1966, p. 78), that the process of self-formation is carried out. The case studies presented in the second part of this book, each in their own way provide empirical illustrations of how the multiplicity of collective practices that characterize contemporary youth culture are the product of such ongoing engagement between individual subjectivity and the objective facilities of everyday surroundings.

CHAPTER 2

Fragmented Culture and Subcultures

DAVID CHANEY

Subcultures and Cultural Diversity

My intention in this chapter is to explore the implications of cultural change in order to suggest that a notion of subculture as a name for one type of cultural diversity is no longer relevant. In the context of the years following the Second World War it seemed that established lines of class division and identity were being re-formulated; particularly in the perhaps unlikely arena of an increasingly confident and strident generational or youth culture that was being established. Displayed in themes such as music, dress, sexual behaviour, drug use and generally more relaxed attitudes (Martin, 1981), new modes of self-conscious cultural identification broke up patterns of cultural difference based on region and class. A notion of subculture seemed at that time apposite to capture innovations that pointed to new social differentiations through cultural forms (Hebdige, 1979). The studies in this book take these changes for granted and show in detail in a variety of settings how, as the changes have been built upon, further developments and changes in our conceptual vocabulary have become necessary. In this chapter I consider the more general character of cultural change as the twentieth century ended and the twenty-first began.

My argument will be that concepts such as subculture have been rendered superfluous by specific developments in the character of late-modern culture. This is true whether or not subculture once adequately captured an increasing consciousness of the cultural divisions of generation, gender, ethnicity and sexuality and so on, in the changing social consciousness of a 'revolt into style.'[1]

In fact, although we might assume that our multicultural world is more diverse, one reason for discarding subculture could be because our assumptions of diversity are illusory; that there has in reality been an increase in cultural orthodoxy (a view that could be supported by Ritzer's (1993; 1998) account of 'McDonaldization'. A deduction along these line would, however, be superficial, because in an important sense the notion of subculture has always been counter-intuitive. It implies the existence of deep-rooted cultural differences within an over-arching parent culture. And yet an idea of subcultures began to seem necessary in an era when there was an unprecedented degree of cultural integration, at least in relation to the forms of popular culture. It would be inappropriate to digress into a history of popular culture at this point, so I shall merely say that when the forms of mass culture – the cinema, broadcasting in radio and television, recorded music, mass publications, and not least mass marketing and so on[2] – began to dominate the diversity of urban popular cultures, national cultures became more homogeneous than they ever had been before. Subcultures were not then instances of the sort of variety in sporting traditions that marked modernizing society; they were not primarily ways of referring to a spatially distributed heterogeneity in cultural practices.[3] Rather, they dramatized different ways of investing in cultural identities and how these involvements can be symbolized or articulated. Instead, my argument is that the idea of subculture is redundant because the type of investment that the notion of subculture labelled is becoming more general, and therefore the varieties of modes of symbolization and involvement are more common in everyday life. It is this variety of modes that I try to capture in what I describe as a fragmentation of culture.

Changing Forms of Culture

In order to explain more clearly what I mean, I shall outline what I take to have been some of the most significant features of cultural change at the end of the twentieth century and in the initial years of the twenty-first. In this section I shall discuss four aspects of the ways in which the forms of culture have changed. In some cases these may not seem immediately to be very relevant to the character of subcultures, but I shall try to show that, in combination, these changes amount to a transformed 'parent' culture, of which subcultures might be adaptations.

Generally, I think the direction of change is away from what typically has been presumed to be a global collection of unique, identifiable and distinctive cultures. This could suggest that culture is becoming less important, although my argument is that the reverse is, in fact, true. Of course, to suggest that culture is becoming more important is itself a bit puzzling. If culture is our whole way of life (Williams, 1958), comprising the patterns of discourse and representation through which we order and understand experience, then it is clearly central to social consciousness and cannot become more important. And yet culture is both the institutions of custom and ingrained understandings characteristic of a people, and possibly a locality, *and* the ways that distinctive identity is dramatized and represented in cultural forms. It is in relation to the production and character of cultural forms that culture has become increasingly important in the era of late-modernity.

I shall mention briefly three ways in which culture has become more important. The first is the economic significance of the production, distribution and consumption of industries of entertainment. All the activities we group loosely under a heading of the media have become larger and more central economically, but we should also include here other forms of information and entertainment, such as advertizing and the tourism industries. Both in terms of selling images and performance, and through a reframing of other commodities to emphasize their semiotic significance has the cultural economy become central to post-industrial prosperity (du Gay and Pryke, 2001). The second dimension of increasing importance is the ways in which more generally economic activity has turned from trading in material artefacts to symbolic ones. As examples of this process I can point to the significance of fashion in every aspect of material culture, and not just clothes (Gronow, 1997; Dant, 1999), and the massive expansion in the acceptance of eating out as a leisure activity which is both a focus of social life and an important medium for the display of taste and cultural skills (Warde and Martens, 2000). More generally, all sorts of goods, activities and environments are evaluated and marketed as representations of condensed meaning and association (Lash and Urry, 1994).

The idea of importance at this point is then based in the ways in which culture can act as a focus for commodity relationships,[4] and how the economic significance of cultural dimensions to those relationships has changed in recent years. The third way in which such a focus for commodity relationships has become more important concerns how culture is being used as both a theme and an instrument of public policy. It might seem surprising to label this a commodity relationship, but I am thinking of how culture has been used increasingly in recent years as an instrument of economic regeneration and community development (more generally on this, see Selwood, 2001). Principally by attracting tourists to areas that had not been seen as tourist sites, such as Bilbao in Northern Spain and Salford in greater Manchester or Gateshead in Tyneside, through the building of prestigious galleries, museums and cultural centres, culture has stimulated a wide range of economic activities. In addition to restaurants, hotels, transport facilities and so on, one would also want to mention here how a change in cultural status affects the area as a residential site for local people and brings all sorts of other entertainment and leisure facilities (a process discussed in Chaney,

2002b). More generally, these developments are part of change in the understanding of the rights of citizenship, with culture becoming of central significance (Stevenson, 2001).

I hope to have been able to sustain an argument that the first aspect of change relevant to subcultures is that cultural activities and concerns have become more self-evidently important in the everyday lives of the majority of individuals, not merely those for whom cultural activities are accentuated through visual appearance or musical preference. The second aspect of change concerns an 'opening-up' of culture. The central theme of this aspect is that a good deal of the stratification of culture that became so massively institutionalized in the course of modernization is being discarded. What I mean by the stratification of culture is the highly differentiated vocabularies of cultural taste correlated with a hierarchy of class and status that was so ably dissected by Bourdieu (1984) in his study of French taste. To say that such a hierarchy of cultural taste is being discarded is not to say that inequalities of cultural capital have disappeared, or that we are entering a golden age of popular cultural sophistication (for further information on everyday cultures, see Bennett *et al.*, 1999). There are, however, at least three trends which, in combination, are transforming established cultural distinctions. The first is an all-pervasive populism that is usually expressed as an overwhelming concern with market considerations. The consequence of this is, for example, that new novels continue to be published but bookshops prefer to rely on established names, books that are linked to other media (preferably television), and books that are backed by extensive marketing by their publishers. The further consequence is that the range of literature available is squeezed towards a middle- to low-brow of fictional narratives supplemented by a range of self-help books in hobby areas such as cooking, gardening and personal health.

The trend I have described in literature is not, of course, unique to this cultural form, but can be seen to be operating in other cultural forms such as music, television, films and theatre. A widespread conviction that it is elitist and therefore necessarily highly objectionable to fail to respond to popular taste is of a piece with a second trend, which I shall describe as a loss of confidence by cultural elites. This is necessarily hard to quantify, but I think it can be detected in a shift in public discourse concerning support through various forms of subvention by public funds for elite tastes. In areas such as opera, music generally, theatre and literature there is a greater defensiveness about justifying support in terms of intrinsic quality, and a more widely recognized need to spread a net of social inclusion as widely possible. In this respect, the device of using subventions from public gambling has been relatively successful in being used to justify a new form of taxation while deflecting attention from using public resources to support cultural elites. Increasingly, however, even this sleight of hand is being adapted to goals of wider communal support. This leads on to my third aspect of changing cultural hierarchies, which I can label loosely as a process of informalization. Here the conventions of polite behaviour in public cultural settings are gradually being discarded in favour of broader, less socially-differentiated forms of informality in dress, speech, customs around eating and other modes of public behaviour (a process more fully discussed in Chaney, 2002a, esp. ch. 5; see also Warde, 1997).

The third aspect of change in the forms of culture in recent years concerns the trend towards becoming a more multicultural society. Although the phrase is used quite widely in public discourse, there is a good deal of controversy as to whether the trend is to be welcomed. I think this is largely because the term is interpreted to refer to a less deferential immigration, by which I mean that cultural and ethnic minorities are less willing, and – to be fair – are less likely to be expected, to subordinate their identities in the 'parent' culture. It is in this sense that an ideal of assimilation is less likely to be an aim of public policy, except among conservative groups opposed to immigration and what they often see as the 'dilution' of a national culture. For the latter, multiculturalism is often depicted as both a form of conspiracy by liberals seeking to undermine national traditions and a misconceived project that will inevitably end in conflict between incompatible cultures. More generally, though, the cultural diversity of multi-ethnic society is seen as an obligation of contemporary diversity, and indeed welcomed as part of the trend towards a greater recognition of the rights and needs of minorities, whether they stem from gendered, ethnic, sexual, physical or age-based differentiation.

It is in this sense that the idea of a multicultural world is an acceptance that a normative cultural homogeneity within a national context is no longer possible. Even the most bigoted conservatives would probably accept that developments in global cultural industries have meant that distinctiveness in national cultural styles in areas such as popular music, film, fashion, and even local culinary tastes, is being overwhelmed by borrowings and imports facilitated by global marketing. The inevitability of this process is recognized as stemming from the logic of mass cultural industries which in the past have only arbitrarily been restrained by national cultural boundaries. Of course, a recognition of the inevitability of globalization does not preclude widespread hostility with a multiculturalism that involves a forced adaptation to, and acceptance of, the glamour and garishness of American cultural industries in food, clothing, entertainment and so on (Hannerz, 1996). While the force of, and resistance to, cultural imperialism should not be underestimated, it is also important to recognize, as Lull, among others, has persuasively argued (2000, especially Chapter 9) that hybridity has bred forms of cultural melding and mediation such as transculturation, indigenisation and glocalization (see also Gonzalez, 2001; Lull, 2001a). In brief, these terms refer to the active use of culture by its inhabitants who, refusing to be governed solely by nostalgia and tradition, select and re-combine in order to let the panoply of cultural choices available function as resources for new forms of creative expression.

I have so far in this section reviewed three aspects of changing forms of culture – culture becoming more important, becoming less stratified, and becoming more 'balkanised' in that a greater heterogeneity of cultural styles and identities is both visible to, and can be adopted by, ordinary people. I said in the opening section that a subculture was distinguished by a distinctive cultural involvement on the part of its members, and that such a degree of involvement was becoming more general. I hope it is now apparent how the aspects of change I have been describing all contribute to a more widespread involvement – that the qualities of appropriation and innovation once applied to subcultures can be seen in relation to a range of consumer and leisure-based groupings across the social spectrum.

The idea that the diversity of cultural choices available in the intensively media-saturated environments of contemporary popular culture can be experienced as emancipating through greater involvement is continued in the fourth and last aspect of changing forms of culture that I shall mention in this section. This is the aspect of cultural change I have previously discussed as a move from ways of life to lifestyles as the frameworks on which notions of identity, community, affiliation and difference are negotiated (Chaney, 2001a). Briefly, the ways of life are the local customs, traditions, attitudes and values that have given an environment both a distinctive character and a weight of expectation to which individuals necessarily adapt. Such a sense of culture as lived environment informed what Williams (1961) meant by his famous injunction that 'culture is ordinary', and was based in a recognition that a complex modern society had developed fissured by deep structural divisions – principally those between class cultures.

While recognizing the strength of this traditional account, I have also argued (Chaney, 1998) that a new sort of materialism in cultural history has proved necessary. This has to consider how accounts of social structure based on divisions deriving from the organization of production have to adapt to more fluid differentiations based in consumption practices (see also Miller, 1995). In a culture of consumerism, goods, experiences, places and social actors are all valued for their semiotic meanings and associations rather than their functional utility. To say that the material culture of ordinary life is being treated increasingly as a corpus of signs might suggest that it is becoming fixed less tangibly in physical givens and thus is in an important way being dematerialized. Although this is true, if it also means that if values, relationships and identities are being constructed in the manipulation of vocabularies of style, then material culture becomes the terrain – albeit an unstable, relative terrain – through which social order is constituted.[5] This, it seems to me, is one of the most important aspects of the rise of lifestyles as 'sites and strategies' for new forms of affiliation and identification (Chaney, 1996a, esp. parts 3 and 4): that is, culture becomes more clearly a resource than an inheritance. Thus, what were once described as subcultures could now be regarded as collective lifestyle statements, which reflexively negotiate rather than directly mirror the structural experience of social class.

Two further aspects of this process of transition in the structures of culture are worth bringing out at this point, as they are relevant to the general theme of the significance of subcultures. The first is that, if the framework of meanings that culture embodies is in important ways destabilized, then the authority of intellectuals to control or legislate for cultural value is crucially undermined. This does not mean that there is an anarchy of value, or that expertise loses any role. Indeed, the reverse is true, as expertise in a culture of mass entertainment seems to proliferate, taking up an increasingly large proportion of public discourse, and to be offered at a variety of levels of complexity (Bauman, 1992a). It is rather that the authority of expertise needs to be renewed continually, and is endlessly contestable in relation to different audiences and contexts. Second, and this is a corollary of the first point, an investment of personal meaning and desire for control over the organization of material culture will lead to what has been called an 'aestheticisation of everyday life' (Featherstone, 1991a,b; Chaney, 1996a). Although the idea has been criticized for being restricted effectively to specific beneficiaries of new cultural industries and for heralding a loss of any distinction between representation and reality, it does suggest that the politics of culture is less a conflict between a parent and its subcultures, and more a general feature of everyday life in contemporary society. It seems necessary, then, to cast around for new terms for the diversity of contemporary culture.

The Changing Character of Culture

In the first two sections I have set out the general theme of my approach, and then described four aspects of cultural change in later modernity in order to bring out how they have facilitated a greater involvement in cultural issues. I have been particularly concerned with the ways in which the status and organization of culture have been changing. What I mean by this is changes in how cultural practices inter-relate with other aspects of social order; in effect the character and delineation of the cultural sphere. They do, however, essentially leave the imaginative purchase of characteristic cultural experience unexplored.

What I mean here are the sorts of fictional experience that are conjured in different cultural forms. How forms of social life are represented in performance so that a distinctive 'way of seeing' is being provided (Chaney, 1996b). In this third section I shall therefore address this issue of the character of representation in later modernity. In particular, I shall attempt to show that the boundaries that mark fictional performance from 'reality' have become blurred and cultural idioms have bled into everyday life in a variety of ways, with the further implication that cultural experience has changed its status in the constitution of everyday life. I believe that, in grasping how distinctions between culture and reality have been blurred, we can more easily understand how the sorts of cultural involvement once deemed to be characteristic of subcultures have become more general.

I have suggested previously that the dominant impulse in the more self-conscious or high cultural forms of the modern era (modernism) has been a pursuit of authentic representation, which I have characterized as an aesthetics of realism (Chaney, 1994, ch. 5). In this project, the fictional (that is, any mode of representation) enjoys a different status from its subject matter – the real – a difference that is sustained by a variety of framing devices. Examples of such devices would be the stage on which a performance is set, and the frame that marks the boundary – and thus the edge of representation – of a painted work. Summarizing a complex process extremely simplistically, I can say that in the changing market circumstances of cultural production in the modern era, artists (cultural producers, more generally) have become increasingly self-conscious about the authenticity of their creative labour, and have therefore deployed in their representations ways of undermining or destabilizing the framing devices of fictional experience (see also Clark, 1999, on the ultimate impossibility of authentic representation in modernity). More technically, we can say that artists in modernism have – in response to perceived difficulties in authentic representation – explored myriad ways of ironicising or making more explicit the reflexivity of the process of representation.

It is important to appreciate that the crisis of confidence in modernism over the aesthetics of realism was set in the context of the establishment of a hugely commercially successful mass culture. The popular culture that spilled out of the enclaves of class culture was essentially based in an alternative tradition of an aesthetics of representation (again, discussed more fully in Chaney, 1994, ch. 5). This alternative tradition privileged communal experience over personal expression, it valued spectacular show over complexities of individual character, and it aimed for an all-embracing experience rather than a controlled or tightly-framed fictional experience (Stallybrass and White, 1986). If an aesthetics of realism is concerned essentially with the validity of representation, then the aesthetics of representation is, in contrast, more concerned with the elaboration of reality.

In brief, the argument is that, in the developments of later modernity the aesthetics of realism has lost its privileged position and gradually been supplanted by an all-pervasive aesthetics of representation. This has meant, in a development of the characteristics already mentioned, the frequently identified features of an emphasis upon surface and show rather than complexity and depth, an exploration of association and likeness typically expressed through playful disorder rather than narrative coherence, and an enormous sophistication in awareness of stylistic allusion which is used for effects of shock and humour, glorying in fictional artifice rather than a more agonised exploration of authenticity. In effect, then, what I am arguing is that what are usually taken to be the innovations of postmodernism are an elaboration of older cultural traditions undoubtedly given greater force by technological developments in means of representation. In their most recent form, boundaries between the different media of representation, and between representation and reality, have become ever harder to grasp and sustain in the virtual realities of digital culture (Bell and Kennedy, 2000; Webster, 2002). Two further contextual factors are also important. First, that the dismantling of traditional hierarchies of culture to which I have already referred was taking place; and, second, that advances in production meant that hardware in variety of cultural forms was becoming ever cheaper in real terms, with a consequent emphasis by cultural industries on marketing software with complex effects.

Another way of describing the shift in the character of cultural experience has been provided by Lash's (1991) formulation that we are moving from a discursive to a figural paradigm. At its simplest, this thesis suggests that the process of modernization was managed – in the discursive paradigm – through a rationality grounded in the linear coherence of prose. The ways of describing the world and experience were conceived in the abstract symbolism of language, and were thus dependent on the syntactical conventions of grammatical utterance. While this is an extremely powerful means of representation, it is essentially disembodied in the sense that it could be used by anyone in any context, and subjects reality to the continuous consideration of rational discourse. In contrast, in later modernity the dominant framework for conceptualizing reality has shifted gradually from the linearity of prose to a profusion of pictorial imagery linked by connotative associations rather than their denoted content – the figural paradigm. This alternative is made possible by what Messaris (1997) has called the 'syntactic indeterminacy' of pictorial imagery. In this means of representation, pictures can be assembled in any order and acquire their rhetorical force through a multiplicity of levels of association, playful punning and complex allusion. As a collagistic repertoire, their use is necessarily embodied and situational.

Perhaps the best example of the creation of powerful accumulations of meaning through pictorial conjunction is in the use of montage in film narratives. In this cultural form, though, the power of pictorial association is to a large extent constrained by the logic of narrative order. In the wider society, imagery drawn from newspapers, posters, advertizing imagery, television, films and a myriad other forms of marketing is in random and indiscriminate profusion. The lack of logic or rationality in this cornucopia of representation creates both a very dense visual environment for everyday life, and new ways of conceiving reality and experience (Lash, 1999). If the most powerful exemplar of the discursive paradigm is the library book, in which an interpretation is stored for abstract and repeated engagement in ways that facilitate elaborations of rational development; the contrasting exemplar of the figurative paradigm is the collage of graffiti-esque advertising imagery on the margins of objects, places and performances. Advertising is ephemeral, associative, literally superficial and metaphorical in that it represents artifice and illusion but is unconstrained by narrative and thus content with only a rhetoric of style and allusion.

More recently, James Lull (2001b) has suggested that it would be helpful to think of a wealth of representation in which there is a profound looseness of meaning and reference as a superculture. Among the reasons for this is a desire for a term which indicates a situation where culture has burst its banks with an abundance of content and media, and in which all sorts of overlaps and penetrations between symbolic materials provide yet further layers of meaning and representation. Two further aspects of a superculture for Lull should, however, be mentioned. These are that the profusion and openness of a superculture allows ordinary people to become their own authors in the way they combine and enjoy different types of performance and representation (and in this way further develop the concept of the aestheticisation of everyday life); and, second, that superculture facilitates the emergence of distinctive communities of taste, because: 'The superculture's creativity, hybridity, and interactivity open up possibilities for establishing, maintaining, and linking meaningful "virtual cultural communities", and for inventing and managing other new encounters and mediations in ways that are positive and productive' (Lull, 2001b, p. 137). I think this suggestion is valuable, because it both helps to make clear how the changing character of culture represents different forms of engagement with 'reality' and the democratization of creativity this facilitates. Both of these mean that the type of engagement with the products of the media and consumer industries that the word subculture originally signified has become more widespread, resulting in a pluralistic and fragmentary everyday cultural sphere.

I have suggested previously that contemporary intellectuals are in the contradictory situation of having both endlessly expanding opportunities for comment and interpretation, faced with the proliferation of representation and stylistic resonance, and yet also losing the privileges of inherited privilege because their authority is continually being challenged and assumed to be partial, selective and time-limited (Eyerman, 1994). In coping with the complexities of this contradictory situation, intellectuals are shifting their role (as Bauman (1987) has said) from legislators to interpreters, and having to find new conceptual resources to represent their domain.

I think that subculture is one of the conceptual resources that is being reconsidered. A simple and unique cultural identity no longer seems feasible. Hetherington (1998a) has argued that more traditional concepts of social theory, including subculture, which labelled a world out there with a series of denotations, are not sustainable. All the blurrings and dissolutions of category boundaries I have been describing mean that social theory needs a more connotative approach which: 'while it does not dispense with narrative and theoretical work, challenges [any] attempt to represent the world as a single and simple picture rather than in its multiple state' (Hetherington, 1998a, p. 10). A further consequence of this challenge is that a distinctive practical consciousness or – in Williams' (1961; 1977) powerful phrase 'structure of feeling' – is emerging, orientated to the hybridity of contemporary culture. In this, individual units of social action are less like the isolated rationalists of traditional social theory agonizing over personal authenticity than overlapping networks orientated towards: 'diversity, polyculturalism and much more disparate forms of identification that support the condition of de-individualization' (Hetherington, 1998a, p. 52).

The Fragmentation of Culture

I have been describing changes in the organization, status, use and character of contemporary culture to illustrate my thesis that not only has culture become considerably more diverse, but also that the character of diversity is more far-reaching than before. I hope to have shown that diversity now means something more than the fact that there are a lot of different traditions, and styles of performance and representation, from among which individual consumers can choose. Indeed, I hope to have shown that it is more relevant to think of diversity as having reached such a pitch that it is appropriately thought of as a process of fragmentation (although other terms that might be used are post-culture or superculture or multi-culture[6]). The name of the process is less important than its role in signalling that the ways in which cultural objects and experiences typically mediate and articulate themes in everyday social experience are changing.

I hope that it will by now be becoming clear why the account of changes in contemporary culture that has taken up the greater part of this chapter leads to the conclusion that the concept of subculture has become redundant. This idea – subculture – developed as a way of trying to describe a distinctive type of structural conflict in modern societies. There were, as the introduction has shown, two distinct sources for this idea. One was the discovery in studies of criminality that young men felt drawn to dramatize their frustration and anger in commitments to largely age-based social groups. These groups both grew out of traditional structural patterning of ways of life that had become institutionalized in urban society, and yet were still independent of and in conflict with those traditions of identity (Cohen, 1955; Whyte, 1993). A second source has taken the study of the imagery of identification, whether it is in clothes, music, gendered relationships or values, further, thus accentuating the cultural motifs, but still seeing the meaning of style as deriving from a search for a means of articulating tensions and conflicts that had arisen in the changing social formations of later modernity (Willis, 1978; Hebdige, 1979). As I noted in the first section of this chapter, the idea of subculture was a way of taking seriously the meanings of those among the largely inarticulate and non-intellectual young who invested in cultural adaptation – usually by parodying and making grotesque themes and imagery in the public culture of their social context.

In saying that subculture has become superfluous I am not meaning to imply that structural conflicts have disappeared, or that there are not still confused conflicts over adaptations to social change. Clearly, the cultural is still political in every tissue of its being, and it is the general theme of this chapter that the cultural, as it is generally understood, has become more significant as the means through which the raw materials of everyday life can be handled. It is rather that it is not sufficient to assume that elements in a dominant culture can be appropriated or adapted as a means of distinctive 'counter-cultural' revolt. That is, as public culture has lost its warrant and authority, and as the scope for adaptive investments in modes of cultural diversity has increased, so the idea that cultural objects, practices or icons can be identified so distinctively with a dominant culture as to be adapted or transformed is no longer sustainable. To put this another way, the once-accepted distinction between 'sub' and 'dominant' culture can no longer be said to hold true in a world where the so-called dominant culture has fragmented into a plurality of lifestyle sensibilities and preferences.

In what became a famous phrase when developing the subcultural theorizations of cultural diversity, Clarke *et al.* (1976, p. 10) referred to a culture as providing 'a map of meaning'; in his development of the phrase, Jackson (1989) has pointed out the salience of geographical metaphors for subcultural writing at the time. While initially an attractive metaphor, the idea of map has at least two unfortunate connotations. First, maps are, as we have come to realize, instruments of power. They lay down modes of description and use that are necessarily authoritative and suppress alternative modes of habitation. Second, a map implies a distinctive space with recognizable features – in effect, a common terrain. As will have become clear in my account of cultural change, neither of these connotations may seem appropriate. Contests over how to describe cultural change have become endemic to the extent that there is no longer the possibility of authoritative representation, and any confidence in a shared space with commonly recognized features has also evaporated. In such a situation, all cultural practices are adaptations, and the idea of core and subcultures is no longer necessary. In a fragmented culture, the tensions between diversity and conformity require newer and more sophisticated metaphors of representation.

Notes

1   I have appropriated the title of George Melly's (1972) path-breaking account of new types of cultural conflict as a shorthand way of characterizing earlier forms of cultural change; some of the critical discussion concerning the adequacy of a notion of subculture have been rehearsed in the introduction to this collection, although it is worth noting that subculture is one of those terms that captured an idea for a broader public than those just concerned with more academic studies of contemporary culture.

2   A fuller account of eras in popular culture as a basis for a view that culture is now fragmenting has been presented in the final chapter of Chaney (2002a).

3   Although, as I note in my concluding remarks, spatial metaphors were powerfully attractive to many subculture theorists.

4   A number of distinguished writers have deplored the commodification of culture as a recent development; in its literal sense this is a nonsensical view, as culture has always been a commodity, among other things, even when revered primarily as a ritual object. In the mass marketing of culture, inevitably it has become increasingly populist and market-orientated, and while I accept that this has many deplorable features it may be that a more explicit concern with its commodity character has involved stripping away many of the privileges of those who controlled ritual status.

5   A terrain that Harris (1992) has called, in a happy phrase, 'the politics of pleasure'.

6   See also Featherstone (1995) on 'undoing culture'.

PART 2
CASE STUDIES

CHAPTER 3

'It's Like Canada Reduced': Setting the Scene in Montreal

GEOFF STAHL

In the field of popular music studies, examinations of the social dimensions of music-making have led to a number of valuable discussions about what descriptive categories might best account for socio-musical experiences. Recently, one particular debate has emerged that centres on the sociological value and usefulness of the terms 'subculture' and 'scene'. One specific aspect of subcultural theory, namely the creative response to exclusion and marginalization as 'making' or 'winning space', has been revisited in recent literature focused on music-making. There are various reasons as to why this might be, but two related developments stand out here: the emergence of place studies, and a renewed emphasis on the conceptualization of urban space. In the case of place studies, this shift has in many ways to do with the stress placed on locality, or 'the local', taking up issues that relate to civic politics, cultural policy, or the microeconomics associated with regional cultural production (Gay, 1995; Street, 1995; Mitchell, 1996). This development complements the second trend prevalent in studies of music-making, one that tends toward Henri Lefebvre-inspired discussions of urban space, spatial relations, spatial representations and spatial practices, noting how these might then bear upon cultural practice in the city (and vice versa). Cultural geographers, sociologists, social anthropologists and others have taken up both of these trends in analyzing musical cultures (Finnegan, 1989; Cohen, 1991, 1998; Straw, 1991, 2001a; Olson, 1998; Skelton and Valentine, 1998). As a result, this so-called 'spatial turn' has meant that a different interpretative schema for the study of musical practice has come to the fore, one that revolves around the more theoretically compelling notion of scene. Thus, at the same time that the notion of subculture was being reinvigorated or refashioned, it was also being eclipsed by the ubiquity of scene.

51

Salient aspects of these debates will be highlighted in the discussion that follows. The first part of this chapter will examine some of the theoretical and analytical issues raised by the notion of scene. However, the object is not to dispense with subcultural theory; rather, it is to suggest ways of expanding the conceptual possibilities that music-making in the city has introduced to cultural analysis. The second half of the chapter briefly considers the Montreal anglophone independent rock scene; specifically, the aesthetic strategies of one record label, 'derivative records', using this as an entry point into an exploration of the analytical value of scene over that of subculture. The various infrastructures that make up the Montreal scene are explored as a way of getting at the deep imbrication of musical practice in the cultural space of the city. The process through which these infrastructures define each other reciprocally will be considered in relation to the socio-spatial properties of the term scene, primarily as a way of accentuating its applicability to the study of urban music-making.

Setting the Scene

When it comes to describing the more informal social organization associated with a majority of music-making, it is evident that an emphasis on the spectacular nature of subcultures obscures, rather than illuminates, the complexity of contemporary musical practice. The shift towards scenes taken by some scholars acknowledges that different interpretive tools are called for in order to account for the many-layered circuits, loose affiliations, networks, contexts and points of contact determining the socio-musical experience. The notion of scene might be mobilized more readily to incorporate these elements, allowing an expanded consideration of the industrial, institutional, historical, social and economic contexts alongside the ideological and aesthetic strategies that underpin music-making. Scene's elasticity enables a more nuanced analysis of the webs of connectivity that define musical practice in a manner that the more rigid category 'subculture' generally resists.

If we want to consider a particular context for music-making – the city, for example – scene carries with it a semantic latitude that can widen the scope of analysis. For example, at a semiotic level, certain questions emerge when considering the theoretical efficacy of the term 'subcultures', many of which become much more insistent when grounded in the kind of urban context that 'scene' necessarily implies. In thinking about the pluralistic nature of cultural life in a city, for example, how do we begin to explain the significance of what we might call, for lack of a better term, not-so-spectacular subcultures? It is easy, on the one hand, to single out punks or goths, as they wear their difference in the form of 'semiotic guerilla warfare', the ostentatious display of which is taken as the standard hallmark of subcultural style; they are so much semantic disorder or 'noise' in the system (Hebdige, 1979, p. 90). What, on the other hand, can we make of those not-so-spectacular subcultures that are just as insistent and industrious in mapping out their difference, albeit on a less visible plane? How do we begin to discern or distinguish between those many groups that make up the background, the *white* noise of the city? And how do we account, in both a semiotic and sociological sense, for their significance? By not addressing these sorts of questions, accounts that read subcultural practice as a kind of urban costume drama, while they may be rich, risk mapping out social typologies as only so much surface noise. The danger here is the reduction of subcultural studies to a taxonomy of stylistic gestures and mannerisms abstracted from the materiality of the urban milieux which both shape and are shaped by them. Thus, thinking about collective cultural expression and informal social formations in terms of city life, noting also how signifying practices reflect its socio-spatial properties, requires a more flexible definition of context. Scene, understood here as a specific kind of urban cultural context and practice of spatial coding, has become a salient descriptive category, one which, for the purposes of this chapter at least, has more explanatory power.

The different socio-spatial connotations of scene – its allusions to flexibility and transience, of temporary, *ad hoc* and strategic associations, a cultural space notable as much for its restricted as well as its porous sociality, its connotations of flux and flow, movement and mutability – suggest that the significance of musical life might be better seen as occurring at the juncture of spatial relations and social praxis. In other words, a diversity of conditions should be considered and examined that are constituted and inflected as much by local circumstance as they are by trans-local demands and desires. Scene used as an interpretive tool can encourage analyses of the interconnectivity of a city's cultural spaces, its industries, institutions and media, emphasizing its heterogeneity as well its unifying elements, and thereby challenge the subcultural model with its stress on homology and homogeneity. It can enable considerations of the shifting roles that any music-maker may take on in the scene, either simultaneously or over time (from fan to musician, to DJ, graphic designer, zine writer, promoter, from amateur to professional). It can also provide a richer cartography of the relationships music scenes share with other scenes (film, theatre, literary, art and so on). Framing musical activity in these ways can prompt a suppler analysis of the social mechanics associated with music-making, allowing for a fuller account of the dynamic range of forces – social, economic, institutional – affecting the kinds of collective expression found in the city.

This is not to ascribe too much explanatory power to the notion of scene, which according to these terms might otherwise be taken as being all-encompassing (and thus theoretically meaningless). However, the 'fundamental ambiguity' of the term scene (Blum, 2001, p. 33) can be made to give way to a sharper focus. In order to impose some limits, we can consider two salient aspects of scene: at a semiotic level, an emphasis on scene over subculture would not do away with style necessarily, but reposition it within a more complex set of shifting and mobile practices which could then be considered in relation to specifically urban sensibilities, something more akin to lifestyles;[1] and, in terms of the symbolic and material infrastructures in the city, the broader scope of the term 'scene' would incorporate more effectively modes of cultural production, aesthetic strategies, kinds and degrees of social mobility, affective states and ideologies which have pronounced spatial consequences. In this way, an emphasis on the multivalent character of local scenes/cultural spaces would complicate any notion of a single determinant (that is, class, gender, race and so on) acting as the over-arching organizing principle of collective cultural expression. In a related sense, thinking of the scene as both a context for enactment and point of contact means that one can consider cultural phenomena generated at the juncture of various trajectories and vectors. Taking this a step further, these can then be placed alongside the institutional and infrastructural mechanisms affecting cultural practices and creative expression, in order to facilitate a more nuanced description of the role they play in the creation and maintenance of extensive inter-related networks, circuits and alliances found both inside and outside the city. In this capacity, the notion of scene allows a thicker description of the many resources marshalled together to support cultural activity in the city.

'Scene' will be used here to denote the formal and informal arrangement of industries, institutions, audiences and infrastructures (see Straw, 1991). Over time, any scene becomes spatially embedded according to a dense array of social, industrial and institutional infrastructures, all of which operate at a local and trans-local level. Using the anglophone music scene in Montreal as a backdrop, the following discussion places in relief one such 'not-so-spectacular subculture': anglophone independent ('indie') rock (see also Hesmondhalgh, 1999). The means by which certain Montreal-based industries and institutions serve to cross-subsidise and reinforce this particular music scene's cultural economy, shaping also the socio-musical experience of the city, are exemplified by the brief history of one of the city's relatively successful independent record labels, 'derivative records' (which operated from 1992 to 1998). The label's creative practices, as well as their aesthetic strategies, can be positioned in relation to the overlapping social, industrial and institutional networks and economies which serve to co-ordinate, albeit loosely, the actors involved in Montreal's music scene, and at the same time foster a particular sense of attachment to place.

Borrowing the terms 'hard' and 'soft' infrastructures from Charles Landry (2000) in his study of urban creative milieus, what follows is an examination of the industrial and institutional networks underpinning musical activity and their bearing on the soft infrastructure – that is, the affective dimensions associated with the socio-musical experience of Montreal. Hard infrastructure is made up of the built environment, educational institutions, cultural centres, meeting places and so on; soft infrastructure is composed of 'the associative structures and social networks, connections, human interactions that encourages the flow of ideas between individuals and institutions' (Landry, 2000, p. 133). Landry reminds us that the successful combination of these sorts of criteria – and we can include here the cross-subsidization of music-making through the kind of 'institutional thickness' Amin and Thrift (1994) describe – is contingent on an amenable social atmosphere: 'This thickness,' Landry notes, 'is what continues to stimulate entrepreneurship and consolidates the local embeddedness of industry while at the same time fostering relations of trust, exchange of information and urban "buzz"' (Landry, 2000, p. 141). The symbiotic relationship between the hard and soft infrastructures of the music scene, with a stress placed on their unevenness, means that Montreal could figure in the imagination and musical activities of 'derivative' as a model space in which to be culturally productive. The relationship is a complicated one because, as the case of the Montreal music-making demonstrates, the 'buzz' generated by the unevenness of hard and soft infrastructure figures prominently in the symbolic frameworks and material practices of music-makers, in a manner that indicates that the city, its identity, its ambience and its semiotic resonances are inextricably linked.

Keeping this tension in mind, it should be noted that the cultural apparatus underpinning indie rock scenes should be understood as a matrix of sites, routines, networks, practices, events and participants, a dense complex of activities and actors that produce discursive frameworks notable, as John Street suggests, for their emphasis on 'place-ness'. Taken together, they produce regional identities (Street, 1995, p. 255). Where bands come from and where they produce their music are significant aspects of how they register in the imaginations of fans and other music-makers. For example, the Olympia scene, the Seattle scene, the Dunedin scene and the Manchester scene are all signifiers that draw explicit links between the urban referent and images of a vibrant subcultural hub. Spatially coded in this way, city-as-sign and city-as-scene are often conflated in a manner that privileges an aesthetic experience of, and commitment to, the city. Indie bands and their music are understood by fans and artists alike to be deeply connected with specific places, a sign of their unwavering allegiance to an ideology of small-scale production, a deep sense of commitment to their region's underground, and an awareness of their role as bearers of its subterranean values, which takes the form of (an often ironic, as we shall see) civic boosterism. There is in this a kind of moral economy that emerges, significant for the way in which an ethics of commitment (to both a sense of place and other music-makers) is articulated, as the example of 'derivative records' will ably demonstrate.

Montreal

Discourses informing Montreal musical practices are determined in large part by a number of conflicting social, institutional and material practices that affect the scene, in turn shaping how its members articulate a sense of belonging to both the scene and the city, how the scene gains its socio-semiotic shape, and thus, how the scene and the city's meaningful, or affective, dimensions are intertwined. Broadly speaking, the discursive envelope containing the socio-musical experience of the city is heavily determined by the linguistic specificity of Montreal. It would be disingenuous to talk of Montreal music-makers without at least a cursory consideration of language and how it bears on all aspects of musical practice and social life. Anglophones are a minority in the city, currently making up a smaller percentage of the population than allophones (immigrants whose first language/mother tongue is neither French nor English). Among 18–24 year olds, out-migration is highest, with those who graduated from either of the city's two English universities (McGill and Concordia) forming the largest percentage of those leaving the city and the province (Statistics Canada, 1996). The high turnover of young anglophones has frustrated the growth and success of local independent anglophone record industries and underlined the instability of the city's music scenes. For those music-makers who choose to stay, the diminished economic state of the city has encouraged, and in many ways compelled, them to produce an image of Montreal as an ideal place in which to be culturally productive (Stahl, 2001). The degree and kind of commitment to the scene is framed accordingly and, as a result, the anglophone socio-musical experience in Montreal is articulated within a dense cluster of cultural activities inflected by demographically deter-mined contingencies.

These multiple factors both shape and are shaped by the city's soft infra-structure, inflecting sometimes dramatically, sometimes subtly, the tenor and ambience of the city's cultural life. What this means at the level of the everyday is that routes and routines are intimately connected, that the use of the scene's hard infrastructure has a reciprocal relationship to the textures associated with its soft infrastructure, and that the affective dimension of the scene reinforces its structural aspects (and vice versa). Montreal remains a city where the soft infrastructure compensates for the hard infrastructure, but the industries and institutions that do exist are utilized to insulate many of the music-makers from many of the forces that have an impact on other aspects of life in the city. These institutional and industrial contexts, in turn, foster selective perceptions, attitudes and actions (a habitus in other words), and regulating and regular sets of improvizations, which, as Bourdieu states, 'produces practices which in turn tend to reproduce the objective conditions which produced the ... habitus in the first place' (Bourdieu, 1997, p. 95). As exemplified by 'derivative records', the socio-musical experience of Montreal becomes intimately bound up with, and inextricable from, those institutions that support musical activity. In this capacity, Montreal music-makers work to reproduce, rhetorically and materially, the conditions deemed necessary or appropriate for effective creative expression.

'derivative records'

> Making music in Montreal means understanding that you're a little fish in a little pond. In Toronto, it means thinking that you're a littler fish in a bigger pond.
>
> (Patti, 'derivative records')[2]

Patti and Kevin established 'derivative records' in 1992 as a cassette/7-inch-only label, and when distribution increased to meet demand in the USA and Europe, they brought in Gen and Pat and expanded their format to include CDs. 'derivative records' remained active until 1998, when, with the collapse of Cargo Canada (discussed below), the label quietly shut down. 'derivative' and its brand of indie rock emerged out of a typical indie rock sensibility: boredom, bedrooms, vanity and a sense of urgency that something must be done to offer a healthy antidote to what was seen as an anaemic local scene. Even as their reputation in Montreal grew, the label's greatest sales were outside the city and increasingly outside Canada, a modest sign of success that established 'derivative records' reputation among North American and European indie rock fans. Eventually, they formed distribution and licensing deals with a number of labels in the USA and the UK.

'derivative records' members brought to the label a wider aesthetic perspective combined with personal and professional histories whereby label activity remained relatively unaffected by the limited resources of the Montreal scene. Their musical sensibilities allowed them to respond instead to local and non-local needs in ways that confirm, as Street suggests, that 'local identities are constructed out of resources (both material and symbolic) which may well not be at all local in their origin' (Street, 1995, p. 257). The complexity of this position was managed by 'derivative' through a dexterous combination of aesthetic and industrial strategies, which was fostered by their positions in local circuits and trans-local networks. 'derivative' put to good use the material and symbolic resources at hand in Montreal, but also confirmed their commitment to a number of similarly inclined music-makers in a geographically dispersed indie rock scene.

The solution 'derivative' assembled out of the Montreal musical milieu relied, in part, on the label owners' musical biographies and reputations both inside and outside the city. The status of 'derivative' and its band, Pest 5000, in Montreal's scene, their value as independent cultural producers, as well as the various positions the members held in the scene's hard infrastructure, allowed multiple forms of access to new music the circuits through which it could be heard and disseminated. Of derivative's place in Montreal, it can be said that the label fits into a larger scheme of local/global cultural frameworks that clearly are dependent on Montreal-specific features for their success. The nature of the position 'derivative' occupied in the trans-local system of musical networks relates well to the three criteria that Scott Lash and John Urry use to define the success of the 'local' and its relation to what is being described here as a scenic sense of place. The first is that of interpretation: 'derivative', in their role as cultural intermediaries, exemplified how 'local production complexes can provide the context in which discourses and accounts develop by which these apparently distant systems can be made sense of and interpreted' (Lash and Urry, 1994, p. 284; see also Negus, 1996, p. 62). Their place in Montreal-based institutional and industrial networks fostered an ideal interpretive and organizational frame of mind, supported also by their diverse musical experiences and workplace connections, all of which served to cross-subsidise derivative's operation. Of these various networks, two significant points of contact in the music scene's hard infrastructure made much of derivative's label operation possible: CBC Radio and the one-stop distributor, Cargo Canada.

The first point of contact with both the Montreal scene and the broader music community centred on Kevin, Gen and Patti's involvement with 'Brave New Waves', a programme on CBC-FM (Radio 2), The programme's bearing on derivative's operation depended on a symbiotic relationship struck between the formal requirements of a bureaucratic government institution such as the CBC-FM and the informal, laissez-faire, qualities of an independent ethos. 'Brave New Waves', established in 1984, has played a crucial role in shaping the indie rock community in Canada (and given the signal reach of the CBC, even to some northern US states). Broadcast after midnight, from Sunday to Thursday, from Montreal, 'Brave New Waves' has been a showcase for new, independent, experimental and avant-garde music, profiling bands, airing lengthy interviews with musicians and providing some space for cultural commentary. It remains the longest-running show on Radio 2, with a target demographic age group of 18–35, an anomaly in a radio schedule generally offering programming that is decidedly high-brow and classical/jazz based, interspersed with 'adult' news and current affairs. However, it is a show notable for the programmer's refined taste, as borne out by the esoteric eclecticism of its programming. Thus the role of the staff of 'Brave New Waves' as cultural custodians can be contextualized according to the cultural biases of a network such as the CBC, which ' "builds its programs in its own image of the public interest" persuading itself "that apathy shown towards its offerings is due to listeners" bad taste rather than its own poor judgment' (Hodgetts, cited in Raboy, 1990, p. 10). Set within a government-subsidized broadcast institution which views itself as a vehicle for the promotion of 'good taste', 'Brave New Waves' has an official sanction to be 'alternative', affording the programmers an ideal position and perspective from which to select and organize musical choices, accessing new demo cassettes, singles and albums delivered daily. The prestige associated with this position feeds an aural space where cultural capital can be displayed through the tasteful choice and arrangement of difficult or obscure music, thereby confirming the show's place within the CBC's preferred refined culture mandate, and at the same time conferring on the programmers a preferential status within the local and national scene.

The second point of contact is Cargo Canada, where some members of 'derivative' worked. This is a significant contact point, as it typifies the tensions found between the social value of a shared workspace and the difficulty of establishing and maintaining the local arm of a global distribution network. Since the mid-1980s, Montreal had been the base for the one-stop distributor, Cargo Canada. Not only did Cargo serve as the distribution wing for a number of international labels, it also demonstrated a commitment to local indie labels by funding them, typically in the form of fronting the capital that would allow labels to support numerous music projects simultaneously. Cargo also employed a number of musically inclined anglophones who could not otherwise find work, given the French-language requirements of retail in Montreal. In 1998, Cargo Canada collapsed, mainly as a result of mismanagement, over-zealous promotion strategies, failed restructuring and the caprices of the global recording industry. Consequently, a number of labels in Montreal were crippled. Although other companies stepped in to fill the gap, Cargo fits into a pattern of Montreal-based distributors notable for their short and troubled life-cycle – a standard narrative trajectory: a brief flurry of concentrated activity and promise, followed by mismanagement, restructuring, decline, and disappearance – thereby contributing in a direct way to the waxing and waning vigour of Montreal's scene.

Both the CBC and Cargo Canada provided indirect support to what Lash and Urry identify as the second criterion for local success which, they suggest, depends on the context for social interaction, the ability to gather and disseminate information, make contacts and contracts. The hard infrastructure of the indie scene in Montreal, as noted above, is determined by a complex set of economic, linguistic and social factors, and as a result is often understood to be inadequate, partial or unstable. In order to function effectively, 'derivative' relied on connections, touring (with their band, Pest 5000), and licensing agreements fostered through their access to trans-regional networks, thereby orientating their activity outwards, and away from the city. At the same time, they also mobilized locally-based resources and contacts to strengthen their distribution network. As Patti suggested:

> If we transplanted the label with exactly the same contacts and with the networks we know to Winnipeg, I think we would die. You're just geographically far away and psychically too. So this is the perfect isolation – we're still so close to New York and Boston. We get bands coming up here because derivative's here and we get a nice little exchange of musics just out of the network. (Patti, 'derivative records')

The ideological affinity and geographic proximity to other (mainly American) scenes also favoured the role of 'derivative' as a cultural intermediary, reinforcing the image of Montreal as both strategically placed (its 'perfect isolation') and a place to strategize.

At a more prosaic level, Cargo Canada and CBC-Radio served as industrial and institutional contexts that allowed 'derivative' to support and expand their activity, putting them in daily contact with other musicians, record and distribution labels while allowing them to remain based in Montreal, reinforcing and strengthening the scene's soft infrastructure. The lack of distance between work and leisure doubly consecrated the ensemble's status as cultural intermediaries. Gen commented: 'We're committed to making these (label and band) activities work while having jobs we enjoy';[3] and Patti has said: 'I think it's the most brilliant privilege in the world to play the kind of music we do and talk to the people we talk to, because I don't think enough people know about it or care' (Barclay *et al.*, 2001, p. 40). The suggestion of a tighter relationship between work and leisure is indicative of a desire to appear ideologically and aesthetically consistent; cultivating a coherent lifestyle notable as much for its distinctively alternative and artful character as it is for its unity and apparent lack of contradiction. As Gen suggested:

> Hobby is somewhat derogatory, but I do think of it as a hobby. Only because I never assumed to make money from this. This may be a privileged way to think about it, but in my way of thinking about the minute you expect to make money out of dinky little rock music you're setting yourself up for major disappointment and pressure for what is a source of enjoyment, and I don't want that to be taken away.

It's not that I wouldn't ever consider doing this professionally, but my bands are not designed for that. (Gen, 'derivative records')

The final and related criterion for continued local success, according to Lash and Urry, rests on the ability to enable innovation to take place in relatively decentralized systems. A complement to this is the ability of entrepreneurs to take advantage of local amenities and the 'critical mass of knowledgeable people which enable gaps in the market to be identified' (Lash and Urry, 1994, p. 284); 'derivative' did this by using both local and non-local experts. As one node in the centreless web of the indie rock network, 'derivative' built their musical roster through intra-scene and inter-scene contacts made with music-makers who shared their aesthetic perspective. While the members of 'derivative' were not as calculating as this final criterion might otherwise suggest, their positions at Cargo Canada and the CBC allowed receptive markets and audiences to be identified easily, and put them in constant contact with other musicians, label owners and radio stations, maintaining the scene's associative structures. Gen claimed: 'We focused a lot on trying to make friends with bands in other cities, and the job (at the CBC) did help that a lot.' Combined with their urban sensibility and musical acumen, these strategies guided derivative's musical practices, shaping, and later reinforcing, the kind of habitus formed out of the very specificity of Montreal and its institutions and industries, confirming for them the singularity of the city's cultural life. Patti again:

Montreal appeals to me because it's isolated already. I like lower-expectation complex, so it's kind of like Canada reduced even more. So if you can hang on to an aesthetic sensibility against the odds it makes you even stronger. That's a really backwards and noble way to think about it, but it appeals to me on a really 'primal' level.

(Patti, 'derivative records')

The three criteria proposed by Lash and Urry highlight aspects of the scene's hard infrastructure, but elide the role the soft infrastructure plays in shaping the socio-musical experience of place. Often, the nature of a scene and its attendant sense of locality depend on two elements, as Street contends (which can be roughly correlated to hard and soft infrastructures, respectively): place-as-infrastructure and place-as-identity (1995, p. 257), Patti's earlier little pond/big pond analogy about Montreal versus Toronto, is a typical reading of Montreal, evoking an implicit political economy of the scene by linking the 'communal ambience' of the city's vibrant alternative cultural life to its diminished economic state (Maffesoli, 1996, p. 23). For Patti and others, the robustness of the scene is inversely proportional to the city's financial state. The city's weak hard infrastructure defines its anaemic identity for many music-makers and yet it also animates music-making in the city. In Montreal, the entrenched sense of anomie, where a desire to be musically active is heavily determined by the lack of industrial and/or institutional means to achieve that goal, has become a standard trope associated with music-making in the city (see Stahl, 2001). A typical response among some musicians has been to visualize other musical horizons, imagining a fuller musical life in cities where the relationship between hard and soft infrastructure might appear less asymmetrical (that is, in Toronto, or the USA). In these symbolic gestures, members of a scene articulate an affective affinity with a broader imagined community that shares a set of aesthetic ideologies, perspectives and strategies. The strategy of 'derivative' was bifocal, however. On the one hand, the orientation of musical activity at 'derivative records' demonstrated one of the many ways local resources could be mobilized to anchor music-making firmly in Montreal; and on the other, the industrial and institutional ties of 'derivative' reinforced an ability to identify and utilize the extensive networks to support the outward orientation of their label's operation. This linked them in both a material and symbolic sense to a larger network of affiliations, simultaneously confirming and complicating their commitment to Montreal and its music scene.

Conclusion

Montreal is often seen by music-makers as a city that supplies specific resource pools, a knowledge base and a suitably grey economic climate that is more than agreeable to the demands of the cultural production associated with indie rock. For the majority of music-makers in Montreal, their relationship to the city is founded on an aesthetic experience of place. In this sense, music-making in Montreal is about the relationship of aesthetic politics to the creation of an ideal urban experience and the cultivation and maintenance of a chosen lifestyle. Montreal is cast by local anglophone music-makers and represented to outsiders as a city more willing to accommodate modest musical aspirations, where careerist impulses are curbed, and where threats of artistic compromize are rendered moot. As we have seen, in terms of the political economy of the scene, for many music-makers, the success of the scene is inversely proportional to Montreal's economic status. For a number of music-makers in the city, the fraught quality of life in Montreal is transformed into an animated life of quality via the music scene. Here, instability and isolation are valorized, strengtened, and gain a positive valence, imparting to the city its continuing allure as a kind of bohemia as well as instituting a range of expectations on the part of local and non-local music-makers as to the creative possibilities offered by Montreal. That said, in order to negotiate the space of the scene properly requires having the wherewithal to utilize the amenities at hand, both material and symbolic, in an effort to realise the desire for living an artistic life in the city. It also means having the frame of mind, the kind of urban sensibility that interprets the city as a space of creative possibility, keenly attuned to its potentialities, able to identify and mobilize these resources strategically. One has to manipulate both the hard and soft infrastructures of the scene and the city in order to guarantee 'success'.

This last point perhaps allows us to fold the discussion back on subcultural theory. The anglo-music scene in Montreal appears marked less by the drama of *resistance*, less by an antagonistic relation to urban space and the others who live there, and more by an *insistence*, what Blum (2001) identifies as the scene's 'social persistence' (p. 9), a demand and desire that cultural life in the city be made meaningful in a different way. The provocation posed by the relationship of the scene to the city, versus that posed by the notion of subcultures, is one that suggests more forcefully the role played by urban infrastructures, soft and hard, in shaping important aspects of a city's cultural life. Subcultural theory tends to render the city a backdrop, rather than an active spatial trope figuring into the socio-musical experience. Scenes, on the other hand, perhaps tell us too much, and perhaps not enough, about musical life's deep-rootedness in the city. Descriptions of the socio-musical dimensions of city life, however, require precisely this paradox in order to provoke examinations of urban music-making's many presences and absences, it polyvalences, the struggle over its social and cultural value. The study of the contemporary socio-musical experience necessitates a thicker account of musical and social practice, one incorporating a mode of analysis that can better attend to the fixity and flow, the scalar relationships and the multiple dimensions that define urban music-making. Employing the notion of scenes moves the description of socio-musical experiences beyond the strict attention paid to class mechanics by widening the scope of analysis to consider the broad network of affiliations underpinning musical activity. Scene used as an analytical framework captures more fully, even in their fleetingness, the dynamic range of forces at play that affect current musical practice in the city.

Acknowledgements

I would like to thank the members of 'derivative records' for their contribution and insights into the experience of music-making in Montreal.

Notes

1 For more on this, see Chaney (1996a).
2 Personal interview with author 16/5/98. All other interviews with author are from the same interview unless noted.
3 'Pest is Best without Pipe Dream', *Toronto Sun*, 10 October 1996, p. 65.

CHAPTER 4

Dance Nations: Rethinking Youth Subcultural Theory

BEN CARRINGTON AND BRIAN WILSON

Dance music and its attendant cultures now form a central part of the leisure lifestyles of many young people. The emergence in the USA during the 1980s of 'house music', the phenomenon of large-scale 'acid house' raves in Britain during the late 1980s, and the subsequent rise of a globalized club culture have reshaped the cultural landscapes and social geographies of many metropolitan cities. For sociologists who study youth, these developments in dance music signified a shift not only in the way those subcultures were organized, but also in what subcultural participation meant for young people. What emerged was a series of studies and theoretical treatises that attempted to update existing explanations of youth cultural activity in the light of the rave/club phenomenon. The 'classical' approaches to studying subcultures espoused by those at the University of Birmingham's Centre for Contemporary Cultural Studies (CCCS) in the 1970s were revisited, and new models intended to account for the more fragmented, consumer-orientated nature of contemporary life proposed.

These recent revisions, however, also reveal some shortcomings. For example, some theorists have dismissed CCCS approaches without considering adequately what aspects of social life the earlier works continue to explain. In some cases this has meant discarding conventional analytical factors altogether and thus disregarding the potential for a more nuanced understanding of social class in contemporary youth formations and identity constructs. In the same way, issues relating to social inequality remain undertheorized in many contemporary works because of a tendency to over-emphasize a view of rave as a postmodern hyper-individualized scene (that is, a temporal and transient culture defined by, among other features, a blurring of conventional social categories). This has had the effect of playing down the *political* significance of dance cultures, particularly in relation to the reworking of racial and ethnic identities that dance music has produced during the 1990s and later.

This chapter examines these issues by analyzing contemporary perspectives on youth culture critically in the context of dance-music culture. Our central argument is that, if we want to understand one of the most important global youth formations of the 1990s then a rethinking, as opposed to a repudiation, of earlier accounts is required. This requires theoretical constructs that retain a materialist account of subcultural formation and that acknowledge the intersectionality of difference as constitutive of social identities. More specifically, we argue for the need to re-centre discussions of 'race' and ethnicity within contemporary accounts on dance-music cultures as a way to rethink the relationship between politics and music.

Dance Music and Subcultural Theory

Dance culture is a broad term that encapsulates the diffuse styles, fashions, venues and scenes associated with the various music cultures of electronic house music that have dominated European and some North American youth cultures and most major metropolitan cities since the late 1980s.[1] Initially associated with the large, illegal warehouse parties that were held in and around London, Manchester and other cities across England during the summers of 1988 and 1989, 'rave' has since transformed into a multi-million pound global phenomenon that operates alongside, within and sometimes against the global circuits of capital. Rejecting an overt and easily identifiable mode of signification, dance music and its attendant club culture is seen by many commentators to have marked a profound and seminal shift in youth cultural formation away from seemingly straightforward homological fits between social location and group stylization. As David Hesmondhalgh (1998) noted, the varied nomenclatures of dance music 'refer to a genuinely significant cultural moment, a coming together of new ways of thinking about and using dance, drugs and music technology, which has had important implications for the politics of music-related youth cultures' (p. 247).

For many commentators, rave culture during the late 1980s signalled the demise of the 'oppositional' youth styles of the 1960s and 1970s. Steve Redhead was an early theorist who saw within rave culture the clearest manifestation of the key motifs of postmodern style and culture – pastiche, bricolage, depthlessness, and the promotion of hyper-individualism within a drug-induced Dionysian culture of strobe lights, oxygen smoke and a thumping bass. Redhead's (1990) reading of rave culture as an example of what he termed 'post-subcultural pop' has been influential not only for how dance music in general has subsequently been read, but also for subcultural theory more generally. Redhead argued that Gramscian accounts of subcultural struggle were redundant in a context within which pleasure had displaced politics and where the notion of counter-cultures was 'more resonant of shopping and consumption rather than resistance and deviance' (Redhead, 1990, p. 2).

Work that followed in the 1990s was emphatically post-CCCS in challenging accounts of young people active in the construction of bounded subcultural spaces in contradiction to the market. Sarah Thornton (1995), in her much quoted work on dance music and club cultures, proclaims her text as 'post-Birmingham' (p. 8), arguing that the CCCS's work is no longer relevant, because the static and bounded notion of 'subculture' is 'theoretically unworkable' (ibid.). Other 'post-subculturalists' such as David Muggleton (2000) have argued for neo-Weberian accounts that stress status rather than class, and like Miles (2000), focus on lifestyle patterns over class subcultures within which *consumption* is seen as the key dynamic in the formation of individualized identities. In short, much of the new work operates on the assumption that postmodern societies have broken down binary distinctions such as 'the dominant' and 'the subordinate', rendering the whole notion of *sub*cultures redundant (Muggleton, 2000, p. 48).

It is not surprising, then, that for many post-CCCS theorists the key youth formation that demonstrates the dissolution of class-based resistant forms, and that is most emblematic of these shifts towards subcultural fragmentation, is rave culture. Important in this context is the work of Sarah Thornton (1994, 1995), who is best-known for her adaptation of Pierre Bourdieu's 'cultural capital' concept as a means of theorizing the 'taste-related' subcultural hierarchiz/relationships that exist within the rave scene, and for her critique of Stanley Cohen's moral panic concept to describe relationships between rave and media. Thornton's work on 'subcultural capital' is important because it reminds theorists of youth of the need to remain attentive to the intricacies of micro-level interactions that underlie subcultural group life (that is, attentive to the ways that 'insider' and 'outsider' subgroups are demarcated by youth themselves). That said, the extent to which the concept is a genuine *theoretical* advance is questionable, especially considering that Howard Becker's (1957) early ethnographic work on jazz musicians included succinct descriptions of hierarchies of 'hip' and 'cool' – work that Thornton acknowledged and drew on in her book. However, since the CCCS did not pick up on Becker's hierarchy as much as they did on his ethnographic approach and his substantive understandings of drug users (see Pearson and Twohig, 1976), Thornton's reinvigoration of this aspect of Becker's work remains noteworthy.

However, the concept of subcultural capital is misleading when understood as a derivative of Bourdieu's notions of cultural capital and taste, because

Bourdieu's (1984) depiction of taste was interwoven with a view of (French) society that was structured by social *class-based* difference, refracted through socio-economic status. Yet, in Thornton's *Club Cultures* (1995), class has little to do with the taste cultures she studied, and the role of education in (re)producing social hierarchies within the social field is similarly ignored. As Thornton argued: 'Although it converts into economic capital, subcultural capital is not as class-bound as cultural capital. This is not to say that class is irrelevant, simply that it does not correlate in any one-to-one way with levels of subcultural capital' (pp. 12–13). If class is 'barely relevant' for Thornton, then the subcultural capital concept is little more than a descriptive term (that is, a slight revision of Becker).

Thornton's contributions to our understandings of the relationships between media and subcultures are far more pertinent and original than her subcultural capital concept (see also McRobbie and Thornton, 1995). That is to say, while Thornton recognized effectively the still-relevant notions of 'moral panics' and 'incorporation' that the CCCS and others used to explain how the mainstream neutralizes subcultures in order to recuperate and repair the 'fractured order' (Hebdige, 1979, p. 94), she also describes how the mass media both 'confirms the transgression' of subcultures (that is, enhancing the deviant status that some youth desire) and, most perceptively, how subcultures' interests 'are also defended by their own niche and micro-media' (McRobbie and Thornton, 1995, p. 559). This emphasis on alternative media and subcultures is not only a necessary update to traditional work, but also a pivotal precursor to emerging work on the relationships between subcultures and Internet media (Wilson, 2002a).

Unlike Thornton's analysis of rave culture that emphasized subcultural capital and mass media, Maria Pini (1997), following the early critiques of the CCCS made by McRobbie, provides a theoretical and empirical examination of rave that is an important contribution to a CCCS-derived body of work that seldom engaged issues of gender. Pini offers a feminist analysis of the early rave scene, describing an 'erosion of sexual difference' among sub-culture members, characterized by unisex 'dress to sweat/dance' clothing and a (drug-induced) feeling of euphoria that magnified an already-existing attitude of respect and good feelings. At the same time, Pini acknowledged that rave promoters and DJs were almost exclusively male, reflecting a still-gendered power structure 'behind the party'. In *Clubcultures and Female Subjectivity*, Pini critiques Thornton's work in particular because the exclu-sion of females in her analysis was not explored beyond a discussion of event organization and music production. Pini argues that Thornton's 'failure to go *beyond* the levels of production and organization, to say *more* about other levels of event participation and other experiential sites, amounts to a failure to address the significance of club cultural involvement for the hundreds of thousands of women who participate regularly in dance cultures, and who claim that such participation is central to their lives, their friendships and their identities' (Pini, 2001, p. 7).

Pini responds directly to those who might view her work as a 'simple cele-bration of femininity', arguing that contemporary club cultures are places where 'important questions about femininity are being asked' and 'statements are being made about new femininities' (2001, p. 15). She goes on to suggest that the traditional images and connotations of femininity, linked to notions of 'home', motherhood and submissiveness, are dislocated within club culture:

> As a landscape, femininity is rearranged ... [Within club culture] lie adventure and the possibilities for experiences of the self, which are new, exhilarating and some-times frightening. And within it lie the opportunities for challenges to the confines of normative heterosexual femininity, the potential for the playing out of what are arguably more 'auto-erotic' and fluid pleasures and senses of self. (2001, pp. 15–16)

Although it could be argued that Pini *is* celebrating temporarily empowering rave-related experiences, her work moves well beyond relatively simplistic depictions of the 'invisible female' that underlay early CCCS work (and indeed much recent work on dance cultures) and reveals the complex ways in which rave culture has reconfigured new modes of feminine and masculine perfor-mativity. That is to say, and as Pini (1997) pointedly suggests, the open displays of pleasure, friendliness and enjoyment derived from and associated with rave (dance) that traditionally are linked with femininity and gay male culture, 'can be read as a challenge to heterosexual masculinity's traditional centrality' (p. 155). At the same time, Pini (2001) responds to and critiques less grounded postmodern interpretations that over-emphasize the extent to which sex/race/class-bound identities tend to 'disappear' within the liminal spaces of the rave (pp. 6–7) by suggesting instead that these identities remain intact although they are reworked within these spaces.

Andy Bennett's (2000, 2001) work on urban dance music follows Thornton's in its concern with taste, and to an extent Pini's in its engagement with gender issues. Bennett's work is important because it is based on detailed ethno-graphic study across a range of music cultures and is informed by a systematic engagement with social theory. A number of themes emerge from this work. First, Bennett's (2000) view of localization and popular music, which works from the premise that local music scenes are contested territories that are 'crossed by different forms of collective life and the competing sensibilities that the latter bring to bear on the interpretation and social realization of a particular place' (p. 53), is an innovative move beyond the more ethnocentric view of 'the local' proposed by those at the CCCS. More pertinently, by marrying a concern with globalization processes to a methodological approach that privileged participant observation and other qualitative approaches, Bennett has undertaken a 'global ethnography' in the same spirit as the works conducted by Michael Buraway and others at the University of Berkeley in recent years (Buraway *et al.*, 2000). This is an important advancement in youth subcultural studies, although the theory itself, which advocates sensitivity to (the range of) local interpretations of broader cultural forces – be they global in origin or otherwise – is akin to perspectives that have long been engaged in audience studies (Morley, 1980; Jhally and Lewis, 1992), and more recently in work on rave culture in Canada (Wilson, 2002b). In other important ways, though, Bennett's research is a natural complement to the work of Lipsitz and others, who describe how global flows of culture resulting from immigration and accelerated by (new) technologies have led to the existence of 'complicated and complex new cultural fusions with profound political implications' (Lipsitz, 1994, p. 13).

Bennett's other key argument is for theorising urban dance-music cultures as 'neo-tribal' formations (drawing on Maffesoli's *tribus* concept) as a way to describe the shifting and *fluid* nature of collective associations between young people and the associated tendencies of youth to move between different sites of consumption (that is, to associate more with a mix of cultural spaces and less with stable class/race/gender-defined groups). This is a notable update to classical subcultural analyses, because it recognizes an (apparent) shift from the more class-based analyses of the CCCS, where subcultural participation was viewed, at least in part, as a working-class response to feelings of alienation and marginalization. This view of the neo-tribe (akin to Straw's (1991) description of dance-music 'scenes') suggests that the urban dance music scene is 'increasingly a matter of individual choice, the type of music heard and the setting in which it is heard and danced to being very much the decision of the individual consumer' (Bennett, 1999a, p. 611). However, one of the key omissions from such accounts is any extended discussion of social class and its relevance in framing the taste cultures that consumption allows. In other words, it is necessary to acknowledge the fact that 'consumer choice is highly constructed' (Tomlinson, 1990, p. 13). Not everybody is 'free to choose' their neo-tribal identities in the same way, and those very 'choices' are often determined in a complex way by forms of social capital in the first instance, which in turn reveal patterns that can be traced back to broader (structurally conditioned) identities. Despite this under-theorization of class dynamics, the strength of this work lies in the ethnographic explication of how identities are formed and re-made within particular music cultures. Dance culture for these authors has therefore allowed new insights into the ways in which subcultural identity is, via the media, produced and marked, how new forms of femininity are created and lived, and how the very nature of subcultural affiliation and identification has shifted.

Racing the Argument

Despite some of the strengths noted above, what is of the most concern about many contemporary accounts of subcultural theory is the surprising lack of attention paid to issues relating to racial formation, ethnic identity construction, and the articulation of racism within and between 'subcultures'. While acknowledging that the CCCS work was 'late' in fully exploring the importance of 'race' and racism to the study of cultural politics (Carrington, 2001), the work of Dick Hebdige (1979) and Iain Chambers (1985), the publication of *The Empire Strikes Back* in the early 1980s, the work during the 1980s of writers such as Paul Gilroy (2002), Simon Jones (1988) and, latterly, Les Back (1996), clearly demonstrates that it is no longer tenable to continue to produce studies that either ignore the structuring effects of racism or that fail to show how 'race' acts as a modality for the expression of gendered and classed identities. In America, authors such as Tricia Rose (1994), William Perkins (1996) and George Lipsitz (1994) have produced similar arguments. Despite the work that has been done, surprisingly few studies exist that describe or map the racial fragmentation of club cultures during the 1990s, or trace how 'white' dance-music cultures have relied on traditions of black subaltern musical organization. It is worth repeating that the use of pirate radio stations, the networks of independent music production and distribution, the centrality of 'the DJ', the antiphonic nature of the rave experience, and even the term 'rave' itself derive from pre-existing forms of cultural communication that have formed a central part of black vernacular music cultures in Britain since at least the 1950s.

We are arguing here not just that an important 'variable' has been missed out, but also that the very nature of cultural formation cannot be understood within racialized societies such as Britain, America and Canada *without* an account of how the processes of racialization mediate taste cultures, give value to certain styles above others, and how these are often used to maintain, and occasionally challenge, social hierarchies. Some post-CCCS theorists do seem aware of these issues, but do not fully engage them. Thornton (1995), for example, acknowledges that subcultural identities 'are often inflected by issues of nation, race and ethnicity' (p. 30). Yet her observation that the subcultural ideologies she investigates 'are those of predominantly straight and white club and rave cultures' (ibid.) is a weak attempt to unpack the ways that 'compulsory heterosexuality' and the normative assumptions of whiteness have been articulated within dance cultures. In a similar way, Pini (1997), in her account of the gendered nature of dance culture, seems oblivious to the fact that her subjects are, for the most part, articulating particular forms of *white* femininity.

Even today, rave and club culture remains absent from most 'race' and ethnicity-related analyses and, in the same way, studies of dance culture in general seldom engage with issues of 'race' and ethnic identity construction in any meaningful way.[2] This is no doubt a result in part of the wider neglect of discussions concerning black musicians' contribution to British music, and, more generally, black music's relationship to British national identity (Bakari, 1999; Hall, 2002). As Hesmondhalgh (1998) notes, such narrations of the history of house fail to theorize fully the nature of racial construction within these spaces. Such histories often acknowledge dance music's debts to black and gay musical sounds from the USA:

> but by treating them merely as 'roots', relegates these sources to the status of hallowed but primitive predecessors (Frankie Knuckles as Muddy Waters), and uses them to validate the alternative status of the ensuing British subculture. These originators disappear from the story as soon as ecstasy hits Ibiza. We are left with little sense of what happens to these post-disco black music traditions after 1988. (p. 249)

Simon Reynolds' (1998) interrogation of the history of rave and ecstasy culture in *Generation Ecstasy: Into the World of Techno and Rave Culture* is unique in this context for addressing issues to do with 'race' and the formation of new black identities, while interweaving the related histories of 'techno' music in Britain and America up to the late 1990s. His description of the state of jungle and of intra-cultural discord and (sub)cultural development is evidence of this:

> jungle's mainstream breakthrough in Britain and critical recognition in America... saw jungle torn every which way in conflict between two rival modes of blackness: elegant urbanity (the opulence and finesse of fusion/garage/funk-jazz/quiet storm) and ruffneck tribalism (the raw, percussive minimalism of dub/raga/hip-hop/electro). Lurking beneath this smooth/ruff dialectic was a covert class struggle: upwardly mobile gentrification versus ghettocentricity, crossover versus undergroundism. (p. 347)

Reynolds' analysis notwithstanding, the still widespread disavowal of 'race' in studies of electronic music, rave and club cultures means that important work that explores, for example, how music cultures can offer new modes and spaces for forms of black femininity to be expressed and reworked within music cultures such as raregroove (Bakare-Yusuf, 1997) and ragga (Noble, 2000), is simply ignored in much of the dance-music literature. This is a serious neglect, as we would argue that in important ways dance culture has contested both the dominant narratives of Britishness (Hesmondhalgh, 2001) and the political forms of ethnic absolutist politics (Gilroy, 1993) that flow from this position.[3] Thus, while Blur, Oasis and the rest of the Britpop collective have entered into the pantheon of pivotal cultural intermediaries in reshaping notions of late-twentieth-century New Britannia (see Bennett, 1997a), black dance-music pioneers such as Fabio and Grooverider are simply left off the cultural compass altogether. Dance music, particularly in its garage/drum and bass/broken beat variants, has produced effective forms of everyday anti-racism that make the populist appeals of the far right both redundant and anachronistic. These seemingly innocuous encounters, particularly for white working-class youth, have been important in developing a 'new ethnicity that contains a high degree of egalitarianism and anti-racism' (Back, 1996, p. 123; 2002). As Paul Gilroy (2002) notes, it is within the 'convivial metropolitan cultures' that Britain's young have provided the main 'bulwark against the machinations of racial politics' (p. xxix), thus rendering any 'strong commitment to racial difference absurd to the point of unthinkability' (ibid.).

Just as we must avoid any utopian notions of inter-racial love across the turntables, it is important to note that the embrace of 'difference' and 'marginality' has itself now become a key marketing motif for multicultural corporate capital (Sharma *et al.*, 1996, p. 1). It could be argued that since the 1990s Asian dance music in particular has disrupted the formal patterns of cultural politics within which Britain's story of racial progress has been refracted through a black/white binary. The embrace of Asian culture – ranging from the comedic success of the BBC's 'Goodness Gracious Me' and 'The Kumars at Number 42,' to the lauding of artists such as Hanif Kureishi and Anish Kapoor, through to the prominence of performers such as Talvin Singh and the Asian dance 'underground' more generally – has been read as a sign of Britain's multicultural maturation. However, as Koushik Banerjea (2000) points out:

> cross-cultural musical flows...do not of themselves hijack the power structures of corporate hegemony; or the mobile terrors of white supremacy. Eulogizing Talvin Singh on a Sunday afternoon at his club in Brick Lane does little to hide white distaste for the large Asian community which actually lives there...Similarly, showering the Asian Dub Foundation with praise across Europe has not meant a decrease in the vilification of and violence against people of colour, 'guest workers' or immigrants struggling to establish themselves in that continent. (p. 65)

There is a truth, of course, in Banerjea's, and similar critics', arguments concerning the neo-orientalist construction of the cool Asian other – Asians as the new blacks. However, such critiques come close to substituting one totalizing discourse – that of music as a pure modality for racial harmony – with its opposite – music as a form of false racial consciousness. Those who dismiss the politics of popular music too readily miss out on the nuanced ways in which racialized and gendered identities have been reformed in these increasingly globalized urban cultural spaces in performing important 'identity work' concerning the collective identities we inhabit. In other words, the forms of 'white distaste' that are not disrupted need to be set alongside the construction of new forms of sensibility from which the claims of the British National Party (BNP) in Britain or Le Pen in France *can* be contested, precisely because such music cultures have helped to form emotive, if fragile, points of cosmopolitan identification. Popular culture, and music culture in particular, has never offered ready-made identikit formulas for oppositional praxis. Rather, it is the potential that dance cultures produce for an alternative public sphere within which new spaces of belonging can be found that is most significant. The inter- and intra-cultural dialogues set in train by dance music mean that appeals to forms of absolutist politics become increasingly less socially tenable. Again, Gilroy (2002) summarizes the contradictory nature of these issues usefully when he notes that it is 'electronic dance music' rather than rap or punk that has been the most important musical form over the past few years in mapping these changes. Dance music's

> technological base and subterranean metropolitan conditions of existence have promoted the same unremarkable, ordinary hybridity which has been alloyed with recreational drug use on an extraordinary scale. If racism is still enacted in these conditions it is largely devoid of any strong belief in integral races. With their turn inwards and their determined pursuit of ecstatic bodily pleasure, the resulting 'sub-cultures' have lost nearly all of their old political flavours. They have also been partially annexed by corporate power and exported around the globe without anyone associated with either politics or government being able to appreciate their worth as political and economic assets. (p. xxix)

Part of the reason why the political significance of dance music has been lost on many post-CCCS writers is their reliance on a narrow account of the post-modern. Within this framework, politics, if it remains at all, is shorn of its emanicpatory potential and reduced to the properties of predictable actors – understood either as expressions of consumer lifestyle choice or as the reshaping and modification of the body. These are undoubtedly important aspects of the contemporary *zeitgeist*, but they do not exhaust the novel ways in which particular subaltern groups continue to (re)negotiate the conditions of post-modernity to other ends. The reworking and recovery of styles and the eclecticism of source material that dance music has produced, particularly through the complex dialogic rituals of MC-inflected styles of garage and drum and bass, should be read more accurately as operating within a longer tradition of black musical styles that narrate self-consciously a diasporic history of black struggles for freedom. Paul Gilroy has shown how the use of samples, new versions and extended mixes of classic reggae sounds is a political process of call and response that does not 'amount to either parody or pastiche' (Gilroy, 1993, p.37). Gilroy extends his critique of the easy embrace of 'the postmodern' when he states:

> It is interesting to note that, at the very moment when celebrated Euro-American cultural theorists have pronounced the collapse of 'grand narratives', the expressive culture of Britain's black poor is dominated by the need to construct them as narratives of redemption and emancipation...all the constitutive features of the post-modern...the new depthlessness, the weakening of historicity, the waning of affect – are not merely absent from black expressive cultures but are explicitly contradicted by their repertoire of complete 'hermeneutic gestures'. These cultural forms use the new technological means at their disposal not to flee from depth but to revel in it, not to abjure public history but to proclaim it. (1993, p. 42)

Our point, then, is not that the postmodern is not an important and even constitutive part of dance cultures. But rather the failure to theorise processes of racialization and to account for the diversity of those black and Asian dance-music forms that operate outside the more commercialized aspects of club culture dominated by the likes of the Ministry of Sound and guest spots on BBC Radio One means that a de-racialized account of dance music's apolitical significance is produced, within which social distinctions, let alone divisions, disappear. Part of the problem is that most of the studies to date have focused on a particular form of dance music, located within a specific locale, at a certain moment in time. Yet the desire to produce a meta-narration of 'dance cultures' in general means that the complexity of a forever moving and fragmented scene is underplayed. As Caspar Melville (2000) reminds us, the 'meanings' of these scenes are markedly different, as the

> politics of buying your way into the 'dancefloor community' at one of the globally branded and meticulously policed 'superclubs' is significantly different than that of illegal raves in Northern Ireland or Sarajevo where 'dancefloor communitarianism' takes on a more convincing tone in the light of fierce religious or ethnic antagonisms that may be overcome, however briefly, on the dancefloor. (p. 41)

Conclusion

It is worth noting that 'the CCCS's work' was never as unified or as coherent as some have claimed it to be – it was always a body of work as much concerned with arguing theoretical difference with itself as it was against certain sociological orthodoxies. We should also remember that the work of the CCCS was produced in the context of, and in relation to, a specific set of political questions concerning the role of culture within late capitalist societies, and thus owed more to an engaged form of intellectual intervention than it did to the project of producing universal sociological truths. As Hebdige (1988) himself noted, theoretical insights and models 'are as tied to their own times as the human bodies that produce them. The idea of subculture-as-negation grew up alongside punk, remained inextricably linked to it and died when it died' (p. 8). It is a point not always fully acknowledged by those claiming the new territory of subcultural analysis, that many of the developments and refinements of class-based models of subcultural formation have come from, albeit ageing, former members of the CCCS itself. 'There is certainly no longer a case to be made,' noted McRobbie (1994),

> for the traditional argument that youth culture is produced somehow in conditions of working-class purity, and that such expressions are authentic and in the first instance at least uncontaminated by an avaricious commercial culture. That argument has long since been replaced by a more complex understanding of the dynamics between subculture, the mass media, commercial culture and the state. (p. 179)

We suggest that arguments within subcultural theory over whether or not the term 'subculture' should be used at all have become increasingly unproductive. The requirement to be seen to have gone beyond 'subculture' by the invocation of new terms sometimes takes place at the expense of such concepts offering genuinely new analytic insight. Rather, the reason for the continuance and necessity to think through the insights of all such work (be it neo-, post-, or even anti-CCCS) is that the central analytical questions remain the same. How can we account for group formations balancing the specificity of the moment against the historical conditions that structure the social field? To what extent do the meanings generated shape identities that can be seen in opposition to both the dominant culture(s) – however defined – and the internal hierarchies of the groups themselves? And what, if anything, does this tell us about the nature of social inequality and cultural change at this specific historical conjuncture? The move towards the use of concepts such as 'lifestyle' to describe the more diffuse aspects of sociality that young people inhabit, and the deployment of ethnography, does not, in itself, solve the complex methodological and theoretical dilemmas that researchers face. Put straightforwardly, invoking the concept of the postmodern does not end theoretical discussion, and simply using ethnography does not resolve the epistemological dilemmas involved regarding the ontology of 'subcultures'. As Hollands (2002) points out, 'the same question that often plagued earlier theorists of youth sub-cultures remains: are post-modern examples any more representative or empirically demonstrable among the young than minority sub-cultures were? Post-modernists do not appear to find inequalities or stratified youth cultures partly because they are not looking for them' (p. 158). While Hollands over-states his case somewhat, the necessity to understand the nature of subcultural formation remains an important sociological task that is weakened if structuralist accounts are negated entirely.

The important work on dance cultures discussed earlier highlights some of these weaknesses. For example, Sarah Thornton's (1995, p. 162) conclusion that 'subcultures are best defined as social groups that have been labelled as such' is no more than a sociological truism that in fact tells us very little about why subcultures emerge when they do, and what politics might derive from them. The danger is that, in moving too far from the over-determined struc-turalist interpretations – be they of a semiotic or Marxist kind – we simply end up with a symbolic interactionist version of labelling theory that is void of sensitivity to social and historical context. On this basis, we suggest that it is crucial to conceptualize the social field more widely in terms of the articulation of competing social identities where relations of ethnicity, sex, class, gender and so on are played out – and to emphasize how it is possible to see how different types of being in the world can be expressed in and through youth cultures that we may want to label as 'resistant'. Not in any simple sense of class politics – although we argue this will always be a part of any social field's construction – but in a more general way in which youth cultures signal a 'staking out of an investment in society' (McRobbie, 1993, p. 407). As Hutnyk and Sharma (2000) note, 'it does not follow that (musical) youth cultures possess an indeterminate politics, or a politics of only taste and dis-tinction as implied by some of the post-subcultures work' (p. 57).

The problem with much of the existing literature on dance music is there-fore twofold. First, despite the embrace of ethnography and the attempt to move beyond earlier myopic class-centred accounts, discussions of 'race' remain remarkable in these accounts only by their absence. There is still a paucity of sociologically informed accounts that have mapped the racial signification of dance music cultures. Second, this shift towards understanding the subjective meanings of actors has had the effect of allowing researchers simply to ignore questions of social stratification and political economy. We still have too few studies that have traced the extent to which the production of dance cultures operate outside, alongside or in contradiction to the formal economic routes of the music industry.[4]

We maintain that dance cultures *are not* just about individual lifestyle choices made by autonomous consumers. While the notion of a clear and direct homological fit between style and social location is clearly much weaker than the early CCCS accounts claimed, contemporary dance cultures do exhibit patterns of class and racial differentiation that necessitate some form of materialist understanding. In this sense, a key goal for contemporary subcultural theory is to remain attentive to the economic determinates of popular culture without reducing all formations to an economic reductionism, while at the same time remaining reflexive about how we make sense of changing cultural forms which, in the last instance, will always be one step ahead of our theorizing of them.

Acknowledgements

Both authors would like to thank the editors of this collection and Caspar Melville for valuable feedback on an earlier draft of this chapter.

Notes

1 Dance music, broadly defined as those forms of music that de-emphasize vocal content and privilege music's relationship to bodily movement, has a genealogy that far exceeds the scope of this chapter. We are concerned here with those music cultures associated with house music's emergence since the early to mid-1980s. For a useful overview of dance music, see Straw (2001b).

2 Journalistic exceptions are Collin's (1997) history, which traces the black, Hispanic and gay roots of the house music scene, and the race-related tensions that similarly inspired the Detroit techno innovations. See also Reynolds (1998), who identifies the influence of American hip-hop and rap on the UK developments of jungle and trip-hop music scenes, and similarly demonstrates the need to consider race, locality and history. Noys (1995) provides a useful summary of drum and bass/jungle's musical aesthetic.

3 Straw (2001b, p. 142) suggests that whereas British club cultures have operated through a creative cultural translation between various racialized music scenes that have redefined multicultural Britain, the relative 'underdevelopment' of a dance club culture in the USA, and to a degree in Canada too, is linked to North America's continued musical segregation of audiences in terms of 'race'.

4 For an analysis of dance music production and distribution, see Smith and Maughan (1998). See also Rowe (1995) and Negus (1998) for analyses of the popular music industry.

CHAPTER 5

Tourists and Travellers? 'Subcultures', Reflexive Identities and Neo-Tribal Sociality

PAUL SWEETMAN[1]

The aim of this chapter is to address some of the ways in which contemporary social theory can allow us to approach 'post-subcultural' practices and formations, given both extensive criticism of the 'classic' work on subcultures associated with the Birmingham Centre for Contemporary Cultural Studies, and the widely accepted idea that such groups have become increasingly heterogeneous and fluid in terms of issues such as membership and style. Even if the unity and internal cohesion of post-war subcultures was exaggerated in CCCS accounts (Clarke, 1981; Bennett, 1999a; Muggleton, 2000), it is still widely agreed that things have become more fragmented, and that 'subcultural' groups and styles – to the extent that these terms are still applicable – no longer exhibit the same degree of internal cohesion and commitment that was once the case (Gottschalk, 1993; Muggleton, 2000).

This chapter proposes that one way to approach such developments is via accounts of reflexive modernization, which – though not specifically aimed at explaining 'subcultural' practices and formations – suggest that consumption and related practices have become more individualized and are dedicated increasingly towards constructing an individual sense of identity. While such work may go some way towards explaining the increasing fragmentation and heterogeneity of 'subcultural' styles, however, like the earlier accounts of subcultures associated with the CCCS (Sweetman, 2001a), it can also be said to overlook the more affectual or experiential aspects of 'subcultural' involvement, including the way in which coming together as a group – however temporary and fragmented the group is – can provide individuals with a sense of belonging and identification *as well as* a sense of individual identity or style.

In the second part of the chapter I outline briefly a potential approach to this particular aspect of 'subcultural' involvement, focusing particularly on Michel Maffesoli's (1988, 1991, 1996) notion of neo-tribal sociality. The chapter then continues by noting that, despite apparent differences between the 'reflexive modernization thesis' (Hetherington, 1998b, p. 47) and Maffesoli's analysis of contemporary sociality, such approaches can be brought together in terms of the elective nature of contemporary patterns of identity *and* identification, and suggesting that while each approach on its own can provide us with only a partial account of the phenomena in question, combining the two may allow us to present a fuller picture of contemporary 'subcultural' formations. I also suggest that we can usefully divide contemporary 'subculturalists' into two distinct metaphorical 'types' – *travellers* and *tourists* – where the former adopt a modernist orientation towards 'subcultural' style, and the latter are happy to play around with the multiple options open to them in what some have referred to as the 'supermarket of style' (Polhemus, 1995, 1997). The chapter draws throughout on my own research on contemporary body modification (Sweetman, 1999a, 1999b, 1999c), as well as on illustrations taken from recent studies of 'club culture' and other relevant publications.

Before going on to discuss accounts of reflexive identity, it is worth noting that there is an inevitable difficulty in discussions of this sort over the appropriate use of terminology. As has already been indicated, the argument presented here supports the wider contention, as represented elsewhere in this volume and within the wider literature, that the concept of subculture is increasingly problematic, not least because of the increasing heterogeneity and fragmentation already identified. Despite its support for this position, however, the term subculture is retained throughout the chapter – albeit in inverted commas when referring to contemporary practices and formations – in part for convenience and ease of expression, but also because an adequate and widely accepted replacement has yet to be clearly established. The term – if not the concept to which it is attached – also retains some utility in pointing to particular sorts of groups, styles, practices or forms of behaviour that are recognizably 'subcultural' in at least *some* sense of the term, even if they also differ substantially from previous subcultural formations, or do not display the full range of characteristics identified by CCCS writers as being central to what the concept of subculture implies.

Reflexivity and Identity

According to writers such as Anthony Giddens (1991, 1994) and Ulrich Beck (1992, 1994), identity has become increasingly reflexive and is now actively constructed through privatised patterns of consumption. In pre-modern social contexts, identity was taken as given, and even in simple or organized modernity identity was relatively stable – a fairly unambiguous reflection of factors such as occupation or familial status. In late, high or *reflexive* modernity, however, identity is increasingly ambiguous, and has to be worked at individually in the context of more-or-less freely chosen possibilities.

Accounts differ, but the essential argument is that in simple or organized-modernity, identities were 'comparatively stable', because they were 'firmly bound into coherent and integrative social practices' (Wagner, 1994, p. 170). Thus, as Wagner observes:

> You were German and a white-collar employee, or English and a worker, but whatever you were it was not by your own choice. Ambivalences had been eliminated by comprehensive classificatory orders and the enforcing of these orders in practice. (ibid., p. 159)

In this sense, simple or organized modernity was 'only partly modern' (Lash, 1993, p. 5) because identity remained largely ascriptive – one's 'place' may have been less fixed than in pre-modern social contexts, but one still knew who one was according to the position one occupied in familial, occupational or nationalistic terms.

With the continued 'decline of traditional ties' (Warde, 1994, p. 881), however, and the rise of individualized patterns of consumption, identity has increasingly become a matter of choice. 'De-traditionalization' means that 'the monitoring by the other of traditional conventions' has been 'replaced by the necessary self-monitoring, or reflexivity' of late modernity (Lash, 1993, p. 5) and individuals must now choose their identities from the range of possibilities on offer. Self-identity has become 'a reflexively organized endeavour' (Giddens, 1991, p. 5) and 'individuals must [now] produce, stage and cobble together their biographies themselves' (Beck, 1994, p. 13).

'The break-up of organized modernity' has thus involved a 'shift from socialized to privatized modes of consumption', which in turn offers 'greater choice in consumer practices and greater diversity and variability in defining and creating one's social identity' (Wagner, 1994, p. 165). This also involves an element of risk: because individuals are 'deemed to have chosen their self-images ... they can [now] be held to account for the end-result' (Warde, 1994, p. 883). At the same time, however, consumer practices offer the potential for some form of security in this respect. For Giddens (1991) at least, the adoption of a chosen lifestyle can 'give material form to a particular narrative of self-identity' (p. 81), and thus stabilize one's chosen narrative through the confirmation of 'self-image' (Warde, 1994, p. 882).

While associated with writers who stress the continuities between simple or organized modernity and what is variously termed late, high or reflexive modernity, this analysis shares considerable affinities with work on identity in *post* modernity. While certain theorists of post rather than late, high or reflexive modernity have adopted a rather pessimistic tone, however – questioning the possibility of stable or ontologically secure identities forged through consumption (Angus, 1989) – and others have been more ambivalent (Kellner, 1992), certain postmodern theorists have been more optimistic, stressing the playful and creative freedoms that such a situation might be said to afford (see, for example, McRobbie, 1994).

Aside from differences in terminology, then, perhaps the key difference between proponents of the 'reflexive-modernization thesis' and their postmodern counterparts lies in their respective interpretations of the consequences and effects of the flexibility and ambiguity that both identify. For the latter group, this may be seen as cause for celebration, and the implication is that at least some individuals revel in the creative and/or resistant opportunities afforded by the new-found freedoms on offer. While proponents of reflexive modernization also emphasize the choices and potential freedoms available to contemporary individuals, however, these are also seen to entail new risks and responsibilities. The implication here is that consumer practices are less geared towards creative play, and more towards an attempt to ground one's identity in a coherent lifestyle that accords with the reflexive narrative one has chosen to adopt.

Accounts of reflexive identity have been criticized – with Alan Warde, for example, questioning the extent to which individuals really are free to choose, and suggesting that an over-emphasis on individual choice 'ignores the sense in which consumption exhibits a not inconsiderable degree of *social* discipline' (Warde, 1994, p. 896, emphasis in original). A further, related, difficulty is that such approaches tend to overlook the way in which lifestyle choices may be guided not so much by reflexivity as by *habitus* – the deeply embedded (or *embodied*) set of pre-dispositions which, according to Pierre Bourdieu, 'governs all forms of incorporation, choosing and modifying everything that the body ingests...digests and assimilates, physiologically and psychologically' (Bourdieu, 1984, p. 190). It may be that certain forms of contemporary habitus themselves encourage a reflexive orientation towards consumption and related practices (Sweetman, 2001b). At the same time, however, it can still be argued that, in their failure 'to consider fully the recalcitrance of embodied existence' (McNay, 1999, p. 97), 'theories of reflexive identity transformation' overstress their case, and that self-identity may be 'less amenable to emancipatory processes of refashioning' (ibid, p. 95) than such approaches suggest.

Such difficulties notwithstanding, accounts of reflexive modernization and postmodern identity share considerable affinities with the idea that both contemporary fashion and 'subcultural' style have become increasingly heterogeneous, fragmented and diffuse, with mainstream fashion, for example, no longer referring unambiguously to standard sociological variables such as gender, ethnicity and class. Contemporary fashion is regarded by many as an eclectic and self-referential system, which quotes freely from multiple sources, transforming the phenomena thus appropriated into more-or-less meaningless cultural ephemera: 'floating signifiers' that refer to nothing but themselves (Falk, 1995, p. 103). As Efrat Tseëlon points out, for writers such as Jean Baudrillard, postmodern fashion can be characterized as 'a carnival of signs with no meanings attached' (Tseëlon, 1995, p. 124); an eclectic mish-mash of once potent styles and devices appropriated from a variety of sources in a vain attempt to lend authenticity to what is no longer imbued with meaning. Postmodern fashion no longer refers to anything but itself, and this lack of external referentiality means that everything is available: we can all wear what we want, with the proviso that what we wear is no longer indexical of anything other than our participation in the fashion system. Even among those who reject the more extreme position occupied by writers such as Jean Baudrillard, it is generally accepted that contemporary fashion can be described, as 'a field of stylistic and discursive heterogeneity without a norm' (Frederic Jameson, in Wilson, 1990, p. 223), that we have witnessed 'a blurring between mainstream and counter-cultural fashions', and that 'all fashion has become "stagey", self-conscious about its own status as discourse' (Wilson, 1990, p. 222).

This clearly problematizes the notion of subcultural style: if everything is 'quotable' and more or less divested of meaning, if there is no dominant dress code or hegemonic standard by which one's sartorial conduct might be judged, then arguably it makes little sense to speak of subcultural or counter-cultural styles of dress (Wilson, 1990). In this context it may be that certain 'subcultural' groups now practise alternative strategies, 'such as the tactic of making themselves invisible ... through the ordinariness of their bland and baggy' clothes (Evans, 1997, p. 170). To the extent that a valid distinction *can* still be made, however, 'subcultural' styles are also argued to have become increasingly fragmented and diffuse, with contemporary 'subculturalists' displaying less commitment to particular styles, and themselves quoting ironically from a plurality of sources, while freely exchanging one look for another in the 'supermarket of style' (Polhemus, 1995, 1997). As David Muggleton points out, such *stylistic* promiscuity is also argued to reflect a wider degree of superficiality: postmodern subculturalists 'do not have to worry about contradictions between their selected subcultural identities, for there are no rules, there is no authenticity, no ideological commitment, merely a stylistic game to be played' (Muggleton, 2000, p. 47).

In combination with the work on identity outlined above, such perspectives on fashion and style suggest, therefore, that we might regard the contemporary adoption of 'subcultural' style as an individual lifestyle choice; a more-or-less superficial attempt to lend outward substance to a particular vision – or version – of the self. Where classic post-war subcultures such as the Teds and skinheads arguably displayed a greater degree of homogeneity and commitment, and reflected – to at least some extent – the difficulties and preoccupations of a particular *class*, an involvement with contemporary 'subcultural' style may be dedicated less towards the symbolic, magical or imaginary resolution of 'class contradictions' (Cohen, 1997; see also Clarke *et al.*, 1976) than to a more individualistic expression of identity.

This is supported by my own work on contemporary body modification (Sweetman, 1999a; see also DeMello, 1995a, 1995b; Pitts, 1998).[2] Few of those interviewed for this project linked their tattoos or piercings to membership of specific 'subcultural' groups, instead tending to emphasize the personal nature of the modifications acquired. Several tattooees told me that they had chosen motifs that were expressive of personal interests or their own biographies, and many noted that they had opted for custom designs in order to ensure that 'no one else would ever have the same tattoos'. As one lightly-tattooed female interviewee put it: 'I saw various designs I liked, but I thought it would be more personal if I had something that was a design of my own.' It was also common for interviewees to refer to such forms of body modification as marks of individuality; as 'a way of standing out [and] saying, "Look, I'm me, I'm an individual"'. Some also suggested that becoming tattooed or pierced could be seen as an act of 'self-creation'. As one heavily-tattooed interviewee put it:

> it makes you feel individual... You know, like, everyone's born with roughly the same bodies, but you've created yours in your own image, [in line with] what your imagination wants your body to look like. It's like someone's given you something, and then you've made it your own, so you're not like everyone else any more.

Elsewhere, Muggleton (2000) points out that his own 'subcultural' informants 'demonstrate[d] a fragmented, heterogeneous and individualistic stylistic identification' (p. 158), and provided 'little evidence... of what the CCCS approach has led us to believe is typical of a working-class subcultural sensibility – a definite sense of group solidarity, a "them and us" perception of society, a collectivist value system' (p. 161). As will be explored more fully below, however, while such examples provide support for the idea that 'subcultural' style may have become increasingly individualized, and be both dedicated towards, and explicable in terms of, efforts to construct an individual sense of self-identity, neither Muggleton's nor many of my own informants displayed the ironic and playful stance characteristic of certain accounts of postmodern identity or of 'subcultural' involvement within the 'supermarket of style'

(Sweetman, 1999a; Muggleton, 2000). In this sense, such examples arguably provide more support for Giddens' interpretation of reflexive projects of the self as modern*ist* attempts to lend stability and coherency to the individual's chosen narrative, than for the idea that contemporary 'subculturalists' necessarily revel in the playful inconstancy of Baudrillard's 'carnival of signs'.

Neo-tribes and Emergent Socialities

While theories of 'reflexive modernity' may allow us to address the increasing fragmentation and diffusion of 'subcultural' style, such approaches do not, however, allow for an engagement with the more affectual or experiential aspects of what an involvement with 'subcultural' formations can entail. Even in some of the recent work that ostensibly brings the body into centre stage – suggesting that work on the 'outer body' (Featherstone, 1991a, p. 171) is central to contemporary projects of individualized identity-construction – the body itself is regarded not so much in terms of its lived-sensuality as a 'topic of reflexivity' (Turner, 1992, p. 7): a cognitively apprehended phenomenon that is worked *on* as part of a wider project of the self (see, for example, Giddens, 1991, Shilling, 1993). In this sense, theories of reflexive modernity share certain affinities with the overly textual accounts of subcultures associated with the CCCS, but, as I have argued elsewhere, there is more to 'subcultural' practices than simply playing with signs (Sweetman, 2001a).

While certain theorists have argued that we are all becoming increasingly reflexive, however, others have suggested that we are currently witnessing a resurgence of sensuality and the emergence of affectually based forms of sociality. These writers include Michel Maffesoli (1988, 1991, 1996) and Zygmunt Bauman (1992b), both of whom have referred to an emergent form of *'neo-tribal'* sociality, and Philip Mellor and Chris Shilling (1997), whose work talks of both a resurgent sensuality and the extra-discursive or affectual bases of contemporary solidarities (see also Hetherington, 1998b; Bennett, 1999a).

In various works, including *The Time of the Tribes* (1996), Maffesoli argues that we are currently witnessing a resurgence of basic forms of community, a move away from rational, contractual social relationships towards an empathetic form of *sociality*, where what is important is not some abstract, idealized goal, but rather the feeling of togetherness engendered by one's direct involvement with the social group. Where modernity was characterized by the proliferation of associational forms of relationship – which were 'drained . . . of any real content' – 'postmodernity has tended to favour . . . [a] withdrawal into the group as well as a deepening of relationships within these groups' (Maffesoli, 1996, p. 89).

Neo-tribal groupings are informal, dynamic and frequently temporary alliances, centred around 'their members' shared lifestyles and tastes' (Shields, 1996, p. x): around *feelings* rather than a commitment to particular ideologies or beliefs. Built around tactility and proxemics, these are non-instrumental, apolitical allegiances 'whose sole *raison d'être* is a preoccupation with the collective present' (Maffesoli: 1996, p. 75). Tribal collectivities may have an *ostensible* goal, but 'this is not essential; what is important is the energy expended on constituting the group *as such*' (ibid., p. 96, emphasis in original). They represent, in other words, a form of 'undirected being-together' (ibid., p. 81), or 'sociality-for-sociality's-sake', and it is this that allows them to generate a certain *puissance* or 'affective warmth'. Such 'affective warmth' in turn allows for that 'loss of self in the group' or 'ex-static attitude', that sense of 'collective effervescence', 'immanent transcendence' or 'shared sentiment', which 'is the true social bond' (Maffesoli, 1996, p. 43).

For Maffesoli, the rise of tribal sociality corresponds with both the 'saturation of the political' and 'the saturation of individualism' (ibid., p. 64), and in this sense his work links to much of the literature outlined above in referring to the loss of once-secure forms of identity. Where Giddens and others regard the loss of secure and stable 'ideological identities' as having contributed to an ongoing process of *individualization*, Maffesoli argues instead that we are witnessing a period of *'disindividuation'*, or *'indifferentiation'*: 'the 'losing' of self into a collective subject' (1988, p. 145). And where the 'reflexive modernization thesis' suggests that individuals respond to the loss of 'ideological identities' by grounding themselves in a reflexively constructed narrative of the self, Maffesoli – like certain other theorists of *post*modernity – argues that members of the sociality revel in the superficiality of the neo-tribal *persona* (ibid., p. 148).

Neo-tribalism can ultimately be seen as an *aesthetic* form of sociality, favouring 'appearance and form' (Maffesoli, 1996, p. 98) – as an expression of shared feelings and experiences – above, for example, formalised membership criteria, or a commitment to particular (ideological) beliefs. In this context, particular places, things, or behaviours can assume *iconic* significance, acting as badges of recognition, confirmation of the group's existence, and strengthening communal ties. An 'elaborate hairstyle', for instance, or 'an original tattoo', acts not only as a mask, but also reinforces social cohesion, 'subordinating' the person concerned to their 'chosen affinity group' (ibid., p. 91).

The emphasis on 'the near and affectual' (ibid., p. 128), on tactility, proxemics and shared *bodily* experiences, lends contemporary sociality 'an orgiastic or... dionysiac tendency' (ibid., p. 75). On the other side of the 'affectual nebula', however, one's experience of 'the social divine' may take the form of apparently trivial or unimportant encounters: 'sitting in the café', 'having a few drinks', or 'chatting with friends' (ibid., p. 25). Examples of groups displaying neo-tribal tendencies thus range from simple 'friendship networks' to those attendant at sports events as well as 'festivals, carnivals and other effervescent moments' (ibid., p. 77). No longer 'marginal', such tribal sociality 'is now the ordinary reality of everyday life' (ibid., p. 75).

This work has been criticized on several counts. David Evans, for example, argues that Maffesoli underplays the continuing importance of 'work, productivity, science, technology, and so forth' (Evans, 1997, p. 231), and in over-emphasising the shift to an empathetic and dionysiac postmodernity, neglects the double-sided nature of modernity itself, which should not be regarded as being governed solely by an instrumental rationality. In a related criticism, Kevin Hetherington argues that Maffesoli plays down the continuing importance of factors such as class: while such structural characteristics may no longer offer a secure and stable sense of identity, 'we can still talk about class, gender and ethnicity alongside neo-tribes' (Hetherington, 1998b, p. 53). A further difficulty is that, while Maffesoli regards clothing, hairstyles and other iconic devices as being central to the expression of neo-tribal patterns of identification, such factors are still regarded primarily as symbolic devices, as indicative or *expressive* of, rather than themselves *constitutive* of, wider affectual ties (Sweetman, 2001c).

While recent work on identity and consumption treats the body as something to be worked *on*, Maffesoli's work on neo-tribal sociality allows us to address the affectual dimensions of 'subcultural' involvement and the extra-discursive aspects of the forms of identification involved. In this sense, it can help us to redress the overly textual, symbolic or semiotic focus of classic work on subcultures (Cohen, 1997 [1980]; Muggleton, 2000; Sweetman, 2001a) and to think instead about what it is that 'subculturalists' in fact do. Equally importantly – in the context of the present discussion – Maffesoli's work also helps to illuminate further the increasing fragmentation of youth and/or 'subcultural' styles, while resonating well with the emphasis on the affectual and experiential in both academic accounts of contemporary 'subcultures', and the first-hand accounts of certain 'subculturalists' themselves.

In her recent study of club culture, for example, Hillegonda Rietveld emphasizes the way in which the experience of clubbing centres around both physical effects and the 'collective effervescence' generated by the clubbing crowd. Talking about the early house scene in Chicago, she notes that: 'This was not a political movement with manifestos in print. It was an ephemeral cultural event which was experienced through the movements of the body, its sexuality and its emotional reserves': despite the absence of an overt agenda, clubbers were drawn 'together in a sense of community, as though they were attending a religious gathering' (Rietveld, 1997, p. 128; see also Ross, 1994;

Reynolds, 1997; Stanley, 1997). Elsewhere, Larry Harvey, co-founder of Burning Man, an annual 'festival' held in Nevada's Black Rock Desert, explains that:

> The whole point is that from the beginning it was based on activism. It wasn't about community. It *was* community. The one essential notion at that time was that our only salvation was to be had through this activist appeal to immediate experience over doctrine, ideology. We weren't producing a symbol or a spectacle. We were creating an initiation. (Harvey, in Wieners, 1997, p. 132, emphasis in original)

Harvey goes on to point out that: 'with ... Burning Man we aren't creating art about society. It's art that *generates society*, which, by a magical process, convenes society around itself' (Harvey, in Wieners, 1997, p. 134, my emphasis):

> You can communicate with anybody in the world on the internet, but so what? Here we've resorted to a kind of primal psychology, a level of experience that lies at the heart of all ritual – primordial, preverbal, prehistoric. The genesis of that feeling is standing around a campfire. You have to reach back that far to find something that's going to bring people together. And we're going at it in a very American, very pragmatic way. We're doing it because it works. (Harvey, in Wieners, 1997, p. 137)

Tourists and Travellers?

Maffesoli's work suggests that 'the logic of identity' has given way to 'the logic of identification' (Hetherington, 1998b, p. 68), or what Maffesoli refers to as a process of *disindividuation*, and, as Simon Williams (1998) has pointed out, from this perspective, 'Giddens's emphasis on late modernity as a detraditional order based on a reflexively mobilized self, appears, at the very least, problematic' (p. 760). That this 'opposition between "individualism" and "neo-tribalism" is not as stark ... as might be thought', however, has been noted by David Evans, who points out that ' "neo-tribalism" depends upon a highly individualized society where people are released from the chains of tradition and are therefore in a position to ... choose between the "life-style" alternatives offered up to them' (Evans, 1997, p. 239).

Hetherington (1998b), similarly, points out that 'the elective basis to neo-tribal identifications means that they create a sociation that is affectual rather than traditional', and which relies on a 'reflexive process' of self-identification, even if this is subsequently *realized* 'in the context of emotional identification with others' (p. 101). For Hetherington, neo-tribal forms of sociality 'act to promote individuality as well as provide an intense experience of communion into which that individuality is subsumed' (1998b, p. 95). Bauman (1992b), meanwhile, argues that 'tribes' are not 'unambiguously anti-individualiztic', but are key to the construction of individual identities, helping to sanction lifestyle choices, and offering a guide through the bewildering array of options people now face (p. 25).

Taken together, these points suggest that we might view certain contemporary 'subcultural' practices and formations as manifestations of *both* a reflexive process of identity-construction *and* of a resurgent sensuality or neo-tribal sociality. Indeed, if such is the case, then in analyzing such practices one might also consider breaking them down into a reflexive component – the decision to act – and an affectual component – the action's extra-discursive effects. The issues raised above also suggest that it might be profitable to avoid either Giddens' rather exclusive focus on individualization, or Maffesoli's equally one-sided insistence on disindividuation, instead adopting an approach – such as that proposed by Bauman or Hetherington – that allows for both processes to be recognized adequately.

In my own work on contemporary body modification, while becoming tattooed or pierced can be seen in part as a reflexive process of identity construction, the concept of neo-tribalism has proved useful in examining the emphasis many of those involved place on the importance of the modificatory *process*, and the sense in which this can lead to an affectual link between those concerned. As one interviewee explained, when you become tattooed or pierced you can feel like part of a club or community that in some ways is like any other lifestyle group, 'but because it's permanent and it's painful and it's all these things, and you feel *special* somehow – you know, it's quite strong – it's maybe more close, and more passionate, than golf, say'. Another interviewee pointed out that, whatever you are like, 'you have to go through...a similar amount of pain...so I think there is a common, sort of, denominator there', and that this shared experience of the modificatory procedure means that, 'it's hard to talk to people about [tattoos and piercings] unless they've had 'em done'.

As these examples also illustrate, however, there may be certain difficulties in describing such affinities as temporary and superficial, given the degree of commitment that is sometimes displayed. Indeed, to return to my own work on body modification, factors such as the pain and relative permanence of tattoos and piercings mean that one cannot simply go and purchase a complete tattoo or piercing as one might acquire a new tee-shirt, nor can such 'corporeal artefacts' necessarily be discarded easily if one wishes to adopt a new 'persona'. As another interviewee pointed out:

I do find there's a similar consciousness among people who've got a tattoo...It's like anybody who has a love of something – like antiques dealers, or people with old cars – they all get together in the end, and that's modern day tribes...[But] I think it's quite special among people who have tattoos, 'cause you cannot run away from them. You can't stop being a tattooed person. (Harvey, 21 year old tattooee)

It was also common for my interviewees to value their tattoos – in particular – for precisely this reason. While several informants told me that they had deliberately become tattooed or pierced in order to mark specific turning-points or events, others pointed out that, once acquired, their tattoos served as an indelible connection with particular periods in their lives (Sweetman, 1999a). One interviewee told me that he regarded his tattoos as a permanent 'diary' that 'no one can take off you', while the informant quoted above – who had noted that 'you cannot run away from' your tattoos – also told me that he regarded the two designs on his upper arms as 'a commitment to [him]self', and explained that:

By marking myself I thought I could... keep... what I felt when I was eighteen, nineteen, for the rest of my life, cause I'd always remember the time. Because having a tattoo done is such a special thing. There's the pain to begin with, and then there's like the high you get afterwards when you first have it done...But, just looking at them reminds me of that time, and hopefully it will stop me from forgetting who I am, when life starts to get, you know, kick the door in a bit more. The older you get...mortgage, kids, whatever. (Harvey, 21 year old tattooee)

As Hetherington (1998b) points out, then, we might wish to question Maffesoli's depiction of the 'tragic superficiality' of contemporary sociality, and the ensuing implication that people revel in the playful opportunities that the problematization of identity might be said to afford, instead regarding certain forms of 'tribal' identification as an attempt to re-ground or anchor the self through a more or less specific commitment to a particular narrative.

I have indicated elsewhere that contemporary tattooing and piercing can be regarded as 'postmodern practices' in the sense that they involve the 'refashioning of personal identities out of cultural materials' (Tseëlon, 1995, p. 123; Sweetman, 1999a). Muggleton (2000) also refers to his informants as 'postmodern' in relation to the 'fragmented, heterogeneous and individualistic' nature of the forms of stylistic identification they displayed (p. 158). In both cases, however, such reflexive projects can be regarded as modern*ist* in their attempts to secure 'an authentic sense of self amidst the uncertainty that is the [contemporary] social terrain' (Hetherington, 1998b, p. 54).

This is not necessarily true of all contemporary 'subculturalists', however. While his informants were drawn exclusively from the former group, Muggleton (2000) suggests that a distinction can be made between 'full- and part-time' subculturalists (p. 151), with the latter group displaying a greater degree of stylistic promiscuity than the former, and regarded accordingly as superficial by his 'full-time' respondents (p. 93). Despite a number of significant caveats, it should also be noted that several of my own interviewees appeared to regard their tattoos and piercings as little more than 'accessories' (Sweetman, 1999a).[3] Elsewhere, Gregson *et al.* (2001) identify two distinct 'modes of appreciation' for '70s retro fashion' – the 'knowing' and the 'carnivalesque'. While the knowing mode of appreciation is characterized by a degree of seriousness and commitment that is arguably modernist in form, the carnivalesque mode is characterized by fun, irony, and the 'temporariness' of the appropriations, performances, and identifications involved.

In an article on identity, Bauman (1996) proposes that the modern *pilgrim* – as a seeker of truth, authenticity, commitment and stability – has given way to a number of increasingly prevalent metaphorical figures – the *stroller*, the *vagabond*, the *tourist* and the *player* – each of whom is either denied, or they themselves deny, the commitment and stability that the pilgrim sought. Bryan Turner (1999), meanwhile, suggests that we now inhabit the metaphorical space of the 'airport departure lounge', a superficial and transient environment in which few display commitment or attachment, and everyone is 'passing through'. There are, as I have argued elsewhere, difficulties with Turner's accompanying depiction of contemporary body modification as playful and ironic (Sweetman, 1999a). Both sets of metaphors are instructive, however, and in the context of the present discussion can usefully be extended by introducing a further metaphorical figure – the *traveller*.

Both tourist and traveller inhabit – or at least regularly pass through – Turner's departure lounge. But where the tourist accepts, acknowledges and openly celebrates this superficial, postmodern environment the traveller seeks – and *claims* – authenticity on the basis of a greater depth of involvement – whether real or imagined – with the various stop-off points on his or her itinerary (the global circuit of 'local' departure lounges; an arbitrary selection of which informs the individual's 'route'). The traveller, in other words, adopts a modernist orientation to this postmodern environment, or – to use Gregson *et al.*'s (2001) distinction – a 'knowing' mode of appreciation rather than the tourist's 'carnivalesque'. In relation to contemporary 'subculturalists', it may be, therefore, that we can distinguish usefully between 'travellers' and 'tourists'. Both groups inhabit the same metaphorical space, but where the tourist playfully celebrates, happily rummaging in the dressing-up-box of past subcultural styles, the traveller chooses a costume and sticks to it – *at least for a short while*. Where the traveller corresponds most directly to Giddens' understanding of the reflexive consumer, however, and where the tourist may seem to be the epitome of Maffesolian neo-tribalism – revelling in the superficiality of the neo-tribal persona – part of the purpose of this chapter has been to suggest that both types of involvement or orientation may be characterized by reflexivity and sociality – that for both travellers *and* tourists, issues of identity *and* identification may apply. It should also be reiterated that, despite the traveller's modernist orientation to the contemporary social terrain, he or she is not a pilgrim in the sense that Bauman employs the term: unlike the Teds, skinheads and other post-war subcultures, both tourists and travellers inhabit Turner's departure lounge, and both – to run the risk of further mixing my metaphors – shop in Polhemus's 'supermarket of style'.

Conclusion

The foregoing has suggested that two distinct strands of contemporary social theory – accounts of reflexivity and identity, on the one hand, and accounts of neo-tribal sociality, on the other – may provide us with helpful ways of exploring 'post-subcultural' practices and formations in an era when established forms of subcultural analysis can no longer be applied so readily. It has also suggested that, despite their apparent differences, these two approaches can usefully be brought together on the basis of the elective forms of identity and identification involved, and that contemporary 'subcultural' practices and formations may be regarded as both explicable in terms of, and as providing the basis for, both the construction of individual identities *and* the wider forms of identification that Maffesoli and others have explored.

In making these suggestions, however, it has also been argued that we can distinguish usefully between two apparent 'post-subcultural' types – the tourist and the traveller. While the former most clearly approximates to Maffesoli's neo-tribal persona, however, and the latter to Giddens' understanding of the reflexive consumer, each stance involves both the construction of individual identities and wider forms of identification, and neither can be regarded as true 'subculturalists' in the CCCS sense of the term. Although contemporary travellers may *regard themselves* as 'authentic' subculturalists – on the basis of their knowledgeability and degree of commitment to a particular style – theirs is an individual choice rather than a collective response: a choice made from a plurality of options which, however long the traveller commits to his or her chosen 'destination' – learning the language, mixing with the locals, and avoiding tacky tourist traps and cheap souvenirs – remains an arbitrary selection from the variety of options available. While the class-based analysis of the CCCS may no longer be applicable, however, and while the concept of neo-tribal sociality may be helpful in exploring contemporary practices of a 'subcultural' type, the distinction between tourists and travellers suggests that we should be wary of adopting Maffesoli's analysis in its entirety, and simply and uncritically replacing the term subculture with the looser concept of the neo-tribe. It also suggests that the term subculture retains a degree of relevance – as well as a certain descriptive utility – if only in exploring the way in which certain 'travellers' – rather than 'tourists' – may continue to regard themselves.

Notes

1   I am grateful to Andy Bennett and Keith Kahn-Harris for their helpful editorial comments.
2   This took the form of a qualitative study of contemporary body modification, for which in-depth, semi-structured interviews were conducted with thirty-five tattooed and/or pierced informants, as well as with several professional tattooists, body piercers, and other key respondents (for further details, see Sweetman, 1999a, 1999b, 1999c).
3   When asked what she most liked about having her navel pierced, for example, one young interviewee noted the way in which 'we like to change our bodies', before adding, 'all girls like jewellery, don't they, and it's sort of an extension of that I think'. The same interviewee also pointed out that, for her, getting the piercing done was something of a 'treat': 'a bit like going into a really posh salon and having your hair done'. Nor were such views confined to those with piercings. One young woman with two small tattoos, for example, referred to the design on her back as follows: 'it's nice choosing your outfit depending on whether you want to show off your tattoo or whatever, and, I dunno . . . I just think it's kind of like an extra accessory kind of thing.'

CHAPTER 6

Teenage Girls' 'Bedroom Culture': Codes versus Zones

SIAN LINCOLN

The concept of a 'bedroom culture' (McRobbie: 1978) first emerged as a response to traditional youth research conducted by the Centre for Contemporary Cultural Studies (CCCS) in the 1970s (see Cohen: 1972; Clarke: 1976; Hall and Jefferson: 1976; Willis: 1977; Hebdige: 1979). Primarily, this concept was developed as a means of addressing the alternative ways in which girls organize their cultural lives, and to account for their absence from street-based, male-dominated youth cultural activities which 'Predispose[d] [girls] to retreat, especially when it is also a situation in which they [we]re being assessed and labelled according to their sexual attributes' (McRobbie and Garber, 1997, p. 113).

McRobbie was highly critical of research conducted on British youth sub-cultures, and in her paper (written with Jenny Garber) 'Girls and Subcultures' (McRobbie and Garber, 1976) suggested that significant 'gaps' in CCCS commentaries were apparent. The most notable gap was that of young women; one of her major criticisms being of the male-dominated nature of the research, researched and researchers that rendered girls invisible, and the oversight that, structurally, girls could be pivotal and central to alternative spheres (for example, the home), hence their absence from the streets. Crucially, though, McRobbie did not consider the concept of 'subculture' itself to be flawed; therefore she understood that the role of girls in culture could be 'added on' to CCCS's subcultural theory, thus remaining within the 'subcultural' paradigm. In doing this she maintained the central themes of subcultural analysis, these being class and the spheres of school, work and family. She then added the dimension of sex and gender as a way of enhancing and enriching the theory already in existence.

The theoretical discussion in this chapter draws on a study of the youth cultural interests of teenage girls in relation to the physical, social and intimate space of the bedroom as representing their cultural histories. Since McRobbie's work was published in the 1970s, her idea of a bedroom culture has remained unchallenged, and no further research specific to this area has been published. Here it is updated, using the concepts of 'zoning', 'spatial fluidity' and 'socio-spatial configuration'. My ideas, alongside McRobbie's, are grounded in more contemporary cultural theory to take into account the much changed worlds of teenage girls since the 1970s, within both public and private realms. These concepts are used to explore the existence of a bedroom culture in the social-life worlds of teenage girls in the late 1990s that allow for 'fluid boundaries and floating memberships' (Bennett, 1999a, p. 600), produced both culturally and physically through different activities, and to explore whether there are elements of McRobbie's definition that remain a part of teenage girls' social-life world.

Researching Bedroom Culture

The discussion below is based on an analysis of a small, intensive ethnographic study of teenage cultural life. Primarily, this analysis draws on data relating to four girls – Leila, Miranda, Eve and Kate – each aged 16 or 17 and living in Greater Manchester[1]. In order to build on our understanding of bedroom culture, I used specific methods of research and concepts of analysis that challenged those of McRobbie. For example, my recorded interviews with the girls took place *within* the culture itself – one of the participants' bedrooms – rather than in a youth club, which is where McRobbie conducted her interviews. I used a diverse range of data collection, including visual and written diaries, so I was able to produce a more complete picture of what the girls' lives are really like, and what they means to young people as part of the culture. This approach contrasts with McRobbie's method of 'coding' based around a teen magazine super-imposed *on to* the culture through which teenage girls supposedly lived out their cultural lives, and takes into account the different ways that teenage girls live their social lives in the 1990s. Finally, I felt it was important to consider boys' roles in bedroom culture as part of this research, to avoid falling into the subcultural tradition of marginalizing specific groups of people, although I do not refer to this data, as they were not of sufficiently close age for comparison in this chapter.

Codes and Zones

Codes

For teenage girls in the late 1990s, the bedroom is often the only space within the home that is personal, personalized and intimate. It is a space over which teenagers are able to gain privacy from parents and siblings alike, often displayed on the bedroom door with signs such as 'knock before entering!' It is a room that provides respite from the public world, from the demands of peers, siblings and parents, in which unmediated activities such as sleeping, reading books and magazines, daydreaming and 'chilling out' take place. The teenager can exent control over what level of 'the public' can filter into bedroom space through zones. The bedroom also exists as a central 'meeting' place in a teenage girl's social-life world. It is the space into which friends are invited to listen to music, chat (either to each other or on the (mobile) phone), smoke, drink alcohol, experiment with hair, make-up and clothes, and get ready for a night out. The bedroom is a biographical space in that the posters, flyers, photographs, framed pictures, books, magazines and CDs tell stories of a teenage girl's youth cultural interests and, ultimately, cultural identity. This brings together past and present experiences of both the present occupant of the bedroom and previous occupants – for example, older brothers and sisters. The reorganization and accumulation of 'things' contained within the space means that, biographically, the bedroom is continually being reconstructed around changing and age-related tastes in cultural activities and uses of bedroom space.

McRobbie's study of bedroom culture focused essentially on the bedroom as an exclusive female sphere within which teenage girls could feel safe from the sexual humiliation of the streets, with 'no chance of being stood up or bombed out' (McRobbie and Garber, 1976, p. 220). Teenage girls could indulge in their unique subculture of fantasy and romance: a 'teeny-bopper' culture, while remaining within their traditional culture of domesticity.

The activities that McRobbie (1981) discusses as taking place within this space are primarily those linked to the pursuit of beauty and finding a husband. This included experimenting with make-up, hair and clothes, gossiping with a couple of friends about pop idols and 'boys they fancy', and reading *Jackie* magazine, particularly the love photo-stories or the problem pages, activities that could be: Easily appropriated into the traditionally defined cultural space of the home or the peer-centred 'girls' culture – operated mainly within the home, or visiting a girl friend's home (McRobbie and Garber, 1976, p. 213).

In her original study, McRobbie's bedroom culture was based around a set of codes: 'the code of romance', 'the code of fashion and beauty', 'the code of personal life' and 'the code of pop music' (McRobbie, 1991, p. 94). These ideological codes were based primarily around the pursuit of romance, and ultimately 'finding a husband' and 'keeping him', and relied heavily on the fantasy worlds of teenage girls 'mapped out' by *Jackie* magazine and the like on to their romantic lives. Although important, these codes remained abstract and were not developed further to consider the importance of the bedroom as an intimate space into which young women's cultural ideals were integrated. Therefore, this chapter updates and revises some of these fundamental ideas and developments in a contemporary setting.

The 'traditional' activities that made up a distinctly female bedroom culture in the 1970s are also found in a 1990s version of the culture. It can be argued, though, that the extended range of activities (such as using the mobile phone, Internet or the stereo system) and the fluid nature by which contemporary youth activities are understood, bedroom culture is no longer 'almost totally packaged' (McRobbie, 1991, p. 11). The culture is not, and it is questionable whether it ever was, learned through magazines aimed at teenage girls, as McRobbie suggests.

Zones

> It is not only the codes – the map's legend, the conventional signs of map-making and map-reading – that are liable to change, but also the objects represented, the lens through which they are viewed. (Lefebvre, 1991, p. 85)

The concept of 'zoning' in bedroom culture works alongside contemporary post-subcultural debates and critiques that re-examine the place of subculture in the study of young people and youth culture: for example, Muggleton's notion of 'postmodern codes' and the adaptation of subculture (including style and 'the visual') by its 'members' creating 'subcultural choice' (1997, p. 198); Bennett's 'neo-tribes' (1999a) and his re-thinking of the 'local' in post-subcultures (2000); and Thornton's (1995) use of the term 'subcultural capital' as a form of representation and cultural knowledge, specifically in club cultures. The concept of zoning in this chapter relates well to Muggleton's suggestion that: 'Post-subculturalists will experience all the signs of the subculture of their choosing time and time again … Choosing is the operative word here, for post-subculturalists revel in their availability of subcultural choice' (1997, p. 198).

When researching bedroom culture, a zone is a physical and visible arrangement of furniture, technical equipment, beauty products, school books, in fact any item that is 'contained' (Lefebvre, 1991, p. 83) within bedroom space. It is orientated by the social activities that take place within the space, therefore it may not be fixed in physical or cognitive activities; zones can over-lap and integrate. The zone can also become a mediated and fluid construction, enhanced through technologies such as the TV or the sound system, the mobile phone and the Internet; therefore, the space of the bedroom is a fluid and dynamic cultural domain. As a conceptual tool, the zone, unlike McRobbie's 'code' and the CCCS's concept of 'subculture', is material rather than abstract, and is constructed by the teenagers themselves who occupy the space of the bedroom and who select from their 'pick and mix' culture and, as mentioned above, their immense 'cultural choices' (Muggleton, 1997, p. 198). This is not to say that McRobbie's girls were not active agents in their social-life worlds, the mere picking up of a magazine such as *Jackie* is a cultural choice. However, girls in the 1990s are more active in the shaping of their social- and cultural-life worlds, and this is an important development that builds on McRobbie's initial ideas about the role of girls in culture.

McRobbie used the notion of a 'map of meaning' to understand girls' bedroom culture as specifically 'mapped out' cognitively and ideologically through the 'codes' presented in *Jackie* magazine. Zones, in contrast, are both physical and cognitive, and are derived from (rather than constructed by) the media. The concept of zoning allows for the 'uniqueness' of each bedroom space as opposed to being a 'subcultural' space that is rigidly defined through 'style' and 'membership'. I would argue that one teenage girl's bedroom is never the same as another, but is specific to the individual teenager in relation to her 'social labour' (Lefebvre, 1991, p. 77) imposed on bedroom space to maintain it as a representation of contemporary cultural and social life.

Bedroom Culture in the 1990s

Eve, a research participant, indicates the amount of time she spends in her bedroom by saying 'I just go downstairs for food.' The private space of the bedroom accommodates and offers her every other need in terms of entertainment and communication. The rest of the house, occupied regularly by various family members, is entered only for necessities such as food (often taken straight back up into the bedroom). This is a useful example of the ways in which fluidity of 'zoning' works in bedroom culture, and how other 'home' spaces can, from time to time, drift into private space – for example, when Eve takes coffee cups and plates into her bedroom. Eve also explains why some of her friends may spend more or less time in their bedrooms:

> *Eve*: Well, I think I know why we do [to Leila]. [To Miranda] You work a lot and [to Kate] you've just moved into a new bedroom, your bedroom is kind of smaller, and your mum's not around as much, there's not really anyone there so you spend more time downstairs.

Time not spent in their bedrooms is largely spent in the public sphere of work or college. The bedroom is a 'lived in' and personalized space, although the new bedroom which Miranda has just moved into is not initially an individualized space. More time is spent in other rooms in the house, such as the living room or the kitchen when parents are not around, but the girls retreat to their bedrooms when parents return. There are activities that only take place within the private sphere of the bedroom, beyond the parental gaze; chatting and gossiping, drinking or smoking cigarettes.

The bedroom also accommodates non-leisure activities such as doing (or not doing) college work; it is the room in which to 'pretend' to do homework, or it is a place to go 'when you can't be bothered':

> *Leila*: If I pretend to study I do it up here!
>
> . . .
>
> *Kate*: Sometimes I go up because I can't be bothered, just to get away, I just get into bed and start thinking . . . .

Watching television in the bedroom is preferred, as it is private space in which other activities such as chatting on the phone can take place without being disturbed or disturbing other family members. Again, this also means that the teenager has ultimate control over which 'bits' of public culture to allow into the bedroom. The television in the bedroom is sometimes used by Eve as a distraction for her boyfriend who is waiting to go on a night out with her, or with her and her friends. It is used as a guarantee of minimum distraction for Eve and her 'going out ritual' (Hollands, 1995):

> *Eve*: Well, if I'm going out with the girls, then I usually get ready with them. But if I'm going out with my boyfriend, then he usually comes round about seven o'clock and he'll sit and watch telly while I get ready. He'll have to sit there for about three hours whilst I do my hair in different ways, then we'll go out.

Here the role of the teenage girl in contemporary youth culture is very different from her role in traditional CCCS discussions. For McRobbie, the bedroom was an exclusively female domain in which the boyfriend was embraced purely as a romantic character found only in her fantasies and daydreaming, and made up from the pop idol of 'teeny-bopper culture' and the *Jackie* love stories. The bedroom was never opened up to the potential threat of 'sexual danger', as it was primarily the sphere that protected teenage girls from the threats of 'boys on the streets', violence, sexual degradation and suppression. This was not a place into which to invite boys; it was only a place in which to prepare to meet them, talk about them or read about them. As Eve demonstrates, teenage boys are often invited by teenage girls into their personal space. But rather than mapping or enforcing his masculinity on to the cultural setting of the girl's bedroom into which he has entered, which would reflect the traditional domination of masculinity in subcultural theory (Willis, 1977; McRobbie and Garber, 1997), 'the boyfriend' fits into a controlled and passive aspect of the bedroom's socio-spatial configuration.

Creating Bedroom Spaces

> Social space contains a great diversity of objects... including the networks and path-
> ways which facilitate the exchange of material things and information. (Lefebvre,
> 1991, p. 77)

The physical space of the bedroom unfolds because the fluidity of cultural boundaries (Bennett, 1999a) in both public and private space means that there is an integration of both traditional and media-enhanced activities. In their bedrooms, the girls have the freedom to engage in a number of activities, often at the same time, in ways that vary considerably from day to day. Their choice can depend on whether they are 'having a night in', when the main activities may be doing college work, talking on the phone, watching television or reading magazines, or preparing for 'a night out', when the girls may listen to music, drink alcohol, experiment with clothes and make-up and call friends on the phone to make arrangements for the night ahead.

For the girls I spoke to, music and the way in which it was used was not specific to the 'going out ritual' (Hollands, 1995), but was rather a sound-scape, a constant mediator of the 'emotional tone' of bedroom culture. What this means is that music is not just an important part of their youth cultural activity in the public sphere; it is just as crucial in the production of their culture within the private sphere, and that its significance to the girls is associated primarily with the creation of a specific type of ambience.

The production of social space through music is determined not only by the activities that are taking place at the moment in which the music is selected, but also by the activities that will take place later in the evening, again merging both the public and the private spheres. An example of this is when the girls are going to a club – they may listen to a 'club anthems' CD, but, as Leila explained, when they are getting ready to go out they may listen to 'rap and stuff like that'. But if she and a group of friends are just sitting about, talking, she said: 'I'd rather listen to R&B or soul, it's nice to have it on in the back-ground.' The selection of music is an important part of teenage girls' bedroom culture, particularly because 'gossiping', 'chatting' or 'talking' is a popular female activity. If the girls are staying in, 'ambient' background music accom-modates the chat. Using the remote control to adjust the volume allows the girls to talk without shouting. This means parents do not hear what they are saying because there is enough sound to distract family members from their conversation. Choosing which CDs to listen to is also an interactive part of bedroom culture, and demonstrates how the girls move in and out of different zones and are involved in a number of activities at any one time. When choosing or changing a CD, the girls may still continue chatting without the topic of conversation shifting to which CD to put on, while putting a CD on can also direct the subject of a conversation to a specific type of music, band or DJ. Leila may redirect the conversation if the girls are in her bedroom through questions such as: 'Have you heard this CD?'; or 'What do you think of this DJ?'; 'What shall I put on?' Selecting a particular CD is also a way for any of the girls to confirm music taste: 'Oh I love this', which, again, may direct the conversation to a specific music genre.

New technologies play a significant role in teenage girls' 'bedroom culture' in that the girls all had a TV, video, stereo and CD player in their bedrooms. Predominantly, this equipment provides the main ways of creating the 'sensuous and emotional ethos' of the space through visual and aural enter-tainment (Malbon, 1998, p. 280). Arguably, the most significant piece of new technology in the girls' creation of a 'bedroom culture' is the telephone (both landline and mobile). Each of the girls owned a 'mobile' (some were in fact used during the interviews) and used it as a means of relocating 'bedroom' chat with friends from private into public spaces.

For McRobbie, the bedroom was considered as the prime space in which teenage girls could get together and gossip with as little interruption or intrusion as possible about other social-life worlds and influences such as school, going out, boys, other girls, parents, hair or make-up. 'Gossiping' was still found to be a popular leisure-time activity, with the topics of conversation remaining similar to those of McRobbie's girls:

> *S. L.*: What sort of things do you talk about?
> *Leila*: Well ... males!
> *S. L.*: Men you fancy or want to go out with?
> *Miranda*: Well, just men generally ....
> *Leila*: Yeah ... pretty much any male we've got a sexual interest in, I suppose you could say! Umm ... we talk about ... We do a lot of bitching. If we talk about people we do it in the bedroom.

An important element of contemporary bedroom culture, is this crossover into the 'dangerous' public sphere (McRobbie and Garber, 1997). This demonstrates how public and private spheres can flow into each other, and can interact simultaneously as bedroom culture.

In terms of alternative forms of new communication technologies, this fluidity of bedroom culture does not appear to be extended further through the PC or the Internet. The use of PCs by the girls was categorized primarily within the context of their education, and accessing a PC only when they needed to use one to do college work highlighted the gendered nature of this activity (see McNamee, 1998).

For teenage girls, the bedroom is a place to create a haven of memorabilia that represents their role in social-life worlds (see Figure 6.1). This includes the presence of childhood toys, such as teddy bears, photographs of family and friends, holidays and recent nights out, and posters. The cultural interests of the girls are recorded biographically on their bedroom walls. Eve's bedroom is a good example of this process of biography inscribed on social space (see Fig 6.1). Her bedroom walls and ceiling are covered with posters, post-cards and photographs, which are not only snapshots of her cultural interests, but also of her sister's, who occupied the bedroom before Eve moved in:

Eve: At my Dad's my whole ceiling is covered in flyers... there's some posters up, but they weren't my choice, they were my sister's.

Figure 6.1 Eve's Bedroom

This preference for flyers rather than posters is a representation of how teenage girls' bedroom culture may have shifted from teeny-bopper pop idol 'poster-gazing' to a visual account of nights out that the girls have experienced.

The girls document their 'coolness' through active participation in the public sphere of the pub or club rather than relying on the creation of fantasy 'love affairs' with pop idols. Flyers, though, can be collected from people handing them out in the street and from record shops rather than through the girls in fact insiting a specific club. If this is so, then McRobbie's element of fantasy is still an important concept in bedroom culture. This means an interest in clubbing is represented by the flyers that adorn the bedroom walls and ceiling, and being a clubber may, to a certain extent, rely on the imagination. The display of a flyer from a particularly popular club may also be a form of 'subcultural capital' (Thornton, 1995) in that it lets the girls demonstrate their knowledge of the latest club trends that are rife outside the sphere of the home, but without having to be part of the clubbing scene 'physically' in the public sphere. The girls used photographs of family and friends in collages, on pin-boards or in frames as a way of decorating the walls of their bedroom. The space is used to record holidays, parties, nights out, activities that feature in the cultural and social life worlds of the girls. The girls' bedrooms offered their own cultural histories from their childhood to their teenage years; their own 'representations of youth' (see Griffin, 1993).

Codes or Zones?

The 'doing college work' zone

McRobbie (1991) and Blackman (1998) are among youth researchers who have shown that resistance to the conformities of school and college are not just limited to boys' youth subcultures. McRobbie claimed, in her analysis of *Jackie* magazine, that its reading in the classroom represented the girls being bored, and that this act could be interpreted as them rebelling against the school culture. Blackman's ethnographic account of the 'new wave girls' shows how the girls demonstrated their 'alternativeness' at school through the music they listened to and the clothes they wore: 'a skirt, and Doctor Marten's boots under a "dirty mac" (Blackman, 1998, p. 207). My own research findings suggest that the context of school or college is still rebelled against, and that as a zone in a teenage girl's bedroom, 'doing college work' is often separated from other zones, which are leisure-related. In Kate's bedroom, for example, the 'college work' zone is isolated and compacted onto the desk. The desk is tidy and organized with files, a filing tray, pens and pencils in a glass jar, and college papers, all items that make it look ready to work on. But also on her desk there is an ashtray, arguably an item primarily linked primarily to the 'leisure' zone, which suggests that smoking is one possible distraction for kate from doing her homework. This relates to her confessions that: 'when I pretend to study I do it up here!' so actually doing college work is not the priority in this space.

The pursuit of leisure over doing college work within Kate's bedroom is demonstrated through the display of pub/club flyers on the wall above her desk in the 'college work' zone. The presentation of nights out in the 'doing college work' zone may work as both an incentive to work, leaving the weekends free for nights out, or as a representation of something that Kate would rather be doing. It is a piece of memorabilia that triggers thinking and daydreaming about nights out with friends, and thus creates a form of work avoidance.

The 'fashion and beauty/going out' zone

> Beautification and self-improvement forms...the ideal hobby for girls...The important point is that beauty-work assumes that its subjects are house-bound...And so every moment of the girls' time, not taken up with romance, is devoted to the maintenance and re-upholstery of the self. (McRobbie, 1991, p. 124)

As McRobbie suggests, a teenage girl's bedroom is used as a space in which to experiment with hair, clothes and make-up. Photographs show distinct 'fashion and beauty' zones which centre around a dressing table on which there are cosmetic products such as moisturizers, hairspray, hair mousse, deodorant and perfume that the girls have accumulated, and all contribute to their beauty routine. For the girls interviewed, the bedroom has a central role in beautification or getting ready for a night out, and is a 'pre-going out' space. However, the arrangement of zones and the items within the space of the bedroom are largely related to other leisure pursuits outside the bedroom, and not just restricted to the private sphere. The 'going out ritual' was explained, step-by-step by the girls themselves:

> *Leila*: We come home from college, have a sleep, then have a shower. While one's in the shower, the other one's usually deciding what to wear or drying their hair. We have a few drinks [alcoholic], then try to leave about half an hour just to chill out before we go out...

McRobbie's claim that there is a routine that girls follow in terms of fashion and beauty is theoretically appropriate here, although there is a shift from McRobbie's code of fashion and beauty as being associated primarily with the pursuit of romance (which would often only be lived out in a fantasy world restricted to the bedroom) to simply getting ready for a night out (which involves cultural consumption within the public sphere). This is further justified by other items in the bedroom that make this zone particularly geared to getting ready to go out. This includes items such as packets of cigarettes, ashtrays, money, fizzy drinks bottles (a mixer for spirits) as well as CDs and cassettes.

The 'sleeping' zone: getting in from a night out

Bedroom space is not only significant in getting ready for a night out, but also in 'getting in' from a night out as respite from the public sphere. The activities experienced within the public sphere of the pub or the club are further extended back at home in the bedroom where, the continuation of such activities is unconstrained because of easy access to those consumables such as alcohol and music needed in the re-creation. The importance of zoning is particularly apparent here, as the significance of the bedroom as a social space is central to the integration of public and private spheres. These spheres are often blurred and the integration of them is controlled by the girls rather than imposed on them. The re-created atmosphere of a pub or a club is further enhanced by the configuration of the bedroom in which an integration of the 'new technologies zone' provides access to various media. The girls may even continue to extend the flow of the zone by using their mobile phones to invite other friends over, or to chat about the night's events.

Lighting has a significant effect on the ambience of the bedroom. The girls use table lamps, fairy lights, lava lamps, 'dimmer' switches and candles to provide a 'softer light', which mimics the lighting of a pub or club. The dim light allows the girls to gossip more freely and without embarrassment about the events of the night: who fancied whom, who 'got off' with whom, and so on. It removes inhibitions, which are also lessened by the consumption of alcohol and existing to 'mellow' music, producing a culture that encapsulates both the public and private spheres that make up a teenage girl's social life, rather than the bedroom being the abstract, dislocated and insulated culture that McRobbie described.

Conclusion

This chapter explores the notion that a bedroom culture still exists in the social lives of teenage girls. I have argued that the concept of a 'bedroom culture' can no longer be understood simply in terms of a set of abstract codes 'mapped' on to the social lives of teenage girls (McRobbie and Garber, 1997), but that bedroom culture should be explored and understood in terms of zoning, thus moving on traditional subcultural theory. The zone is an important conceptual tool in the understanding of bedroom culture as its fluidity means that the physical arrangement of the bedroom can be shaped by the activities that take place within the space. I have developed this concept, in the tradition of McRobbie's work, by suggesting that it is possible to categorize activities into specific zones. I have further extended this categorization, as I have demonstrated how a zone is also a socio-spatial configuration drawing on the analysis of a small ethnographic study.

The constant interaction of zones demonstrates the complexity of bedroom culture, as the girls are often involved in a number of different activities at any one time, accessing both the public and the private spheres. This represents the ways in which contemporary bedroom culture can be understood as an important site in which youth and subcultural activities take place, and highlights its continuing importance as a cultural space in the social life worlds of teenage girls.

Note

1   The names of all the research participants have been changed.

CHAPTER 7

Unspectacular Subculture? Transgression and Mundanity in the Global Extreme Metal Scene

KEITH KAHN-HARRIS

In the CCCS model of subculture, 'spectacular' visibility both defines subculture and, through their concomitant exposure to media industries and the state, is also the source of their inevitable destruction. Contemporary critiques of the CCCS have rightly reassessed the value of 'normal', 'unspectacular' youth culture and have shown that even producers of spectacular style may lack an unambiguous commitment to spectacular subculture. Yet spectacular subculture continues to grab the attention of researchers no less than the media and the state. However much we might not wish to use the word 'subculture' to describe spaces within which spectacular practices are produced, and however much those spaces may have changed since the 1970s, the CCCS delineated a topic for research that continues to fascinate. Furthermore, that practice of delineation means that the 'ghost' of subculture remains in research on spaces of spectacular youth cultural production, even if different analytical frameworks and terms are used to define such spaces.

Interactionist researchers have criticized research on the spectacular, on that which stands out, as a distraction from the much more significant mundane ways through which culture is reproduced (Silverman, 1993; Widdicombe and Wooffitt, 1995). They have shown how researchers' desires to study the spectacular may simply reproduce, rather than deconstruct, the social processes that create the phenomenon of spectacularness. Although they are right to point out this risk, I do not believe that it obviates the necessity for analytical attention towards the spectacular, and the extraordinary. Rather, the challenge is not to explain away the spectacular, but to understand its relationship to 'everyday life'. In this chapter I wish to show how the complex relationship

107

between the everyday and the spectacular works within the global Extreme
Metal music scene.

The Extreme Metal Scene

This chapter draws on research carried out on the global Extreme Metal
music 'scene', based on case studies in the UK, Sweden and Israel (Harris,
2001). The genealogy of the concept of scene is discussed in more detail
in the introduction to this book, as well as in Geoff Stahl's contribution
(Chapter 3). What is important to point out here is that the scene's non-
essentialist (Straw, 2001a) opacity means that that no single element of the
phenomena to which the term is applied ever comes to dominate subsequent
analysis. Where subculture was made visible through its spectacle, scene is
made visible through a complexity of interlocking, non-reductive factors.
One such factor may indeed be spectacle – as Blum (2001) shows, spectacle is
part of the connotative vocabulary of scene. However, the wider focus of
the concept of scene may change the way in which spectacular practice is
understood and situated.

The spectacular may well be the most 'visible' aspect of a scene (indeed, the
nature of the spectacular is precisely to become visible), and this is certainly
the case with the Extreme Metal scene. Extreme Metal is an extraordinary,
exceptional departure from conventional musical norms. The term is used to
describe a collection of genres that radicalize the better-known genre of Heavy
Metal (Walser, 1993). Extreme Metal genres such as Death Metal, Black Metal,
Doom Metal and Grindcore, largely dispense with melody, favouring instead
a 'fundamentalist' (Weinstein, 2000) reliance on extremes of speed, growled
or screamed vocals and dense, sometimes unintelligible collections of guitar
'riffs'. Extreme Metal may sound chaotic, with conventional musical structures
breaking down into near-formlessness (Reynolds and Press, 1995) and the use
of bewilderingly complex tonal structures (Berger, 1999a). Extreme Metal
should not be confused with Nu Metal, a genre that has been popularized
since the 1990s by bands such as Limp Bizkit and Korn. Although Extreme
Metal was crucial in the development of Nu Metal, most Extreme Metal scene
members now claim to detest Nu Metal.

Extreme Metal lyrics focus largely on death, mutilation, the occult and
misanthropic denunciations of humanity. Extreme Metal fans and musicians
dress in an identifiably spectacular way, wearing lurid T-shirts of their favourite
bands. Fans and musicians sometimes espouse extremist views, flirting with
(and sometimes embracing) Satanism, anarchism and very occasionally neo-
fascism. 'Deviant' activity is frequently produced within the Extreme Metal

scene, often fuelled by the heavy use of alcohol. On occasion, Extreme Metal scene members have found themselves in trouble with the forces of law and order. Most notoriously, in Norway in the early 1990s there were a spate of murders, church burnings and suicides linked to a circle of Satanic Black Metal musicians (Moynihan and Søderlind, 1998). The musician Varg Vikernes (aka Count Grisnacht), who recorded under the name of Burzum, killed rival musician Euronymous, of the band Mayhem. Mayhem's vocalist, 'Dead', had previously killed himself, an event celebrated within the Black Metal scene at the time. Vikernes was subsequently imprisoned, as was the musician 'Faust' from the band Emperor, who had murdered a homosexual stranger. A number of other scene members were also imprisoned or investigated for a spate of church burnings that took place around the same time.

The violence and anger demonstrated in Extreme Metal music, and in its more spectacular practices, have been analysed by some commentators in ways that recall the CCCS's notion of 'homology' (Willis, 1978). Harris Berger (1996b) argues that the music provides a source of individual empowerment, responsibility and community among people who have suffered as a result of changes in the structure of capitalism. Similarly, Jack Harrell (1994) finds in Death Metal 'an unofficial expression of industrialism's emotional isolation and violence' (p. 91), and Anne Petrov (1995) argues that 'Death Metal could be seen as a direct product of the ongoing urbanization of suburbia, as one of the forms which suburban violence takes' (p. 5).

The danger of such readings of the Extreme Metal scene is that they may reproduce the problems of the CCCS's method of analysis, in which subcultures were defined externally with little attention being paid to the meanings produced by the members themselves. What, then, is the meaning to the members themselves of the spectacular practices produced within the Extreme Metal scene? The question is better put as: How are the practices through which the spectacular is produced 'experienced' (Berger, 1999b) by members? Spectacular practice might better be classed as practice that offers the possibility of 'transgressive' experience. By transgressive, I mean experience produced through practices that cross over or (more usually) straddle the principal boundaries that structure our social reality: death/life, good/evil, pure/impure and so on. Transgressive practice offers 'liminal' (Turner, 1974) possibilities for the experience of the 'abject' (Kristeva, 1982) – the threatening possibility of the dissolution of the self within primal chaos. Transgressive behaviour is 'excessive': it constantly exceeds the boundaries of the body, revelling in the pleasures and pains of embodiment (Bakhtin, 1984; Stallybrass and White, 1986). Transgressive practice is practice not orientated towards utilitarian, rational ends. Rather, it is based on a simultaneous attraction to and repulsion from death. But transgression is not simply the experience of 'losing oneself', of dissolution, it is also at the same time an experience of control over the threat of dissolution. Transgression is an experience of individual 'sovereignty' (Bataille, 1993) over the abject at the same time as it flirts with the possibility of loss within the abject. Transgression is enshrined in art and in ritual practice. In modernity, the possible spaces for transgressive practice have been reduced, resulting in the classification of transgression as 'deviant' behaviour (Jervis, 1999). Music, whether associated with deviance or not, offers the possibility of transgression. Music motivates but also exceeds the body (DeNora, 1997), it allows for the experiencing of the partial dissolution of the self in dance (Reitveld, 1993), and it motivates erotic feelings of joy (Reynolds, 1990).

Transgression is produced within the Extreme Metal scene in ways as various as the production of musical texts that evoke the threatening abjectification of death (Harris, 2002), in violent 'moshing' at gigs, and in alcoholic oblivion – as well as in much more extreme activities such as Satanic murder. Like most transgressive activity, much of what occurs within the Extreme Metal scene could certainly be classed as spectacular. Yet a striking feature of the scene is its obscurity. Other Metal genres, such as Heavy Metal and Nu Metal, are highly culturally visible. Furthermore, Heavy Metal has been the subject of ridicule, disgust, court cases and censorship (Miller, 1988; Richardson, 1991). Unlike other Metal genres, Extreme Metal has rarely faced the threat of censorship and has rarely been the subject of moral panic. This is not because of the decline in the 'shock value' of Metal since the 1980s heyday of Metal – Extreme Metal is simply not exposed enough to engender the possibility of public shock *or* indifference. Extreme Metal is barely even known, much less despised. This is partially the result of much lower record sales than Heavy Metal, meaning that Extreme Metal rarely reaches the mass media, although low sales are not necessarily an impediment to notoriety.

Like the proverbial tree falling in the forest, is spectacular practice that occurs unobserved still spectacular practice? If a scene produces spectacular practice, but you can only see it if you know that it is there, does this still count as spectacular practice? It is here that we must depart from the CCCS definition of spectacle. In the classic subcultural model, spectacle is defined through public visibility. Yet there are other forms of visibility that may be just as potent as public visibility. The scene itself is a space for 'performance' (Butler, 1997), in which the practitioners are visible to each other. The Extreme Metal scene's transgressive practices remain spectacular in that they remain a focus of fascination to the scene itself as an audience. Scene members 'perform' transgression to each other. The scene itself is the focus of the scene's practices.

Everyday Life and Scenic Involvement

The internal directedness of spectacular practice within the Extreme Metal scene changes the nature of spectacle. In the CCCS model of subculture, the relationship of subculture to non-subculture (that is, of spectacular to hegemonic culture) provided the essential motor of subculture's very existence. In the Extreme Metal scene, the relationship of the scene to non-scene is not reducible to the relationship between spectacle and hegemony, or spectacle and non-spectacle. The boundary delineating the scene is not defined by the visibility of the scene but by the relationship of the scene to 'everyday life'.

Henri Lefebvre (1971) argues that everyday life consists of 'recurrences' through which the world is 'reproduced'. He further argues that: 'The quotidian is what is humble and solid, what is taken for granted and that of which all the parts follow each other in such a regular, unvarying succession that those concerned have no call to question their sequence (p. 24).

In members' accounts, the scene frequently is constructed as something removed from the sequential order of the quotidian. A common theme in accounts of entry into the scene is the 'overwhelming' impact of encountering something entirely different from the rest their lives up to that point. Exposure to Extreme Metal generally comes suddenly, unexpectedly; and it is a bewildering and exciting experience, as one British scene member recalls:

> First time I heard Slayer, I couldn't handle it, first time I heard Slayer, the first album Show No Mercy...and I'd heard about it, I knew it was fairly, totally fast, totally manic, hardcore Metal, and I couldn't handle it – man, it was like, all this satanic stuff, it's like whoa, what's going on here? (30 year old British male musician and record label owner)

The first encounter with Extreme Metal is frequently experienced as a shock – a musical experience separate from previous musical experiences. The shock of being 'blown away' by Extreme Metal almost always leads to a frantic search for more of it. The search for more Extreme Metal inevitably brings members into contact with scenic institutions. Becoming part of the scene can be an intoxicating process. The rapid and overwhelming exposure to a new form of music is combined with an exposure to a new social space, new forms of interaction and new institutions. Most scene members end up becoming heavily involved in the scene – there are relatively few 'part time' (Fox, 1987) fans, whose engagement with Extreme Metal is limited simply to listening to music. The scene overwhelms members, leading them to ever-greater involvement and greater pleasures, but involvement also creates complex problems.

Members still need to earn a living and maintain relationships with the non-scenic world. At times, involvement in the scene can cause difficult clashes with other parts of members' lives, forcing members to make difficult choices, sacrifices and compromises within the worlds of work and study, as in the account of this British scene member:

> I just dropped out of university basically and because I was like, I don't know, I think I just didn't take to it really, further education. I was like, had my fill of it and I was just like, I was totally obsessed with early Metal stuff and basically wanted to get involved in music. (mid-30s British male record label owner)

One of the problems of commitment to the scene is that only a tiny minority are able to earn a living from their activities within it. A top-selling Extreme Metal CD may sell around 100,000 copies, but even this only guarantees a bare minimal living. Furthermore, the globally dispersed nature of the scene ensures that only a subsistence level income can be achieved from touring. Of course, the lack of capital that can be made within the scene does not necessarily mean that members cannot 'live' primarily within the scene. In other scenes, such as the hardcore punk scene, members may seek to reduce their contact with the non-scenic world to an absolute minimum. Punk's 'aesthetic of poverty' (O'Conner, 2000) is embodied in institutions such as squatting and living off begging that enable members to engage with the non-scenic world as little as possible. There are indeed some scene members who live lives of alienation from the non-scenic world in this way, but their numbers are relatively few. What is more striking is how the vast majority of scene members earn a living or are supported by non-scenic means. This raises the problem of how to balance scenic and non-scenic involvement.

The Logic of Mundanity

Scene members have learned to limit the difficulties of balancing involvement in the scenic and non-scenic worlds by orientating their practice towards the experience of *mundanity*. The orientation of scenic practice towards the experience of mundanity constitutes an important 'logic' of the scene. The concept of 'logic' is derived from Will Straw's (1991) work on scenes. For Straw, a scene's logic represents the systematic ability of its practices to 'move' the scene in certain consistent directions.

The logic of mundanity moves scene members towards an 'everyday' experience of the scene. Most members attempt to make their experience of the scene 'normal', uncomplicated and suited to dealing with the challenges of being involved in both the Extreme Metal scene and the non-scenic world. At its most developed, this logic ensures that the scenic and non-scenic elements of everyday life are closely integrated. In their accounts, most members do admit to struggling at times with the often-divergent demands of the scenic and non-scenic worlds, but for most the struggle is tolerable. In fact, what is more striking is how successfully the majority of scene members manage the complex relationship between the scenic and non-scenic worlds, even while most scene members emphasize discursively the distinction between the scene and the rest of the world.

Most scene members attend successfully to the multiple spaces within which they are involved. For some scene members, the world of work and study can even be a space of personal fulfilment. While some of the more committed scene members sacrifice promizing careers to become involved in the scene, other's have well-paid and satisfying jobs in a wide variety of industries. It is quite common for scene members to be secure in economic terms. It is also common for scene members to be educated to university level. Scene members also maintain friendships outside the scene and have non-Metal interests and hobbies.

Scene members also attend to the demands of familial relationships. Many accounts of scenes assume that generational conflict is a crucial aspect of them (Gaines, 1990). Whether or not this is the case in other scenes, generational conflict virtually never appears as a theme in Extreme Metal scenic discourse. More prevalent is a ready display of affection for family members. Parents are mentioned frequently as sources of support, both financial and emotional, and even as inspirations. Acknowledgements on album sleeves frequently contain expressions of musicians' gratitude to parents, as in the following example from an album by the US Satanic Death Metal band, Pessimist, entitled *Cult of the Initiated* (Lost Disciple, 1997):

> I endlessly and profusely thank 'Pessi-Mom' and the 'Big Guy' for putting up with practice three times a week, for sleeping through countless parties and noisy late-night load-ins, for feeding and providing a crash pad for countless bands and other assorted derelicts... and for always supporting me 100% in everything I do... I love you both.

It is true that, for some scene members, the most effective way to manage the non-scenic elements of everyday life is to engage with the non-scenic world as little as possible. One scene member told me how he had very few friends, no television and little contact with the non-scenic world, concluding: 'I live in my small world and whatever happens outside, it doesn't bother me.' The experience of mundanity can frequently become the experience of solipsism.

A capacity to be quite content while alone is an important prerequisite for a sustained involvement in the scene. The scene is so small and so globally diffuse that its institutions have developed in such a way that isolated members can participate easily. The backbone of all scenic institutions is writing, by letter or e-mail. Bands develop reputations and obtain deals with record companies by writing fanzine interviews, corresponding with other scene members and by trading demos. With few exceptions, bands cannot get a recording deal or sell their recordings solely by playing live. Live performance can help a band to develop musically and to solidify a reputation, but it is not the principal route to a scenic career. Similarly, a non-musician within the scene finds quickly that greater involvement within the scene cannot come without writing to other members and hunting down CDs, fanzines and websites.

The mundane, solipsistic practice *par excellence* is collecting. Most scene members have extremely large collections of recordings – I saw a listing of one member's collection that totalled nearly 20,000 items. Members frequently have a staggering knowledge of the scene's music, and obscurity is valued for its own sake within the scene. Will Straw (1997) has argued that the pleasure of collecting comes from a masculine desire to order and categorize. Collecting involves a sustained commitment to the development and organization of vast and detailed forms of scenic knowledge. Like other forms of scenic practice, it also involves participation in complex scenic networks, the accessing of which demands considerable commitment and self-discipline. In their homes, members often have desks and filing systems that appear little different from those in other kinds of workspaces. One British scene member admitted to having written 300 letters a month at the peak of his involvement in the scene. The accounts of the more experienced members of the scene, who had established bands and other scenic institutions with good reputations, constantly emphasize the need to be focused, goal-orientated and hardworking, as in this account of the origin of one Swedish band:

> I played with these guys and they were much younger than me, just one year, but still they were in high school very childish, you know, and I had my goals set straight, you know, and they were like they didn't have any goals for their future they were just like playing around, having fun, you know, rehearsing but I was like I want to do good songs I was very, I was very, I knew what I was going to do, you know, and I felt kind of trapped with guys that were so childish and didn't have any goals for their future . . . So when I met (name of musician) and he was also very into very much, making a band, coming up with a band that could get a record deal, you know, so when I met with him I talked lots with him and, you know, he, we decided, to work together instead. (mid 20s Swedish male musician and record producer)

What is striking about this account is the opposition constructed between 'having fun' and having a successful career within the scene. The interviewee uses a discourse of work to describe the development of his band. The demands of work dominate scenic careers. The accounts of those who manage scenic institutions constantly emphasize the need for, and an expectation of, 'professional' standards, although, as one Swedish label manager puts it, this is frequently difficult:

> You have to be tough, you have to be really, really tough, and I have learnt this over the years now. You must not be timid and you must not take any shit, you know. But as long as you're that, you know, that's fine. I mean I've learnt the tricks now. (mid-20s British female scene member)

The necessity of orientating practice towards the experience of mundanity threatens to dominate the experience of the scene to the exclusion of all else. The scene necessitates professionalism and work. The problem is that the experience of mundanity produced by work within the scene always threatens to bring with it the boredom and drudgery of a life outside the scene. One British scene member describes how he became jaded with the scene:

> I was working full-time at that time, coming home and writing all these letters and also doing reviews of demos, interviews with bands and doing selling stuff as well and it just got too much. So basically I told a lot of people that were writing to me that I would be cutting down my mail at the time. So there was a lot of people who got cut out that were just writing letters that were two lines long and stuff like that. It was totally uninteresting just to write back to them all the time. (mid-30s British male scene member)

For this interviewee, the pleasure of contributing to the scene faded as it became simple routine. The pleasure that many scene members feel when they start to write letters and receive demos is threatened when letter writing becomes a daily chore. There is a danger that a scenic career may simply become a job like any other. This is particularly the case for the small minority of members who earn a living from the scene, who may be unable simply to leave. As one Swedish label manager puts it:

> You know before I started with this thing, I played in four bands in the same time, one after the other just, well I stopped playing because it was too much, so I miss that part of it. Actually you shouldn't work with the thing you love...But I don't know what I would do otherwise...I don't want to stand in the car factory.

From being an exciting, transgressive exception to everyday life, the scene may simply become mundane everyday life itself. While this guarantees stability and security, it also presents the danger of the experiential negatives of everyday life in capitalist modernity – boredom, exhaustion and alienation.

One possible *telos* of involvement in the scene is thus the integration of scenic practice into mundane everyday life. The experience of transgression is the experience of something exceptional, removed from mundane everyday experience. It is understandable therefore, that transgression is felt most intensely on entry to the scene. None the less, it is still possible that transgression might be experienced amid the mundane reproduction of the scene. Although the production of transgression may be routinized within the scene, the practice of transgression can never be completely contained. Even long-standing scene members involved in the business side of the scene can still be excited by the experience of music through the body, as in this account from a veteran British scene member:

> I still get fucking off on good records yeah, for sure, yeah. I thought that band the other night were that good I needed, I literally felt the physical need to go and bounce round like a [inaudible] you know, and go down the pit, fucking fall off the stage and all that sort of shit. I'm still well up for that you know.

This quotation demonstrates how transgression rejuvenates, giving new life to those jaded by mundane practice. The mundane production of transgression never completely overwhelms transgression itself. Conversely, transgression never completely overwhelms mundanity. The logics of transgression and mundanity are 'balanced', so that the scene rarely becomes dominated by one or the other. The dominant logic within the scene varies over time and space. The early 1990s Norwegian Black Metal space was committed overtly to transgressive practice, to the point where imprisonment and death almost destroyed it. Yet at the point where the scene was most threatened, the logic of mundanity 'saved' it. Those scene members who were not imprisoned or killed began to concentrate on making music and running labels in an efficient manner.

The balance between mundanity and transgression helps us to explain the scene's obscurity and lack of outward spectacle. The transgressive texts that the scene produces would probably threaten the scene were their existence to be made aware of outside the scene. The scene's obscurity is thus the precondition for its continued existence, and for most scene members the continued existence of the scene is of paramount importance, even if this means that the more intense (and concomitantly destructive) forms of transgression must be curtailed. The mundane logic of the scene thus ensures that the pleasures of transgression can be experienced in safety.

More problematically, the scene's obscurity also ensures that the scene remains insulated from the possibility of certain kinds of change. While in some respects the scene is highly heterogeneous (in terms of global diversity, for example) the scene is highly homogeneous in terms of gender. It is possible that the obscurity of the scene means that women are proportionally less likely to discover it than are men, since female involvement in youth culture tends to be constructed around the consumption of mass mediated texts. Indeed, more popular Metal scenes such as the Nu Metal scene have a much higher proportion of female members. Furthermore, the minority of female Extreme Metal scene members tend not to be as involved in scenic practice as are their male counterparts. The scene's safety and obscurity ensures its insulation from discourses and practices from outside that might challenge sexism within the scene. The result is a kind of stasis in which members' 'comfort zone' is never breached – the scene is how the majority of members want it, and those who are discontented either have to put up with this or not be part of the scene.

Conclusion

Focusing on the relationship of transgressive scenic practice to everyday life opens up new insights into the nature of involvement in youth culture. The Extreme Metal scene does not fit into the CCCS subcultural paradigm – its spectacle is too hidden, its members too adept at negotiating with the demands of everyday life. Yet neither does the Extreme Metal scene fit into a 'post-subcultural' paradigm in which scene membership is fluid and individuals are able to drift in and out of scenes at will. Extreme Metal scene members are deeply committed to the scene and make it a primary site of commitment in their lives. It is precisely *because* of this commitment that they are so adept at balancing everyday life and the scene, transgression and mundanity. The primary concern of scene members is that the Extreme Metal scene should continue. In order to achieve this, they must ensure that the scene does not destroy itself in the pursuit of spectacular transgression. They must ensure that their non-scenic lives remain unproblematic, so as not to make scenic involvement overly difficult.

That the Extreme Metal scene does not fit into the subcultural paradigm does not mean that the CCCS's narrative of spectacle followed by moral panic and destruction is redundant. Youth cultural practice since the 1970s has shown an implicit awareness of the dangers of the exposure that spectacle brings. The Extreme Metal scene, and others such as the hardcore punk scene, developed scenic infrastructures designed to avoid spectacular exposure and to ensure long-term survival. Other scenes developed a more playful and manipulative attitude to media exposure, as with some dance music scenes' courting of controversy (McRobbie and Thornton, 1995; Thornton, 1995). Scenes have therefore developed a variety of reflexive strategies to cope with the problematics of subcultural exposure. Such strategies are a sign of the penetration of the concerns of the CCCS into non-academic discourse (Bennett, 1999a). Present-day youth and popular cultural practice has not simply changed since subcultural studies – it has also changed *as a result of* the experience of 1970s subculture. Present-day scenes represent a range of responses to building youth and popular culture after subculture: some scenes are characterized by fluidity and temporal membership, while others, such as the Extreme Metal scene, are more invested in stability and continuity.

The work of the CCCS remains useful as it alerts us to a very real problem in cultural practice – how to produce a space whose symbolic practices challenge the dominant constructions of the world, without that space being destroyed in the process. Since the 1970s, various forms of youth and popular culture practice have responded to this challenge in various ways. Similarly, post-CCCS studies of youth culture can be read as highlighting the complex ways in which cultural practices have developed as a response to the challenges that CCCS-era subcultures faced. Although I would argue that subculture is an inappropriate concept to use in the analysis of contemporary cultural practice, it none the less illuminates some of the more difficult problematics of creating youth culture.

CHAPTER 8

Youth Strategies for Glocal Living: Space, Power and Communication in Everyday Cultural Practice

HILARY PILKINGTON

This chapter[1] shares the aspiration of other contributions to the volume to re-map the terrain of contemporary youth cultural practice, both theoretically and empirically, in search of what comes 'after subculture'. It takes as its empirical example youth cultural formations in Russia at the end of the 1990s, to suggest that emergent strands of 'post-subcultural'[2] theorizing do not engage adequately with youth cultural practices outside the 'global core'. It is argued that empirical data from the Russian field illustrate that terms such as 'postmodern subcultures', 'post-subculturalists' or 'neo-tribes' – which suggest that youth cultural practice is based on a fundamentally new form of sociation, in which the classic identity markers of modernity have become redundant – have geo-politically limited explanatory power. In order to mobilize data effectively from a wider range of youth cultural experience in the 'post-subculture' debate, however, we also need to challenge 'core' narratives of globalization in which global and local are understood as start- and end-points in a chain of cultural transmission. Greater attention to 'peripheral' youth cultural perspectives, it is suggested, lends weight to the understanding of the global–local nexus as inherently power-*ful*. In this chapter, therefore, it is suggested that global–local positionings are more than the points at which 'global culture' is accessed; they are markers of difference that are mobilized reflexively by young people alongside others (gender, ethnicity, social status) in the production of diverse, locally rooted but globally resourced youth cultural *strategies*.

Alternative Modernities and Subcultural Theories

Subcultural theory was the defining 'other' in the sociological study of youth in the Soviet Union from the late 1970s. 'Subculture' was perceived by Soviet sociologists to be an ideological rather than a theoretical category, and was constructed discursively as being relevant only to capitalist societies. Concepts of both 'sub-' and 'counter-culture' were ritually critiqued by Soviet sociologists as 'bourgeois' because they suggested conflict between generations was replacing class struggle as the motor of history, and thereby distracting young people from their true revolutionary interests. Moreover, their focus on the cultural sphere was criticized for promoting the illusion that economically rooted class antagonisms could be overcome through cultural practice; that is, by changing manner, style or clothes (Ikonnikova, 1974, 1976; Davydov, 1977; Khudaverdian, 1977, 1986; Kurbanova, 1985, 1986). Paradoxically, therefore, Soviet sociologists criticized the work of the CCCS (despite its neo-Marxist origins) and, in their concern to show Soviet society as being free of generational conflict, adopted a structural-functionalist approach to youth culture that emphasized the role of youth cultural practice in the successful socialization of young people and rejected any possibility of rupture between generations (Pilkington, 1994, pp. 74–8).

It was in the mid-1980s that cultural theorists began to reappropriate the notion of 'subculture' as applied to Soviet society (see Kuchmaeva, 1987; Matveeva, 1987; Orlova, 1987). The first empirical studies of Soviet subcultures were undertaken by social psychologists at the end of the *perestroika* period (Fel'dshtein and Radzikhovskii, 1988; Shchepanskaia, 1991). It was not until the late 1990s, however, that the first sociological texts on Russian youth 'subcultures' were published (Islamshina *et al.*, 1997; Kostiusheva, 1999; Omel'chenko, 2000).

The late entrance of Russian sociology to subcultural theorizing has meant that the debate has avoided the class reductionism of earlier Western theories of youth subculture. By the late 1990s, indeed, subcultures were being interpreted by Russian sociologists as constituent parts of late modern society in its 'disintegrative' state, and subcultural affiliation was being portrayed as a lifestyle choice (Godina, 1999; Sokolov, 1999, p. 51) rather than a class destiny. Sokolov's argument that subcultures should be studied in terms of what is being chosen by their members rather than what is 'resisted' through subcultural affiliation (Sokolov: 1999, p. 19), for example, combines a traditional Soviet approach to youth culture (emphasizing continuity rather than conflict between generations) with a post-resistance model of youth subculture. Thus, in line with emergent post-subcultural approaches in the West (see note 2), first attempts to map the post-Soviet youth cultural scene by Russian sociologists recognize, as one of its characteristics, the erasing of borders between, and frequent movement among, subcultural groups (Islamshina *et al.*, 1997, p. 54).

In contrast to Western subcultural theory of the 1970s and 1980s, which tended to ignore the global cultural engagement of young people,[3] Russian writing on 'subcultures' from the post-War period onwards was dominated by discussion of the 'Western' influence on young people. Rock and roll fans (*stiliagi*) were the first youth cultural group to be labelled Western-influenced ideological 'subversives', but in the later Soviet period – as hippies, punks, bikers and pop fans became increasingly visible – young people as a whole were criticized increasingly for their 'blind imitation' of decadent Western cultural forms (music, style, dance and movement trends, and political apathy). This vulnerability to 'Western influence' was attributed to Soviet youth right through to the Gorbachev *perestroika* of the late 1980s (Pilkington, 1998, p. 374). Moreover, when the advent of the post-Soviet regime facilitated research by Western academics into Russian youth cultural practice, the primacy of the West in that practice remained paramount. Rayport Rabodzeenko, for example, argues that, in their cultural practice, 'subcultural' youth in St Petersburg engaged with 'the West' primarily through a process of the enactment of exoticism and mimesis of a 'real culture' felt to be missing in their own society (Rayport Rabodzeenko, 1998, pp. 35, 56).

Modernity, Consumption and Choice: Preconditions for 'Post-subculturalism'?

In Western post-subcultural theorizing, the global context of youth cultural forms is generally accepted as a given rather than the object of investigation.[4] Post-subcultural theory has been developed primarily on the basis of youth cultural practices in Western 'culture producing' societies. In the West, clubbing, for example, has been interpreted as providing a spatial shelter from the speed-driven postmodern city characterized by a deficit of meaningful social interaction. Clubs are simply sites of postmodern tribal gatherings, in which place is everything, and the individual nothing; a space in which 'egocentric' cultures are, albeit temporarily, displaced by 'lococentric' cultures (Maffesoli, 1996, p. 138[5]; Malbon, 1999, p. 183). But do young people experience late modern urban space similarly wherever they are located? Are the meanings of practices such as clubbing transportable across cultural space? And, if not, does this limit the applicability of terms such as 'neo-tribes' to youth cultural practices in a small, though influential, part of the world?

Research into Russian clubbing practices shows that in *form*, the scene (self-consciously) reflects back the inclusivity, 'classlessness', fluidity and diversity

that have been said to characterize dance cultures (or at least members' perceptions of them) in the West. As in the West, 'subcultural' identities among
Russian clubbers are not created through any exclusive style, and the sheer
physical pleasure of dancing is central to the attraction of clubbing. In terms
of the *meanings* attached to clubbing, however, there are striking absences in
young Russians' narratives of the club experience. Most notably, there is little
talk of the pleasure of 'losing oneself' in the crowd, or any sense of 'experiential
consumption', that Malbon argues lies at the centre of the communality of
clubbing on the London scene (Malbon, 1999, pp. 22, 185–7). The sensation
of (temporarily) ceding one's body to the crowd, the music and the atmosphere, or more precisely, of fluctuating between belonging to the crowd and
'differentiation' from it (ibid.) is, indeed, hard to imagine within the physical
constraints of the provincial Russian club scene. The buildings housing the
dance scene in provincial cities are most frequently old 'houses of culture',
'youth palaces', or cinemas constructed to Soviet dimensions and more suited
to their daytime use (such as children's ballet classes) than their night-time
existences as clubs. But the real issue is not the quality of the cultural infrastructure of a society suffering the consequences of the high-cost, low-yield
Soviet version of modernity (Arnason, 1993; Sakwa, 1996, pp. 357–60; Castells,
1998, pp. 9–25), but a more profound disruption of paradigmatic understandings of the logic of modernization. In Russia, modernity has been detached
from two of its most loyal companions – consumption and individualism.

For those who study youth cultural practices in 'modernizing' societies, the
problematization of modernity is commonplace; constraints upon youth cultural
agency are considered inherent in the process by which young people form
modern identities at the intersection of tradition and globalization, development and consumerism (Wulff, 1995, p. 9). The Russian experience, however,
appears to conform neither to 'modernizing' nor (post)modern understandings
of the association between the consumption of material and cultural commodities and the formation of youth cultural ('subcultural' and 'post-subcultural')
identities. In post-Soviet Russia, young people may be engaged primarily as
'consumers' rather than 'producers', in a way characteristic of late modern
society (Bauman, 1998, p. 80), but they do not as yet recognize themselves as
subjects of that consumption (Oushakine, 2000, p. 98). Thus, while Western
theorists anticipated that the post-socialist experience would be a happy fusion
of global cultural consumption and political freedom (Lull, 1995, p. 125;
Beck, 2000, p. 66), in practice, lifestyle construction through consumption,
let alone the progression from commodity to experiential consumption, sheds
little light on the nature of youth cultural practice in post-Soviet Russia.
Consuming practice is experienced rather as an almost perpendicular learning
curve whose negotiation is impeded by a chronic mismatch between disposable

income and goods available, the rendering redundant by globalization of accumulated consumer knowledges,[6] and a Russian narrative of national self that requires the public dissimulation of indifference to 'Western' values centred on individual consumption (Pilkington *et al.*, 2002, p. 219).

The relationship between clubber and crowd in Russia is suggestive also of a peculiar (that is, non-Western) relationship between individualization and modernization. In Russia, individualization occurred through public penitential practices (rather than the private confessional practices), and in the context of mutual surveillance among peers (Kharkhordin, 1999). Late modern society in Russia is not saturated with individualism and, at least outside Moscow and St Petersburg, contemporary city living is not characterized by speed, intensity, organization and punctuality so much as disorganization, negotiation, dysfunctionality and dust. While many people nevertheless share with western city dwellers a desire for greater social interaction, this is rarely expressed in the enjoyment of mass rituals (spectator sports, shopping centres, festivals, political events), since these tend to be associated with thoroughly disembodied, public displays of unity with little intrinsic meaning. Moreover, in the urban Russian context, 'the crowd' is not a temporary euphoric gathering, but a constant and hostile presence – pushing one on, or off, public transport, jostling one in a queue, or shouting slogans at a rally. The tactility of 'the crowd' is uninvited and oppressive, and the prospect of giving one's individual sense of identity up to it is more likely to be associated with the constraining rather than liberating cultural force of 'the mass'.

Readers are therefore asked to engage with this chapter, not simply out of an interest in the peculiarity of youth cultural experience in a country that is 'neither fish nor fowl', and that conforms neither to the 'postmodern' nor 'modernizing' models of society. What is argued here is that, as in the West, in their everyday cultural practice, young people in Russia form micro-groups which constitute an 'emotional community' (Maffesoli, 1996, pp. 9–30) that transcends individualism. The chapter uses empirical data, however, to address the question of what constitutes the *substance* of the affectual quality of such micro groups. In the Russian case, it is argued, this emotional community is rooted neither in 'subcultural style' nor in post-subcultural lifestyle-constituting consuming practices, but in an embodied communicative practice. In tackling the specific question of what comes 'after subculture', it is suggested that the kind of communicative practice engaged in is rooted in specific configurations of spatial, socio-economic, gender and ethnic relations articulated via reworked 'alternative' and 'mainstream' identities on the youth cultural scene. In positioning themselves in this way on the youth scene, moreover, young people mobilize the 'global' and 'the local' differentially in what are referred to below as 'youth cultural strategies' of late modernity.

'Progressives' and 'Normals': Strategies for Glocal Living

The data drawn on in this section of the chapter were gathered under the auspices of a collaborative research project between the University of Birmingham and Ul'ianovsk State University.[7] The project studied the youth cultural scenes in three of Russia's cities: Moscow, Russia's political and economic capital; Samara, a major and relatively economically buoyant city on the Volga river; and Ul'ianovsk, a smaller city in the middle Volga region with a reputation for political and socio-cultural conservatism. The wider research project involved original data collection of both a quantitative (representative survey) and qualitative (in depth interviews, focus groups and ethnographic data collection) nature. It explored the increasingly diverse range of media and cultural products used by young people in Russia at the end of the 1990s, the range of images of the West that were contained in them, the actual images of the West articulated by young people, and the enactment of global and local in everyday youth cultural practice. The empirical data referred to here are drawn from one element of the wider research project, specifically 134 in-depth interviews with young people aged 15–25 in Moscow, Samara and Ul'ianovsk, as well as ethnographic data from a number of scenes in which they participated. Respondents in this part of the research were not selected by sample but accessed by visiting a broad range of sites used by young people for leisure, including: street or yard (*dvor*), organized after-school activities (sports clubs or training sessions, aerobics and 'shaping' classes, modelling courses, choral and skating groups, after-school civic education courses), cafés, discos, night-clubs, well-known *tusovka* sites (squares, yards, underground stations, cafés), pop and rock concerts, folk (*KSP – Klub Samodeiatel'noi Pesni*) clubs and young ramblers' groups (*turisty*), schools and colleges.

Figure 8.1 maps the youth cultural scene of provincial Russia in the late 1990s,[8] as reconstructed by young people's own narratives of their location on the scene. The most striking feature of the youth cultural scene in all three cities studied was the persistent 'alternative-mainstream' distinction in young people's understandings of the scene; this is depicted in Figure 8.1 by the perforated line enclosing micro-groups referred to in Russia traditionally as '*tusovki*' and '*neformaly*'. Both of these terms might be translated in shorthand as 'subcultures'. *Tusovki* are centrally-located, often style- or music-based youth cultural formations, which became particularly visible in urban centres from the mid-1980s. Their members are not necessarily from privileged backgrounds, but their claiming of space in the centre of cities signifies an upwardly- and outwardly-orientated strategy, and desire to escape the territorial gang formations of the periphery. The term '*neformaly*' was used from the mid-1980s to describe 'alternative' youth groups active within 'non-official'

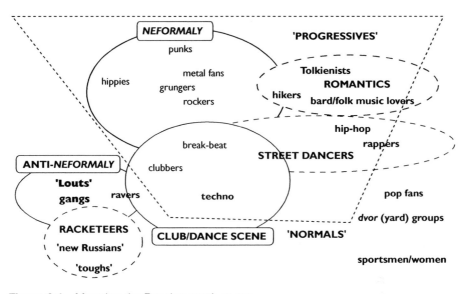

Figure 8.1 Mapping the Russian youth scene
Source: Fieldwork in Samara, Russian Federation, 1998.

spheres of Soviet society. The term was coined to express a horizontal relationship to the dominant social and political institutions – *neformaly* were those who sought expression outside official state structures (the *Komsomol* and the CPSU, for example) – in conscious contrast to the term 'subculture', which intimated a vertical, and resistant, relationship to the 'dominant culture'. However, the '*neformaly*' label was quickly adopted by those on the youth cultural scene, and by the late 1980s had acquired a degree of 'authenticity'.[9]

The perforated nature of the border between alternative and mainstream youth groupings, and the overlapping circles that individual *tusovki* inhabited at the end of the 1990s, confirms the trend noted by others towards 'unstable and shifting cultural affiliations' (Bennett, 1999a, p. 605) in youth sociation. Indeed, movement across and cross-fertilization between groupings on the Russian scene was commonplace (Islamshina *et al.*, 1997, p. 54; Pilkington *et al.*, 2002, pp. 101–32).

Despite this, it is difficult to conceptualize contemporary youth micro-groups in Russia as 'postmodern subcultures', defined by Muggleton, for example, as displaying a limited perception of themselves in collective terms, a transient attachment to any one style, and a failure to recognize divides between the subcultural and the conventional (Muggleton, 2000, pp. 52–3).[10] Studying the Russian scene showed that such 'fleeting' 'subcultural' affiliations were housed within broader, and deeper, youth cultural position referred to here, following young people's own self-identification as 'progressive' and 'normal' (see Figure 8.1). Acknowledging the risk that this attributes too great a degree of agency and self-consciousness to youth cultural affiliation, I suggest that these 'progressive' and 'normal' identifications be conceptualized as 'strategies' (Pilkington *et al.*, 2002, p. xvi). These strategies drew not only on style and musical taste, but also on a wide range of life positions, and had clear (if frequently transgressed) boundaries that were meaningful not only for 'subcultural' ('progressive') but also 'mainstream' ('normal') youth. The term 'strategies' is adopted, therefore, to suggest that these identifications had not been bought at the 'supermarket of style' (Polhemus, 1997, p. 150) but were carved out of the social cleavages (socio-economic, spatial, gender, ethnic and sexual differences) of Soviet modernity. In particular, the term is used to indicate that social structures – in this case the focus is on the global–local nexus – do not necessarily confine young people to pre-ordained destinies, but offer different cultural resources to young people as they negotiate the present and envisage the future.

'Progressives'

Young people adopting a 'progressive' strategy had their roots in the *tusovki* ('subcultural' groupings) of the late Soviet period. The term itself came from the club and dance scene, where members described themselves as 'progressives' – or those who listened to 'progressive music'.[11] Although the term 'progressive' was used by young people to differentiate themselves on the dance scene from 'the mass' of 'mainstream' youth, it was extended to a wide range of 'alternative' youth in an act of inclusivity designed to contrast the perceived particularist practice of older, style-based *tusovki* ('subcultures'). In fact, divisions between individual *tusovki* continued to be recognized (especially by rock-based *neformaly*). Nevertheless, young people across the 'progressive' space shared a number of common cultural practices that distinguished them from the 'mass' of mainstream youth (see Figure 8.2). They sought to create 'individual styles' rather than to 'follow fashion', and professed allegiance to particular styles of music (especially rock, electronic dance, and bard music). More important, since such affiliations were generally temporally constrained, 'progressives' acquired cultural capital via the distinction between 'authentic' and commercial ('pop') music, and they used music in cultural practice in such a way as to align themselves as information-seeking, outward-looking, 'progressive' young people. Thus 'progressives' tended to have more links with, and access to, Western cultural experience and products, and identified themselves consciously as outward-(Westward)looking, forward-moving individuals. The breadth to

	Progressives	Normals
HORIZONS	Outward-looking Translocal orientation Pulled towards 'the centre' Claimed city centre space	Inward-looking Locally rooted and territorially demarcated Used city space diffusely
SOCIATION	Multiple circles of friends and acquaintances Celebrated 'diversity' of their social circle 'Tusovka' was main site of sociability	Single, stable crowd of friends and acquaintances Friends drawn from place of study or residence (*dvor*)
INDIVIDUAL AND SOCIETY	Focused on the individual Emphasized lifestyle 'choice' Drug and alcohol use viewed as personal choice Rejected rigid notions of gender and gender roles	Focused on the group Referred to *group* norms concerning use of drugs or alcohol Employed traditional notions of gender identity and displayed hostility to 'gender-bending'
MUSIC AND STYLE PRACTICE	Allegiance to particular music Cultural capital attributed to musical knowledge and preference Used clothes and attributes to create 'individual styles'	Music did not hold cultural capital Music used as background to other peer group activities Hostile to 'standing out' through style Preferred current 'fashion'

Figure 8.2 'Progressive' and 'normal' strategies for glocal living

the horizons of young 'progressives' – their ability to travel and see beyond the locality – was reflected clearly in their pull towards 'the centre'. They disparaged 'provincialism' and claimed city-centre space for their cultural practice (*tusovki*), that increasingly took place in clubs, cafés and bars rather than on the city streets, in parks and metro stations that were frequented in the late Soviet period. These *tusovki* were the main sites for their social activity, although 'progressives' had multiple circles of friends and acquaintances, and were proud of the 'diversity' of people with whom they mixed. Moreover, these micro-groups were, first and foremost, constituted of *individuals*; 'progressives' emphasized lifestyle 'choice' and prioritized personal choice over 'group norms' in making decisions – for example, about the use of drugs and alcohol.

There is clearly something 'post-' about 'progressives'. The celebration of diversity and temporary transcendence of traditional bonds of community (based on class, social status, ethnicity, gender) has been observed widely in club scenes in the West (McRobbie, 1994; Thornton, 1995, p. 15; Malbon, 1998, pp. 273–7). This was reflected in Russia in the rejection by the 'progressives' of 'sectarian' divisions based on musical allegiances perceived to prevail among *neformaly*, and their replacement by a more fluid sense of commonality rooted not in a new 'style', or even the replacement of style with dancing, but a particular approach to life. Russian clubbers related their corporeal movement to a wider sense of social and cultural movement, or more specifically 'progress': 'the common interest is that we want to move on, we don't want to stay in one place. We want to be developing all the time, there should be no regression...it is movement alone which unites us' (253, Ul'ianovsk).[12] In the context of the ever-present threat of the territorially-rooted, gang-based youth cultural 'other', individual 'progression' marks these young people's movement away, and distinction from, identification with and submergence in to the localized 'mass'.

'Normals'

'Progressive' strategy was articulated, even named, by those who adopted it, and for this reason 'progressives' occupy a disproportionate space in Figure 8.1. In fact, the majority of young people are located towards the bottom half of the figure; they hang out around their place of residence or with school or college friends, listening to music and/or taking part in some kind of organized sport, or musical or other leisure activity. These people generally referred to themselves as 'normal' or 'ordinary' (*obychnie*) youth and rejected explicitly the 'labelling' of young people according to 'style' (see Figure 8.2). Within the 'normals', there were at least two distinct groups of young people – those 'ordinary' kids who hung out in *dvor* (yard) groups or were engaged in more-or-less organized leisure activities; and 'anti-*neformaly*'. Both of these broad groups positioned themselves on the youth scene in conscious opposition to the *neformaly*. The majority of ordinary kids were conscious of their difference from, but were largely indifferent to, those they saw as having 'subcultural' affiliations. However, where *dvor* groups articulated particular hostility towards 'subcultural' groups, they might be considered to be 'louts' (*gopniki*)[13] and to be housed within a broader group of 'anti-*neformaly*'. '*Obychnie*' talked about *neformaly* in general terms, seeing them as an incomprehensible phenomenon with dubious morality, but not as personally threatening to their cultural space. Anti-*neformaly*, in contrast, used the normatively loaded term 'normals' (*normal'nie*) to describe themselves, indicating their belief that their aggression towards the *neformaly* supported the interests of the 'moral majority',[14] and had a conscious sense of the qualities of 'normal' lads: 'We are sportsmen... 'us' is lads who...are normal (*normal'nie*), who understand us...About 70 per cent of youth understand...we are close friends' (3, Ul'ianovsk).

In part, at least, 'normal' strategy did in fact hinge on a rejection of *tusovka* practice. This was most evident in the reluctance, even hostility, expressed by young 'normals' to 'standing out' through style and to 'gender-bending' (see Figure 8.2). Thus a preference for current 'fashion', and a dislike of 'unisex' clothing and long hair reflected not only a set of style tastes, but also an aversion to what they perceived to be the 'non-traditional' gender norms of 'alternative' youth. Although 'normals' expressed musical tastes, they used music neither as cultural capital, nor an end in itself, but as a background to other peer group activities, especially meeting members of the opposite sex or drinking with members of the same sex. Thus, while 'normal' kids were also engaged with electronic dance music, they danced not in clubs but at discos in local Houses of Culture, schools and colleges, or at summer discos, and were referred to disparagingly as 'ravers' (*reivera/y*) by *tusovka* respondents.

'Normals' rejected the division or labelling of young people according to 'subcultural' style and preferred to socialize with a single, stable crowd with whom they studied, or from their place of residence (*dvor*). Although the 'gang' structure of these groups, common in the later 1980s and early 1990s, had largely disappeared, nevertheless the 'group' had an existence over and above its constituent members. 'Normals', for example, referred to *group* norms – rather than personal choice – concerning the use of drugs or alcohol. Perhaps most importantly, and in sharp contrast to 'progressives', 'normal' youth located its cultural practice locally, around home (*dvor*) or place of study. They used city space diffusely through practices of 'going out' (*gul'iat'*) and hanging out in the *dvor* or entrance way (*pod'ezd*). This gave the impression of being in control of one's territory, and was perceived as being intimidating by many 'progressives'. In fact, however, the practice reflected a social background that prohibited claims to central-city space, a narrowness of future horizons, and thus a localised and inward-looking strategy for negotiating the present.

Beneath Style: Space, Power and Communication

From this brief sketch of the Russian youth scene at the end of the 1990s, it is apparent that mainstream-alternative identifications remained strong, that Western music and style preferences were important for many, but the fact that the latter could be found among both groups, did not explain how young people come to adopt 'progressive' or 'normal' strategies. In this final section it is suggested that the micro-groups formed and maintained by young Russians were bound together not by stylistic, musical or other consumer preferences, but by specific practices of 'communication' (*obshchenie*), of which style and music are both elements.

'Progressives' were characterized by a distinctive mode of interaction with society in general, and their peers in particular, central to which was a mode of communication (*obshchenie*) originating in Russian *tusovka* life of the 1980s and early 1990s (Pilkington, 1994; Rayport Rabodzeenko, 1998). At that time, shared musical, dance, style or interest preference often constituted the explicit 'purpose' for getting together, but acted primarily as a setting for the kind of intimate communication central to the creation of the meanings and symbols of *tusovka* life. The wider media and information environment with which *tusovki* of the late 1990s engaged, however, was reflected in a communicative practice that was characterized by increasingly broad horizons and openness to new – global, national and local – flows of information. In particular, 'progressive' strategy incorporated an energy and determination to harness new informational flows for self-development, and 'progressive' young people were characterized by their tendency to look outwards, to maintain broad horizons and to seek new information and cultural stimuli: 'communication (*obshchenie*) is the air, which the brain breathes. When I am getting fresh information I am swimming somehow. If all the information taps were turned off, I would drown [*sic*]...The flow of information is the most valuable thing. It is the main thing in communication' (231, Samara).

While it is tempting to draw parallels here with the information fetishism of the *otaku*,[15] for Russian 'progressives' scouring the information load of late modernity was not an end in itself, but the *means to communication*. Moreover, new information and stimuli were sought not through 'virtual' but through 'real' communication via a cultural practice rooted in the reconfigured *tusovka*. Moreover, unlike the *otaku* – (Grassmuck, 1999), for 'progressives', the *tusovka* provided a vital social context for communication. It facilitated communication with people who were more knowledgeable, more travelled, and who held more cultural capital than oneself. Respondents thus defined the *tusovka* as a constantly-changing group of people who provided stimulation and access to a wider world of 'interesting' people.

In sharp contrast to the 'progressives', in their communicative practice 'normals' valued the security generated by a stable, territorially-rooted friendship network. 'Normals' did not 'revolve' in constantly-changing *tusovki*, but inhabited concentric circles of best friends, small groups of friends (*kompaniia*) based on home or *dvor*, study or leisure activity, and finally a wider group of acquaintances with whom they might 'go out' (*guliat'*). In contrast to *tusovka* youth, who managed multiple identities as a matter of pride, a particular feature of this kind of 'normal' strategy was to bring different friends together in 'one's own gang' (*svoi*). As a practice, it generated a sense of security and control, especially when young people from the periphery were seeking space for leisure on others' territory, such as at a city-centre disco. Thus, whereas 'progressives' described their interaction with each other as purposeful – a frenzied 'exchange of information' – 'normals' described their communication as 'chat' or 'gossip': 'We sit on the bench, sit and smoke, talk about life, with the girls... now the circus has come we will go to the circus... we go to the disco... have fun, smoke dope' (10, Ul'ianovsk).

Thus, in contrast to 'progressives', whose city centre *tusovki* and information-seeking practices marked out symbolically a global communicative space, 'normals' tended to base their get-togethers in each other's flats, or on benches in the *dvor*, indicating a locally demarcated communicative practice in which friendships provided a depth of security measured by its potential for defensive mobilization.

The example of Russian youth cultural practice suggests that 'communication' is not only a structural precondition for the coming together and being together of young people, but is also a set of verbal and embodied practices constitutive of the group. When 'communication' breaks down, either because trust or commitment is lost, or because individuals seek new forms of communication through different styles, music, sports, stimulants and so on, the group is redefined and reconstituted, or disbands. While this confirms the existence of an 'affectual' quality to contemporary youth micro-groups (Maffesoli, 1996, p. 6), it casts doubt on the 'neo-tribal' quality of such groups. The Russian example, it is argued here, suggests that distinctive communicative practices are socially rooted, reinforce alternative ('progressive') and mainstream ('normal') youth cultural identifications, and reflect different strategies adopted by young people in negotiating their location in the global–local nexus.

Conclusion

> Residents of the first world live in *time*; space does not matter for them, since spanning every distance is instantaneous... residents of the second world, on the contrary, live in *space*: heavy, resilient, untouchable, which ties down time and keeps it beyond the residents' control. (Bauman, 1998, p. 88)

Critics of 'subcultural' theories of youth suggest that young people's experience of late-/post-modernity has produced distinctly new forms of youth sociation in the form of tribal gatherings in which young people are (albeit temporarily) radically disconnected from the traditional identity markers (class, gender, ethnicity) of modernity. Where globalization has been discussed in relation to contemporary youth cultural practice, however, debates have tended to focus upon the ability of 'global' youth cultural forms to reach out to youth on the 'periphery', producing 'globalized cultural sensibilities' (Stahl, 1999, p. 2) either in the form of a mainstream, consumer-based 'global youth culture' or trans-local subcultural affiliations. In this chapter, the everyday cultural practice of young people outside the 'global core' has been used to suggest that 'globalized', late-modern society does not liberate young people from their social origins, but in fact reconfigures global–local relations that structure and articulate their experiences.

This is not to suggest that Bauman's notion of the 'globalized' rich and the 'localized' poor should be read as evidence that young people outside the 'core' are condemned to a life of 'despair born of a prospectless existence' (Bauman, 1998, p. 70). The Russian example employed in this chapter illustrates that young people do not live in the shadow of globalization, but rather that the 'global' and the 'local' are resources drawn upon, differentially, by young people in the process of developing youth cultural strategies that manage 'glocal' lives. This means more than the fact that 'global' youth cultural forms are appropriated in culturally distinct ways at the local (for which read 'national' for places outside 'the core') level. It contends that similar music or styles may be appropriated differently within distinct micro-groups to consolidate existing youth cultural markers of difference – producing, for example, both 'progressive' clubbers and 'normal' ravers.

The chapter has charted how the global and the local were drawn upon differentially in the cultural practice of young urban Russians at the end of the 1990s. It has suggested that, for those with the social and cultural capital to permit them to claim a space in 'the centre', the new openness to global cultural flows in Russia has been embraced in the formation of a 'progressive' cultural strategy. 'Progressive' young people were characterized by their tendency to look outwards, to maintain broad horizons and to seek new information and cultural stimuli. They 'looked West' in the sense that trans-local style or music affiliations (in the main produced in the West) were often a source of such information and a focus point on the global horizon to which eyes were turned.[16] In contrast, 'normal' youth located its cultural practice locally, and territorially – around home (*dvor*) or place of study – rather than trans-locally and symbolically (through style or music). In sharp contrast to the 'progressives', in their communicative practice 'normals' valued most highly not new information, diverse people and a sense of perpetual motion, but the security generated by a stable, territorially-rooted friendship network. That their horizons were focused narrowly on their personal locale reflected increasing competition for places in higher education, for professional training that might guarantee a 'real' salary and, above all, a modicum of social security; this required young people to focus intensively on activities – study, work and income supplementation – which continued to require extensive local networking. 'Normal' young people's horizons were severely restricted by the bounds of what was realistically possible, producing a cultural strategy that used the depth of their local connections as a means of securing for them a minimal material security which might facilitate 'global' consumption.

In calling for a more active engagement of social theories of youth with the experiences of young people outside the 'global core', this chapter builds on early critiques of subcultural theory that suggested that, as music and style move out of their original contexts, they develop their own specific cultural significances, often far removed from any original celebration of American (or Western) consumerism (Stratton, 1985, p. 189). However, it suggests that the importance of such engagement goes beyond understanding that youth cultural forms develop multiple meanings depending on the context of their realization. It argues that global–local positions are mobilized reflexively by young people alongside other markers of difference (gender, race, social status) in the production of distinct youth cultural strategies that not only reflect young people's origins, but also help to negotiate their presents and imagine their futures.

Notes

1 This chapter builds on papers presented to the BSA Study Group meeting, Northampton in January 2001, and the (Post)-Subcultural Studies Workshop, Vienna in May 2001. Some of the arguments presented are developed more fully in Pilkington *et al.* (2002, pp. 101–32).

2 By the second half of the 1990s, a series of focused critiques on the applicability of CCCS subcultural theory to contemporary youth cultural practice could be read as an emergent 'post-subcultural' approach to youth cultural practice (see Clarke, 1981; McRobbie, 1994; Thornton, 1995; Gelder and Thornton, 1997; Polhemus, 1997; Redhead, 1997; Hetherington, 1998; Bennett, 1999a; Malbon, 1999; Stahl, 1999; Muggleton, 2000).

3 Exceptions here include the work of Jon Stratton (1985) and Dick Hebdige (1987).

4 Attention to the local meanings invested in global youth cultural forms has been confined largely to writing concerning the local appropriations of popular music (see, for example, Robinson *et al.*, 1991; Taylor, 1997; Bennett, 1999b, 2000; Huq, 1999; Mitchell, 1996; Condry, 2000).

5 Maffesoli (1996), drawing on the linguistic research of Berque, suggests that cultures may be loco-centric – where the immediate surroundings or context are paramount; or egocentric – where the individual's identity and his/her actions take on a primary significance.

6 This knowledge is rooted in the Soviet experience of deficit production of high-quality consumer goods, and thus the fetishisation of Western (*firmennaia*) commodities.

7 The project – entitled 'Looking West? Images of the West among Russian Youth' – was directed by Dr Elena Omel'chenko and the author, and was supported financially by the Leverhulme Trust (F/94/BJ) from March 1996 to June 1999.

8 Of the three cities in which fieldwork was conducted, it is the Samara scene that is depicted here.

9 The collapse of these state institutions in 1991 has led to the designification of this term, although it was still used in Russian provincial cities at the end of the 1990s (Pilkington *et al.*, 2002, pp. 107–10).

10 In fact, Muggleton is developing an 'ideal type' here, and his own empirical work draws more subtle distinctions from the partial confirmation of the original hypotheses.

11 These terms (*progressivy, prodvinutie*) were used widely by scene-leading youth cultural magazines, but had been adopted by those on Russia's club and dance scenes, and extended by them to include other 'alternative' youth.

12 Respondents are referred to by the numbers assigned to them in an anonymized ACES database, plus the name of the city in which they were located at time of interview. A total of 270 respondents were engaged in the qualitative part of the research.

13 This was a term not of self-identification, but one applied by *neformaly* or *progressivy*, who defined the *gopnik* not in individual terms, but as a vodka-swilling, semi-criminalized, grey mass of people who picked fights for the most trivial of reasons, usually on grounds of appearance (hair or clothes), or because they did not like the way somebody else 'stood out'.

14 Although at the end of the 1990s, the anti-*neformaly* continued to articulate hostility towards *neformaly* and 'progressives', the extent and nature of actual conflict between 'progressives' and 'normals' varied significantly between cities and had generally declined since the 1980s.

15 '*Otaku*' was a term coined in the mid-1980s to describe an emergent type of technologically highly-skilled but socially inept young person in Japan who spent large amounts of time at home engaged in or seeking information about his/her particular interest, usually anime (cartoons), manga (comic books), video games or teen-idols (Grassmuck, 1999).

16 Paradoxically, those young people who appeared to be most attuned to Western ways of life were also most critical of them. For a full discussion of these issues, see Pilkington *et al.* (2002, pp. 204–9).

CHAPTER 9

The Goth Scene and (Sub)Cultural Substance

PAUL HODKINSON

The practice of recounting and rejecting subcultural theory has possibly never been more popular than it is now among those who study contemporary popular cultural identities. In particular, the neo-Marxist adaptation of the term by Birmingham University's former Centre for Contemporary Cultural Studies (CCCS) regularly takes extensive criticism at conferences and seminars on the subject, either for being flawed from the start, or merely being out-of-date in a twenty-first-century society saturated by media and commerce. The rejection of the CCCS's particular version of subcultural theory has also prompted some calls for the abandonment of the term 'subculture' itself which, among other things, is deemed to be unable to capture the essential fluidity of contemporary lifestyle patterns (see Bennett, 1999a). This chapter aims to contribute to such discussions in relation to ethnographic research on a music and style grouping known to its participants as the goth scene.[1]

By way of background information, 'goth' emerged in the early 1980s, when a number of bands and their fans merged elements of punk, glam rock and early New Romantic into what became a 'dark', androgynous style of music and fashion. The music, from then until the time of writing, has often been characterized by sinister or sombre sounds and lyrics, while the style has been dominated consistently by black hair and clothing, as well as the tendency for both females and males to wear distinct styles of make-up. During the mid- to late-1980s, the goth scene gained a relatively high media profile, something exemplified by the relative success of bands such as The Sisters of Mercy, The Cure and The Mission in single and album sales charts. From the beginning of the 1990s, however, the record industry and the media lost interest in the dark sounds and styles associated with goth. Since this time, in spite of the emergence of high profile artists such as Marilyn Manson, and the use of elements of goth style by occasional emerging strands of Indie or Metal, a distinct, small-scale and relatively bounded goth scene has survived and developed in and beyond Britain, predominantly outside the realms of mass media and commerce.

From 1996 to 2000, I conducted extensive ethnographic research focused on the British goth scene, a project whose full findings and conclusions are recounted in greater detail elsewhere (Hodkinson, 2002). This chapter seeks to provide a brief illustration of some of the ways that analysis of this case study might inform debates around the future of subcultural theory. While initially we shall see that the example of the goth scene can be used to illustrate some of the problems of the CCCS's perspective, it will be suggested subsequently that the relatively clear, bounded form taken by the group does not fit happily with the emphasis on cultural fluidity often found in the work of those who propose the abandonment of the notion of subculture. For this reason, I have suggested that groupings such as the goth scene may be conceptualized most usefully by using a reworked notion of subculture, which replaces some of the problematic elements of the CCCS's own adaptation of the term with a general emphasis on what I have termed *cultural substance*, a relative quality that can be contrasted with cultural fluidity, and which might be identified primarily through evidence of group distinctiveness, identity, commitment and autonomy (Hodkinson, 2002).

The Goth Scene and Objections to the CCCS

One of the most notable objections to CCCS theory is that its focus on youth subcultures as fixed and bounded symbolic structures had the effect of under-emphasizing internal diversity and instability at the same time as failing to account sufficiently for the flows of differentially committed young people across group boundaries (Clarke, 1981; Bennett, 1999a). Providing a degree of support for the criticism, my research on the goth scene certainly revealed some individual movement into and out of the grouping, as well as instances of contact between its members and the participants of certain other music scenes – for example, at some mixed alternative or rock-based events. There was also some variation in the levels of commitment among insiders themselves. By way of example, some individuals exhibited an extreme goth-orientated appearance virtually every time they left their home, while others only spent a significant amount of time getting 'gothed up' when they went out to particular pubs or nightclubs. Equally, the goth style itself, rather than being static and simple, entailed a degree of dynamism and diversity, as well as drawing on and over-lapping in particular ways with various other styles. This is partially because, in order to earn the respect of their peers, individuals usually sought to develop their own individual 'version' of the goth style rather than to look exactly the same as one another. Indeed, looking too similar to another goth was sometimes liable to be frowned upon as evidence of lack of individual creativity. One of my interviewees explained that, after an initial period of conformity, goths would gradually develop their own individual look through drawing on a variety of influences:

> *Brian*: There's very rarely two people look exactly the same . . . you take things from everywhere – from different types of looks and different people that you see and stuff, and you just make it your own.[2]

Consistent with the emphasis on instances of internal diversity, some other respondents suggested that, as well as individual variations, the goth scene could in fact be divided into identifiable sub-styles:

> *Martin*: You get the Sisters [reference to band, The Sisters of Mercy] goths and the cobwebby goths, or cyber goths . . . and then if you're like us you're stuck in the middle.

While we shall see later that, in the final analysis, they were not overwhelming in the case of the goth scene, such elements of diversity do reinforce the case that theorists should beware of over-simplifying the value systems of music and style groupings.

The case of the goth scene provided more emphatic support for criticisms of the way in which CCCS theorists essentialized the groupings on which they focused, by 'revealing' underlying collective meanings or functions through semiological analysis of subcultural styles (see Cohen, 1972; Hebdige, 1979). This is important because, in spite of the intense criticism CCCS theory has received on this score (for example, Clarke, 1981; Bennett, 1999a; Muggleton, 2000), the general premise that the aesthetic details of particular styles might directly represent and hence reveal particular shared structural circumstances, psychological features or political statements remains influential. Indeed, on many occasions during the process of my own research on the goth scene, colleagues suggested greater emphasis on an analytical interpretation of the distinctive spectacular styles in question. My response was, and is, that reliance on external semiological analysis would construct more than it would reveal. Without necessarily wishing to endorse David Muggleton's rather uncritical subjectivist approach to subcultural research, it is clear that his call for at least some degree of 'fit' between theoretical explanations and subjective realities is worthy of support (Muggleton, 2000, p. 14).

What was revealed by my research approach – which combined data from critical participant observation with the stated views of numerous participants – was the fallaciousness of any notion that the meanings behind the goth scene might in some way have been imprinted neatly in the style its members exhibited. There was little evidence of any distinct shared *raison d'être* embedded within the clothing, music and lifestyle practices of participants. Individuals varied considerably in their views as to what the goth scene was and what it meant, and many suggested that their dark, sometimes ghostly, appearance represented something of a red herring for those seeking to understand their experiences, motivations and meanings. Some respondents to a questionnaire I administered specifically rejected 'common-sense' suggestions that their dark clothes and music reflected any kind of morbid character or outlook, preferring to describe their involvement as a means of enjoying themselves through a celebration of preferred looks and sounds. Here are a few examples:

> *Questionnaire*: In your own words, please explain, what is the goth scene all about?
> *Donna*: Having fun, getting dressed up and getting drunk
> *Pete*: Rejoicing in a high spirited view of the darker side of life ....
> *Jonny*: Wearing black clothes, loads of make-up and bouncing to funky music.
> *Samantha*: It's about dressing up in your best stuff, socialising and making new friends and listening to great music.

A final clear point of divergence between the goth scene and CCCS theory concerns the extent to which the former was directly and positively construc-ted, and facilitated by media and commerce, something that coheres with existing doubts as to the contemporary relevance of Hebdige's notion that conscious packaging and marketing only became associated with subcultural styles some time *after* the groupings had emerged creatively and spontaneously as a response of working-class youth to structural contradictions (Hebdige, 1979, p. 96). As with Thornton's findings on club culture (1995, pp. 122–62), it was clear that the music media alongside both small and large-scale record companies, played a considerable role, both in the initial crystallisation and the subsequent multinational popularity of the goth scene during the 1980s. A number of older respondents to a questionnaire I conducted at a goth festival specifically cited niche and mass media as being responsible for their initial discovery of, and recruitment to, the goth scene:

> *Questionnaire*: Please give details about what or who got you into the goth scene.
> *Dave*: Seeing Sisters of Mercy on TOTP ['Top of the Pops'] and Mission on radio.
> *Sara*: Heard a song by the Cure on television – bought the album, and albums by related bands, then discovered the clothes.
> *Rhian*: 'The Tube' [TV programme] ... and hearing John Peel's radio programme.

Although such medium- and large-scale media coverage evaporated somewhat from the beginning of the 1990s, media and commercial players remained crucial, from well-known labels releasing occasional retrospective compilation CDs, to the expanding phenomenon of small-scale independent companies marketing specialist commodities, often via goth fanzines or websites. Essentially, the goth scene, rather than symbolically subverting capitalism, functioned as a highly specialist consumer grouping whose participants required a variety of media outlets and businesses in order to learn about and purchase the commodities that made them collectively distinctive. While such consumption sometimes did involve the creative appropriation of everyday goods along the lines described by Hebdige (1979, pp. 104–5), music and clothes collections also contained items that were produced and marketed explicitly towards goths. It was clear, more generally, that involvement with the goth scene would be better understood as a particular form of consumer choice influenced by a variety of factors, rather than any kind of spontaneous reaction to structural positionings. In particular, the goth scene was not consistent with the notion of subculture as any form of working-class struggle, symbolic or otherwise. Although it recruited from a mixture of backgrounds, research revealed a middle-class bias in the social make-up of the grouping and, more important, a general tendency for participation in the goth scene to eclipse rather than to reflect or express structural affiliations.

Even from the relatively brief examples provided here, I hope it is clear that it would not be appropriate to attempt to explain the goth scene by means of an unreconstructed version of CCCS subcultural theory. In particular, the extent of the links with media and commerce, and the lack of any absolute meaning, function or class identity signified by the style would invalidate use of the structuralist slant placed on the notion of subculture by the Birmingham theorists. While this much is relatively clear, however, the question as to what might be the most informative, valuable and, above all, accurate alternative way to theorize groupings such as the goth scene in the early twenty-first century, is rather less easy to answer. In the next section we shall examine the case of those whose solution is not only to abandon the writings of the CCCS, but also to avoid, and to try to replace, the notion of subculture itself.

Alternatives to Subculture

The most prominent argument of those who seek removal of the notion of subculture from academic vocabulary is that it will always imply too fixed, inflexible and simplistic a state of affairs to enable us to understand the complexity of contemporary cultural lifestyles. Whether regarded as long-term characteristics 'rooted in the sensibilities of post-war music consumers' (Bennett, 1999a, p. 610), or a symptom of late-twentieth-century cultural developments (Jameson, 1982, 1991; Chambers, 1985; Muggleton, 2000), fluidity and multiplicity are often deemed to be the primary feature of contemporary youth culture, and indeed consumer lifestyles more generally. Rather than being centred around mutually exclusive subcultures, it is argued that identities are assembled through ever-changing individualized selections from an ever-expanding range of commercial artefacts, practices and identities on offer to all (Polhemus, 1997). While incompatibility with such complexity is the primary and most often cited reason for the abandonment of the notion of subculture, Bennett is equally concerned that the term is losing its value as an interpretive device because, in the wake of CCCS's particular explanations, it is used increasingly, by both academics and journalists, as a descriptor for all manner of different cultural formations in a rather vague and ill-defined fashion (Bennett, 1999a, p. 603).

Unfortunately, the considerable consensus on the need to avoid the notion of subculture as it stands does not appear to have been replicated when it comes to the question of alternative ways of conceptualizing the kinds of collective practices and identities to whom it might previously have been applied. A seemingly expanding plethora of differing concepts have emerged which, whether they were originally intended as direct responses to subcultural theory or not, appear to encompass, or at least to include, those cultural formations for whom, until recently, subculture might have been used. Among others, these include *neo-tribe* (Bauman, 1992b; Maffesoli, 1996; Bennett, 1999a); *lifestyle* (Jenkins, 1983; Shields, 1992; Chaney, 1996a); *scene* (Straw, 1991; Harris, 2000); *postmodern subculture* (Muggleton, 2000) and *bünde* (Hetherington, 1998b). There is not room in this relatively short contribution to elaborate extensively on all the individual discussions and justifications for these different terms; suffice it to say that they are often highly compelling and sometimes display notable differences of emphasis.[3]

Notwithstanding individual nuances of explanation or purpose, the key concern for this chapter is that the authors concerned appear relatively united in wishing to focus attention upon loosely-knit transitory forms of culture and on multi-affiliated and ephemeral individual identities and practices. In so doing, they distance themselves – sometimes directly – from the connotations of fixed and clearly bounded groupings or communities which tend to have been invoked by the notion of subculture. Bennett, for example, regards Maffesoli's notion of neo-tribe as preferable to subculture because of its ability to capture 'the shifting nature of youth's musical and stylistic preferences and the essential fluidity of youth cultural groups' (Bennett, 1999a, p. 614). Meanwhile, Muggleton, by invoking the notion of postmodern subculture, emphasizes that the celebration of liminal individual identities and styles is more important to contemporary youth than collective labels or styles (Muggleton, 2000).

In spite of the potential value of some of their individual contributions, the sheer number of terms on offer to us here, and the extent to which they appear to overlap with one another, has a rather confusing overall effect. While the existing tendency for imprecise references to subculture certainly *is* problematic, it is not clear that this apparently ever-expanding array of alternatives brings any greater clarity. While in some cases theorists have distinguished their favoured replacement term clearly from the notion of subculture itself, fewer words have been expended clarifying the similarities and differences between each of the 'alternatives' on offer – or, indeed, justifying the use of one rather than another. As a result, the empirical circumstances in which one should utilize the term 'neo-tribe', for example, rather than 'scene', 'bünde' or 'lifestyle', are less than clear. The potential for confusion can be illustrated by Rob Shields' contributions to his own edited collection *Lifestyle Shopping*, which, in spite of their overall value, are afflicted by what comes across as a somewhat interchangeable use of tribe, bünde, lifestyle and even subculture (Shields, 1992).

Aside from such problems of definition and overlap, a more substantive difficulty shared by the various 'alternatives' cited here is that their common orientation towards an emphasis on fluidity and cross-fertilization may lead to an over-generalized sense of the prevalence of these characteristics. While such features *do* appear to characterize overwhelmingly some contemporary cultural patterns, the current enthusiasm for emphasizing them across the board carries the danger either of misrepresenting or excluding from analysis any collectivities whose empirical reality fails to fit the picture. While there may ultimately be a valuable role for one or more of the 'alternatives' described thus far, it remains necessary to find a way of conceptualizing those elective groupings which, in spite of diverging significantly from the specifics of the CCCS's explanations, may in the final analysis remain less notable for their fluidity than their levels of what may be termed cultural substance.

(Sub)Cultural Substance

Essentially, I mean cultural substance, here, as the relative inverse of the more frequently used notion of fluidity. Therefore, rather than being predominantly characterized by movement and overlap, an elective grouping characterized by significant levels of cultural substance, I suggest, will be relatively stable and bounded in form. Elsewhere, I have elaborated upon this through the use of four indicators that might be applied to groupings in order to assess their level of substance: a *consistent distinctiveness* in group values and tastes, a strong sense of *shared identity*, practical *commitment* among participants, and a significant degree of *automony* in the facilitation and operation of the group (Hodkinson, 2002, pp. 28–33). While none of these relative characteristics is particularly revolutionary or unfamiliar, the hope is that, collectively, they might act as useful yardsticks in the analysis of contemporary consumer culture, for differentiating predominantly fluid elective amalgamations from those displaying greater levels of substance. While the former may be conceptualized using terminology such as that discussed above (if suitably clarified), my suggestion is that the latter – cultural substance – may form the basis for a much-needed reworking and clarification of the notion of subculture (ibid.).

Importantly, while we have illustrated a number of specific problems with the CCCS's neo-Marxist version of subculture, these need not (and ought not to) lead to the abandonment of the term that the Birmingham theorists took up. There is simply no requirement that all the minutiae of that particular adaptation should stand as integral and irremovable components in the definition and use of subculture, now or in the future. In its general usage, the notion of subculture tends to be associated more often with particular substantive types of elective community than with specifics such as class contradictions, symbolic resistance and the like. And such an interpretation, if properly clarified in the ways I have suggested, in fact reflects consistently present (if over-essentialized) definitional traits of subculture which can be found beneath the specifics of the CCCS and its predecessors. Therefore, while there are radical differences with respect to precise explanations, the notion of subculture – whether in its CCCS guise, or that of the earlier writings of Chicago School sociologists such as Albert Cohen (1955) – has been used consistently to infer groupings with distinct sets of values, defiant collective identities, commitment and dependency among participants, and at least some degree of autonomy from the rest of society. Through the notion of cultural substance as defined here, I hope to have extracted such common themes as relative rather than essentialized qualities, and hence clarified existing connotations so as to retain the notion of subculture as a valuable interpretive device. In illustration of its possible relevance, we now return to our case study.

It has already been established that the goth scene did not have a single underlying meaning or function as well as that it was wholly implicated with media and commerce, and largely middle-class. It has also been emphasized that the grouping exhibited examples of diversity, movement and change. In spite of the importance of such indications of fluidity, however, the conceptualization of the goth scene using a term such as neo-tribe, scene or lifestyle would have risked over-emphasizing such features. It will become clear in the following paragraphs that inevitable instances of heterogeneity and dynamism, such as those described earlier, were more than a little overshadowed by the significant levels of (sub)cultural substance exhibited by the group in respect of the four indicators outlined in the proposed reworking of subculture above.

Blending in and standing out

In spite of the already-described absence of directly symbolized functions or meanings, as well as the presence of notable elements of diversity and dynamism, there remained an overall *consistent distinctiveness* to the range of ideals and tastes exhibited by goths. Although participants themselves sometimes preferred to talk about their 'individuality' rather than the features they shared with their peers, critical participant observation emphasized that internal differences usually took the form of creative, yet subtle variations and additions rather than the sort of diversity that would undermine group boundaries significantly. Furthermore, although there *were* some indications of different identifiable sub-styles within the goth scene, the similarities and overlaps between them tended ultimately to outweigh their differences from one another. The collective distinctiveness of the goth style as a whole was illustrated on a daily basis by the ease with which goths were recognized, both by one another and by many outsiders to the group.

The clothing, music and other stylistic artefacts which goths selected, adapted and created tended to reflect two key stylistic themes that were relatively consistent from place to place and year to year. First, a general emphasis on 'darkness' predominated, most obviously in the predominance of the colour black, the deep vocals and gloomy lyrics that pervaded much goth music, and the overt visual references to horror fiction such as vampires, bats, crosses and so on. Second, the display of particular types of femininity by both sexes was a theme that tended to cut across elements of diversity and change. Examples included unisex preferences for particular styles of make-up and significant amounts of mesh, fishnet, lace and PVC clothing. In addition to the significance of these two distinctive themes, there was a take-up by goths of selected artefacts associated with a variety of other music scenes, including Extreme Metal, Indie, New Romantic and dance. Crucially, while diverse in terms of their sources, the particular items likely to be appropriated and the way they were utilized as part of an overall goth assemblage were often relatively consistent and predictable. While they were certainly important features, then, diversity, change and overlap came across as being less significant, in the case of the goth scene, than the overall tendency for goths to blend in with one another and to stand out collectively from those outside the group.

Drawing boundaries of identity

In respect of the subjective perceptions and feelings of participants themselves regarding group membership, Muggleton has pointed out that a lack of clear collective alignment might indicate a fluid or postmodern sensibility (2000, pp. 52–3). The goth scene, though, was characterized by a particularly strong consciousness of group *identity*, and one that tended to cut across any perceived internal differences or subgroups. In spite of a reluctance towards overt self-labelling among some of those I interviewed, the majority displayed very clear feelings of belonging to the goth scene as a whole. In a number of cases, respondents were perfectly happy to describe themselves explicitly as 'a goth', as in this example:

> *Joe*: I dress in black and I'm a goth because that's what I do, I dress in black and I'm a goth – end of story.

Meanwhile, those more reluctant to pigeonhole themselves quite so explicitly tended to talk happily about the extent of their involvement in the goth scene and, crucially, to align themselves alongside others whom they regarded as goths. Notably, there was a clear sense that this shared identity transcended the boundaries of place, with numerous respondents emphasizing a close sense of commonality with goths they didn't know in faraway towns and countries. This *translocal* sense of identity often came out most strongly in the form of expressions of distinction from equally consistent conceptions of 'trendies', a perceived homogenous mainstream grouping who were not only disliked because of the verbal and physical threat to goths that they were felt to pose, but also as a result of the perceived superficiality of their tastes. For the following interviewee, standing apart from the norm was a key aspect of participating in the goth scene:

> *Keith*: I think it's a backlash against the media and general Tom, Dick and Harry. You know, just general low quality, shitty clubs. It's a rejection of that kind of thing – you do feel different.

The strength and consistency of such notions of insiders and outsiders, like the consistency of goths' tastes, seemed not to fit comfortably with an emphasis on fluidity. The following extract illustrates effectively the general sense I gained that involvement with the goth scene tended to be a highly significant component in the sense-of-self of participants:

Tanya: I don't really think about that really, because it is just *me* now.

Susan: I think it is really important.

Tanya: Yeah, it must be very important.

Susan: It's how you are. The way you dress, the music you listen to influences ... other things.

Tanya: I know it's really sad, but [when I went to] Carlisle I just couldn't cope with it because there was no goth scene, I just couldn't cope with it! I had to go back home because I just felt all lost. There were two other goths, maybe three, and guess what – we all sat together! It was purely because we were goths and there were no others so we just suddenly sort of joined.

'Eating, sleeping and breathing' goth?

We have already seen that levels of subcultural commitment did vary, to some extent, from one goth to another. However, consistent with the aforementioned strong subjective sense of affiliation, average levels of practical immersion in the goth scene among its participants were extremely high. Without accounting for *all* their socializing, consumer habits or media use, goth-orientated artefacts, activities and individuals often seemed to dominate. The following estimation about friendships within the subculture was in fact on the conservative side compared with many I received:

Tom: Probably on a close friends level there's about 60 per cent [goths]. On the acquaintances it would probably tip up to about 80 or 90 per cent because of the amount I travel about to other clubs and stuff.

Particular subcultural commitment was also demonstrated by the fact that many goths, like Tom, regularly travelled considerable distances to attend subcultural events, something often induced by the desire to meet up with existing goth friends or to make new ones. In addition, a number of goths had sufficient investment in the grouping to combine cultural preferences with a career, by progressing from being general participants to become specialist producers, organizers and entrepreneurs. Although there certainly were individuals who moved in and out of the goth scene in a relatively short space of time, the norm was for those who became fully involved to stay involved for a significant period. The friendships, status and sense of belonging which was usually experienced by newcomers who embraced the cultural tastes of the group sufficiently, tended to function as a stimulus for the concentration and continuation of their involvement. Although many withdrew a little with the onset of full-time adult responsibilities, increasing numbers remained involved into and well beyond their mid-twenties. Therefore, while few literally 'ate, breathed and slept goth', the levels of group commitment exhibited by most participants would not have been captured by notions such as neo-tribe, which imply a more fickle sensibility.

Self-sufficient and Self-contained?

The importance to the goth scene of media and commerce already mentioned above would clearly make it misleading to present the grouping as being entirely independent or authentic. However, the degree to which the grouping was reliant on specialist operations and services run by participants themselves makes the notion of *relative autonomy* a potentially useful one. Central to the ongoing development and survival of the late 1990s British goth scene, then, were small-scale genre-specific retailers and record labels run by goth enthusiasts. Furthermore, a plethora of semi-commercial or entirely voluntary activities, from organizing gigs to giving out promotional flyers, played a key part in the goth infrastructure. Such volunteers and part-time entrepreneurs often found my questions about whether they made a profit a source of hilarity, and were at pains to emphasize personal enthusiasm for the goth scene as their primary motivation.

Equally, while larger-scale media had played an important part in the construction and initial popularity of goth, the late 1990s scene in Britain received relatively sparse media coverage outside a DIY network of flyers, fanzines, websites and online forums produced by, and for, insiders. In particular, the Internet had become a crucial resource. A wealth of specialist goth websites and discussion forums produced by and for goths formed something of a specialist sub-network on the Internet, providing information and interaction. While very much implicated in media and consumer capitalism, then, the goth scene was relatively self-sufficient in terms of the involvement of its own participants as cultural producers, and relatively self-contained in the sense that specialist events, media and retailers reduced contact between goths and those outside their grouping.

Conclusion

What has been illustrated here is that, while it did not fit with the specifics of the neo-Marxist explanations provided by CCCS theory, the late 1990s British goth scene would not have been described accurately by a term that would have emphasized fluidity and cross-fertilization above all else. While we have seen that the grouping did exhibit certain indications of movement, dynamism and flux, it is clear that these did not prevent it from retaining a relatively substantive overall form. Most notably, the relatively high levels of consistent distinctiveness, identity, commitment and autonomy I have described cohere with the notion of cultural substance as outlined here and prompted my conceptualization of the goth scene, both in this chapter and elsewhere (Hodkinson, 2002) using a reworked notion of subculture.

Notes

1   It should be noted that, in referring to the goth *scene*, I merely replicate the non-academic way in which goths themselves referred to their grouping. Unlike some theorists (Straw, 1991; Harris, 2000), I do not intend the term *scene* as a theoretical or interpretive device.
2   Readers of my book, *Goth: Identity, Style and Subculture* may be interested in why I used codes to refer to interviewees and questionnaire respondents in that text, while pseudonyms are used in this chapter and other one-off articles. Such decisions have been complex, but the relatively small number of respondents referred to in chapters such as this one and, specifically, the lack of reference to well-known individuals, was deemed to make pseudonyms an acceptable option. In my book, there were clear problems with giving false names to high-profile individuals, and hence with deciding precisely who counted as a high-profile individual and who did not among the large number of respondents referred to in that text. In addition, some respondents were specifically unhappy about being given a different name to their own in a book that was likely to receive considerable publicity and attention within the goth scene itself, something that is less of a problem for edited texts addressing a range of case studies such as this one.
3   For greater detail on 'alternatives to subculture' and 'post-subcultural theory', I would refer the reader to the introduction of this volume. To take one example of an apparent difference of emphasis, though, developing use of the notion of 'scene' has tended, in a rather loose fashion, to focus upon collections of practices and identities associated with popular music, whether the basis for these is a particular genre (Harris, 2000) or a geographical locality (Shank, 1994). On the other hand, Maffesoli's notion of neo-tribe appears potentially to have a more general usage, emphasizing a shift in late-modern societies toward the replacement of stable structural identities with new, elective and hence unstable forms of affinity based primarily on consumption (Maffesoli, 1996).

CHAPTER 10

Buffy Night at the Seven Stars: A 'Subcultural' Happening at the 'Glocal' Level

GERRY BLOUSTIEN

Giles. A vampire appears to be completely normal until the feed is upon them, only then do they reveal their true demonic visage. (*Buffy The Vampire Slayer*, Series 1, Episode 1, 'Welcome to the Hell Mouth').[1]

It was so full each week. You would have to queue sometimes for about an hour to even get standing room. At the end of the show – you know when the little cartoon monster goes across the screen in the credits? – all the people at the pub would say 'Grrr! 'arrgh together. It was *sweet*! (William)

Where Have All the Subcultures Gone?

In the middle of the many popular and academic debates about the changing nature of youth cultures (Tait, 1993; Gelder and Thornton, 1997; Epstein, 1998; Miles, 2000) discussions about media fandom often tend to fall between the cracks. This is partly because of the framing and legacy of subcultural theories themselves, and particularly the versions informed by the highly influential, critical analyses of the Birmingham CCCS. With their 'heroic metaphor of resistance, the valorization of the underdog and outsider and the reemergence of the potentially political working class consciousness' (Stahl, 1999, np), subcultures are often positioned socially and analytically as being disaffected or subordinate – apart from and in opposition to 'mainstream' culture. However, such a perspective sits strangely with analyses of what seems at first sight to be excessive engagement with popular cultural texts. After all, such 'addictions'

are rarely seen as being heroic – they are often quite mundane and unspectacular, and they certainly do not appear to be challenging dominant global capitalism. Yet close studies of media fan groupings, usually based on popular
television texts, have a great deal to tell us about the ways that cultural artefacts move beyond their original form to develop new meanings in everyday
life. They tell us how the texts and their fan groupings 'exist in the world, the
ways they occupy space and accumulate' (Straw, 1999, np). Such research
highlights how popular texts function as cultural resources, constituting and
being constituted by shared and personal cultural identities. They also serve to
remind us that most groupings that have been described as 'subcultures' may
not be as bounded, homogenous, spontaneous, and class-based or even as
age-based as many analytical constructs suggest. Indeed, it would seem that
any analytical distinction between fan cultures and 'subcultures' is inappropriate
in today's cultural landscape that is ever-shifting, and defined increasingly by
activities dependent up claiming geographic, symbolic and sonic space.

Youth Cultures, Localities and Spaces to Play

Youth music cultures have been documented and researched extensively, often
in work which describes the importance of the local to youth groupings (see,
for example, Finnegan, 1989; Cohen, 1991; Fornäs *et al.*, 1995; Bennett,
1997b, 2000). Yet very little has been written about the relationship between
media fandom and the informal use of public locales by these social groupings.
Notable exceptions are where the writers are describing spectacular organized
conventions (Jenkins, 1992) or documenting the relationship between fan
hysteria and celebrities (Schickel, 1985). To omit the 'ordinariness' of the
fandom of (cult) TV texts and the fans' more banal appropriation of public
spaces, seems a grave oversight. Clearly, the understanding of media fans' use
of space in this way, as potentially 'free enclaves' (Bey, 1991, pp. 97–9) and as
continually contested 'spaces for (serious) play' (Handelman, 1990; Schechner,
1993; Bloustien, 2000, 2001, 2002), can offer insights into the ways all experiential groupings develop and survive. It is related directly to the ways in
which globalized culture become 'glocal' (Robertson, 1995) – the ways in which
cultural products can be reworked and reinscribed with local meanings in a
local setting (Bennett, 2000). Because it is not simply the primary text that is
important to fan cultures, but the way that the common references facilitate
social interactions and networking, enabling extra-televisual fan activity and
facilitating the carefully-monitored boundaries that separate the 'us' from the
'not us'. In this chapter, I shall draw upon one such regular media fan event,
the *Buffy* night at the 'Seven Stars', as a case study to illustrate this phenomenon.

In so doing, I situate the contested nature of space as being central to all (youth) cultures and experiential communities. I contend that, to understand the nature of contemporary social groupings requires a more complex, 'thicker' (Geertz, 1973) and more multi-layered framework than the usual 'subcultural' theories allow. Rather, I draw on the concepts of 'serious play' to explain the nuances and contradictions of contemporary practices with their fleeting allegiances, 'informal organization, implicit labor and struggles for legitimacy' (Straw, 1999, np).

Buffy the Vampire Slayer (*Buffy*) is a witty American (teen) fantasy series, resonating with the adolescent experience, although with its post-modern reflexivity it clearly appeals to both teenage and much older fans. This broad fascination is reflected in the 3,705 global *Buffy* and *Angel* sites currently on the World Wide Web, and the wealth of popular as well as academic literature on the series growing steadily year by year.[2] I have been a *Buffy* fan since the programme's inception in 1997, yet it was only recently that I learnt about the regular happenings at the Seven Stars Hotel in Adelaide, South Australia. The pub was already well established in Adelaide as a live music venue, particularly for goth and Heavy Metal bands, but I had not realized that it was also being used as a fan venue. At that stage, *Buffy* was just at the end of its fifth year, although fans could read about future episodes or even watch them in advance of the official broadcast, by downloading the material via overseas fans' websites. I learnt about the local 'happenings' through friends, colleagues and some of my students, who were also dedicated followers of the series. Information about such events is not necessarily easy to obtain because, like vampires (on which Giles comments above), media fans and their informal groups are often invisible, 'appearing normal until the feed is upon them'. Publicity for all kinds of fan events is often organized through alternative, sometimes underground, networks rather than through mainstream channels; such informal marketing is often pragmatic but it is also part of the attraction, adding to the sense of exclusivity surrounding such happenings (Thornton, 1995; Gladwell, 1997; Negus, 1999). In the case of media fans, the 'feed' is the opportunity to discuss and share their obsession with their favourite programmes that seems to bring them to life and into the daylight, as it were.

While this chapter is drawn from my wider ethnographic study of the *Buffy* series and its international fan base, I am focusing here on the Adelaide fan group to explore the wider significance of 'space to play' for all (sub)cultural groupings. For five years, regular *Buffy* nights and evenings of live local music were held at The Seven Stars but, despite attracting great crowds and their obvious financial success, both events have now vanished from this particular social space. My inquiry, then, is not only into the nature of the *Buffy* night itself, exploring why it was deemed to be necessary in the first place, but also analyzing the nature of the struggle that ensued to keep the event alive. Essentially, it was a struggle to maintain a significant arena where the fans could experience and celebrate their fandom or, in Hakim Bey's words, their 'right to party' (1991, p. 97).[3] By examining the symbolic centrality of a real space, for all youth (sub)cultures, I am also demonstrating how arbitrary and tenuous the hold on that space can be.

Despite their general invisibility, all self-identifying fans are usually considered to be excessive and potentially deranged (Amersley, 1989; Jenkins, 1992).[4] The literature on fandom, while relatively small, is 'haunted by images of deviance' (Jenson, 1992, p. 9), characterized by the crazed individual or the hysterical mob. For media fans of many popular and cult television programmes, this also means that the object of their affection and interest is often considered to be unworthy of their intense emotional (and sometimes financial) investment. Jenkins describes such fans as people who are defending the 'scandalous category' of bad taste, for they tend to see 'quality and innovation' where others see only formula and convention (Jenkins, 1992, pp. 16–17). At the same time, even *within* fan cultures, fan hierarchies are dichotomized along the usual cultural lines of status, class and gender, holding widely accepted beliefs about what is considered a good or bad affinity, and how that attachment should be expressed (Jenson, 1992, p. 21). Clearly, 'fans discriminate fiercely; the boundaries between what falls within their fandom and what does not are sharply drawn' (Fiske, 1992, p. 34) or, as Alice, one of the Adelaide fans, asserts: 'It's a cool thing to be obsessed about *Buffy*. It's not like *Star Trek* or some weirdo.'

In this respect, many music-based subcultures and media fan groups have the same concerns. They are both deeply committed to aspects of popular culture and social activities which involve the contestation of taste (Bourdieu, 1984, 1998; Jenkins, 1992). Both symbolically appropriate public space (even if it is only temporarily, and sonically) to maintain and affirm their shared cultural identity against outsiders who do not share their lifestyle, enthusiasm or cultural interests.[5] So to find a place where one can share in a cultural activity that is generally regarded as being unworthy is particularly exciting, for social space, never neutral, is always experienced as a space for power relations (Duncan, 1996, p. 4). It is implicitly classed, aged, gendered and, particularly for those regarded as being on the margins of social respectability, frequently exclusive and contradictory (Shields, 1991b; Massey, 1994; Harvey, 1996), an arena of potential struggle for 'symbolic power' (Bourdieu, 1991).

'Fictionalized' Sites or 'A Place Where Everyone Knows Your Name'...

By the time I discovered it, The Seven Stars was clearly not simply a venue, but had come to represent something far more significant to the Adelaide

Buffy fans – both 'a real and *fictionalized* symbolic arena' (Bennett, 2000, p. 63, emphasis in the original). The word 'fictionalized' is not only important for its connotations of utopian possibilities, a stepping into the subjunctive (Bloustien, 2000) but it also points to the inherent drama and ritual that exists in the creation of any 'space to play' (Chaney, 1993, 1996a; Schechner, 1993). On the first Tuesday evening I attended, I crammed into the main bar at the pub along with over sixty others. Together we watched the episode in intense silence on the big screen above the bar, but chatted, laughed, mingled and discussed the programme loudly during the commercial breaks.

The pub itself is an old Victorian hotel sitting in the heart of Adelaide, South Australia, surrounded by established low-rise office blocks, some new apartments and older housing-trust residences, ubiquitous ancient, tiny stone city cottages, so much a part of the nineteenth-century cityscape. Apart from the real-estate sales literature promoting the newly-developed residential investment properties, this is not considered to be a fashionable part of town. Close to the market and the central business district, the area is home mainly to an itinerant population of students and single office workers, with a sizeable population of factory workers and elderly citizens, who have lived nearby all their lives (ABS Census, 1996). It is this population who are the regular customers for the hotel. With its broad verandah, low ceilings and iron roof, the pub looks almost as though it has been displaced from a rural setting, an anachronism in the centre of a city that is trying to smarten itself up. To Australian eyes, in many ways the pub also seems quite English in appearance. One fan described it as the sort of place 'where Giles (Buffy's British watcher) might have gone – quaint, traditional and where magic seemed possible'.

For students and young adults, its original reputation depended on hosting local live bands, at least until 2001, before the gaming machines (the 'pokies') and the city council environmental laws won the day.[6] In 1997, the publican decided to introduce regular *Buffy* nights into his weekly 'fare'. Through regular, though subdued, advertizing in the free street press and the university newspapers, but mainly through word of mouth, the popularity of the event grew. As more people started to attend, fans would have to arrive at least an hour before the programme to obtain even standing room. The main hotel area then was quite large, being a wide, open space between the main bar and the kitchen. In this room were about twenty small, round tables placed across the width of the room. As some of the tables were high, with matching bar stools, up to eight people, at a pinch, could squash around one table – and they often did. To the left, the open kitchen, bordered by the food counter, further separated the bar from a small number of 'pokies' and the small stage used for the live band performances on other nights.

During the *Buffy* evenings, the customers would order drinks and chat during the commercials, but would watch in rapt silence once the programme started. The sudden hush descending on the room was one of the first things that newcomers would notice about the atmosphere on a *Buffy* night, attempting at first to talk through it – but not for long. The will of the many would take over. Silence would reign – that is, except where, after a particularly witty comment or an exciting fight sequence, the audience would spontaneously laugh, sigh or exclaim together, and sometimes at a particularly exciting moment cheer and clap together. These moments of group response were important for the overall enjoyment and understanding of an episode. The same episode watched again, alone at home, was often reported not to seem quite as funny or as dramatic.

Half way through the night, the publican would place trays of hot complementary food – left-over pizzas, pasties and chips – on the kitchen counter, clearly an extra drawing card for students and the unemployed. Sometimes the night would end with quizzes, where people could air their knowledge and hone their skills about the series. Prizes of *Buffy* posters, videos and other artefacts were provided by a local video store owner, who saw such events as good publicity and promotion for his own business. In these ways, the pub became simultaneously a private and an inclusive party (Bey, 1991; Schechner, 1993) providing, as one of the regular fans explained it, 'Beer, Pizza and Buffy', all in one place.

Serious Play and Space

Elsewhere, I have argued that one of the most important ways in which space is created or appropriated, particularly in late modernity, is to mark out safe 'places to play' (Bloustien, 2000, 2001, 2002, 2003). The concept of play used in this paradigm is, first, that all play is serious, often synonymous with pleasure and fun but certainly not with triviality. It is understood to be a fundamental human activity, a process of representation and identification. In popular discourse, play has come to be synonymous with childish behaviour, trivial actions that we (should) outgrow as we reach maturity and adulthood. Yet the play described here is in deadly earnest, and is not limited to this particular group of *Buffy* enthusiasts in Adelaide. It exists in all human activities throughout life, being one of the fundamental ways in which all of us deal with uncertainty (Handelman, 1990). When we trivialize the process, we call it play; when it becomes part of our more formal public institutions, we call it ritual (Schechner, 1993). In Western cultural traditions, as play has become separated from 'the real' work of life, it has become synonymous with escapism, expressing freedom from institutional obligations and structural constraints (Handelman, 1990).[7] Now we talk about playing 'with ideas, words, with fantasies and with social relationships' (Turner, 1982, p. 7). In late modernity, as belief in certainties, science, religion and in concepts of wholeness and 'Truth', has increasingly wavered and fractured, our understandings of self and reality have splintered into incoherence and anxiety, and our reliance on play to deal with these complexities has become even clearer and more urgent.[8]

Within this conceptual framework, the ways in which young people engage with popular culture should be seen as a serious, complex dialectic activity (Willis, 1990; Fornäs *et al.*, 1995). In this paradigm, too, particular 'spaces to play' become more than just a place to hang out with one's friends, because they can enable and legitimate the expression of individual and shared cultural identity. Play becomes part of the process of struggle 'to win and mark out urban spaces' (Bennett, 2000, p. 66), a process which is all the more valuable for being tenuous and arbitrary. A legitimate scepticism interfuses this play – the scepticism of those who know that they too can create images and knowledge, can subvert socially-sanctioned conventions, 'inverting accepted procedures and hierarchies' (Schechner, 1993, pp. 26–7) but that ultimately such a stance is undoubtedly only temporary or illusory.[9]

'Coming Out of the Closet'

Because of the fans' needs to validate their obsessions, The Seven Stars events were important for several reasons. First, they complemented and legitimated rather than replaced other fan activities. For example, most fans were keen collectors of *Buffy* artefacts although, as with all other such activities, they quickly felt the need to qualify and justify their enthusiasm. So, Jen told me that her *Buffy* watch was purchased because she 'needed a new watch and her previous watches were ' "antique" wind up things which you can't really go jogging with'. She had bought a *Buffy* make-up bag because 'it was large and fairly cheap'. When fans did admit to collecting the more expensive artefacts, they recounted this to me with an ironic, self-deprecating laugh: 'There are a set of figurines I wouldn't mind getting sometime. They are about $125 – I can layby.'[10] Their pleasure in the show would regularly be rationalized by noting that the script was 'well written' and clearly 'quality', or that the series used good music from 'not the usual teen pop stuff, more obscure and up-and-coming bands...not "plastic stuff" '(Jason).

Almost all the fans supplemented their viewing with information obtained from books, magazines or through lurking, posting or chatting[11] on the various global *Buffy* websites. Several of the local fans also created their own websites, publishing fan and 'slash' fiction via the Internet. 'Slash' is a term specific to fan fiction and usually refers to a story that centres around the relationship between same-sex characters in a fan fiction story. It originated in Star Trek fan fiction and comes from the actual keyboard symbol '/' used between the names of the characters involved in a story. In spite of 'The Stars', viewing sessions at home were still particularly important, because watching in a group could sometimes be embarrassing. As Alice explained: 'I get very emotional when I watch *Buffy*, I cry, I sigh, I talk to the people (on the screen)'. Shared public viewing can also be particularly difficult when the plots themselves become too intimate:

> The first episode we watched at the Seven Stars was the one when Spike and Buffy first had sex. And we were like going – 'God!' I mean when you are with a group of people it's like watching two people *you know* having sex in front of people. (Emily)

Accumulated knowledge about the series was clearly cultural capital, a currency that was facilitated and exchanged with interest during any shared viewing opportunities. Many fans exchanged text messages (on their cell phones) or spoke on the telephone with their friends while watching, discussing the narrative twists and predicting the outcomes. As Jen articulated, 'The Seven Stars made it okay to admit you watched Buffy as you had other people *of the same persuasion* in the same place. Before (*Buffy* nights) you never admitted you watched to *non-believers*' (emphasis added). Even more significantly, Emily described the *Buffy* nights as 'like coming out of the closet'. Clearly, the open enthusiasm and being overtly part of *Buffy*'s global fan community was felt to be as risky as admitting to membership of an excluded or oppositional socio-economic substructure, or a particular religious or sexual preference. Clearly, too, The Seven Stars evenings offered a safe haven for such anxieties. The active role of the owner was undoubtedly a prime factor in its success. But for space to be appropriated, even temporarily, three related elements have to intertwine successfully: time, place and subjectivity. That is, the timing and duration of the event, the physical structure and ambience of the locale, and how much the participants feel *able* to participate. In the case of The Seven Stars, as these factors changed so did the ability to use the space for a non-mainstream activity. I will look at each of these factors in turn.

The Importance of Time, Place and Subjectivity

First, the question of *when* and *for how long* the broadcast occurred affected the viability of the events. For at least several years, the usual broadcast of

Buffy began at 8.30 pm followed by the spin-off series, *Angel*, so fans would enjoy a two-hour event at the hotel.[12] When the programmes were not broadcast together, because of any sudden change in local scheduling, past episodes of *Angel* would be screened in the pub instead. Re-run tapes were also used during the breaks, when the networks were not broadcasting the series, so the fans could still watch collectively on their regular *Buffy* night. While other years had seen the schedule being arranged according to the previous year's ratings or other pragmatic factors by the network station, 2002 was the first year that the event had started at 10.30 pm, and *Angel* was broadcast on a completely different day.[13]

Second, consideration of *where* the event occurs highlights the importance of the locality and the ambience of the pub. Being in the heart of the city, many of the younger clients would walk to the hotel, strolling in leisurely after a day at work or university. This was their 'local', and on those nights, as in the fictional pub, *Cheers*, it became an extension of home, 'a place where everyone knows your name'. The fact that it was an established hotel, connected with older youth music cultures, meant that it was not seen as 'trendy' or 'yuppie' or connected with more contemporary dance music, as were so many of the other pubs and clubs around town. The internal structure of the open bar space allowed for a greater sense of inclusivity. Although people came in friendship clusters, new alliances and intimacies could easily evolve, either around the tables or at the bar as customers bought drinks, chatted and discussed the night's episode. The mobile nature of the tables and chairs meant that people could drift easily between groups, and many new relationships were formed in that way.

Third, there was the emotional investment and subjectivity of the fans themselves. By mid-2002, most of the original fans had been watching loyally at The Seven Stars for nearly six years. The regular viewers often felt they had developed into maturity along with the protagonists, their real and the fictional worlds both growing more complex year by year. As 22-year-old Haley explained 'When the show first came on air I was in the same year at school as Buffy and her gang. They graduated when I did and started college when I started uni.' Or, as another fan put it, 'Buffy and I have grown up together.' Now, so many years after its inception, many of those same fans, like the characters, had reached early adulthood, gaining more responsibilities and demands. In the real world, this meant it was less easy to participate regularly in late-night, public fan events. In one sense, they had outgrown their own fan culture.

Collectively, these three factors had underpinned the original popularity of the *Buffy* Nights. So, when the ownership of The Seven Stars changed, what had seemed so established and spontaneous suddenly began to unravel, revealing the arbitrary nature of its success.

The Stars Becomes *The Angas*

The new owner of The Seven Stars took over in April 2002, making it clear that he preferred older, quieter and, as he saw it, more lucrative, customers; he was not 'uni student friendly'. As Jason explained: 'The previous owners of The Seven Stars knew how to create an atmosphere. The new owners have changed it into a "yuppie pub". There are more than enough yuppie pubs in Adelaide.'

Not only was the pub renamed The Angas, but the physical space of the hotel was altered too, the stage and sound equipment being rapidly removed.[14] At first, hearing of the change in ownership and anticipating trouble, several of the *Buffy* fans petitioned all the way through the sale to 'keep the *Buffy* night running won't you?' Others approached the issue in a more business-like manner. They designed some publicity flyers from a piece of fan art depicting a cartoon image of the slayer holding her stake. Behind her is a full moon, gnarled tree and obligatory shadowy monsters. The large text to her left reads: 'Get slayed at BUFFY NIGHT, drink specials, prize giveaways, competitions, nibbles. 9pm – midnight, every Monday night.' They also created some complimentary drink cards, complete with Gothic font and iconography (buy four drinks, get one free), suggesting to the owner that he use them to bring him more custom. But these enterprising suggestions were not accepted readily. As Karl explained, 'It would have been an easy market. He could have just inherited so many people. And most of the people were an older crowd now so he wouldn't have had any problem with underage drinking.'

Each week after that, the fans would come to the hotel, only to find more of what they regarded as 'their space' taken over. First, more pokie machines appeared, their clinking electronic noise being a constant reminder that there were other activities planned for the pub. A wall was erected down the middle of the open bar space, making the area narrower, and most of the dining tables were set up on the further side of the wall. Placed in front of the large TV screen was a large pool table, and another large gaming machine was placed just to the right. While the owner still screened *Buffy* on Monday nights, he did not immediately turn down the overhead light or keep down outside noise. Indeed, on some nights he would noisily collect the money from the gaming machines during the programme.

A separate but related problem was the new time and duration of the broadcast. As indicated above, from April 2002, the hour-long *Buffy* episodes were screened at 10.30 pm instead of at the earlier prime-time slot. This timing was clearly not conducive to people to leave the comfort of their own homes, especially in winter and particularly when the atmosphere in the pub was equally chilly and unwelcoming. Most of the fans, who had originally come to The Seven Stars' events, were now in their twenties. Being now in the workforce and with extra family obligations, many were less inclined to have such a late session early in the week for just one hour, not the previous two. Eventually, the numbers of participants started to decline, and the event would clearly die unless a new venue could be found to rekindle the previous interest and enthusiasm.

Other Possibilities: *The Hilton* and *Tavern 540*

The most active of the fan clusters considered three options for a new home for the *Buffy* night. First, there was Charlie's, the front bar at the Hilton International hotel. The headwaiter of the bar, a keen *Buffy* fan, had been advertising to begin a new *Buffy* 'chapter'. Several fans went 'to check it out' but declared it was a 'dud': 'You have to ask them to put on the TV or the videos, and people do not stop talking' explained Emily. A second, more hopeful, possibility was a hotel on Port Road called Tavern 540. This establishment was managed by another, older, *Buffy* fan who, having previously attended The Seven Stars, was keen to create a similar atmosphere – lots of people, soft lights, free food. But this venue was deemed to be too far away from the centre of the city to be really viable, especially, as noted above, the broadcasts were now only lasting for an hour. The third possibility mooted was a modern wine bar, The Bar on Gouger, further down the same road as The Seven Stars. The owner of this bar was well known in the fan community, and it was also well known that he was already running a *Sex in the City* fan night, so, following some negotiation, most of the fan grouping began to go there.[15]

The Bar on Gouger

My first visit to The Bar on Gouger was not a positive one. I found it noisy and devoid of atmosphere compared to the original possibilities of The Seven Stars. Indeed, to my eyes it seemed the very kind of 'yuppie bar' that Jason had been decrying earlier. The social space was certainly very large, with numerous multicoloured sofas around the room, clustered in squares around individual coffee tables. This created several small, exclusive groups rather than the fluid social space of the original fan venue, making it far less accessible for individuals to mingle outside their smaller friendship groupings. However, after several weeks the fans took over. On some nights they would rearrange the sofas into long rows like cinema seats, or move them into semi-circular arrangements so that more people could feel free to drift and chat between the groups.

Jen and her friends were particularly active in recruiting new members and in encouraging previous fans to try out the new venue. Although sometimes outsiders would mistakenly enter the bar on a Monday evening assuming they could just relax and talk, it was made clear that the *Buffy* fans had precedence on these nights by large notices, posted by the manager, requesting silence during the programme. Not all of his patrons were so accommodating, however, and there were several nights when irate non-*Buffy* fans argued with the owner for their own 'right to party'. 'Call this a bar?' argued one man recently as he took his custom elsewhere. But the fans stood firm – this was their space for at least one hour every week – all the more precious for its precarious and uncertain nature, because young people need to construct lifestyles 'as adaptable and flexible as the world around them' (Miles, 2000, p. 160).

A Fuss About Nothing?

Tuesday, 23 August 2002, was the final, two-hour episode of season six of *Buffy*, many of the original fans turning out to mark the event at The Bar. The night was lively but it could not reproduce the original atmosphere of The Seven Stars in terms of numbers of participants or ambience. Yet I am fascinated by why it was so important to try, and by the way that 'practical nostalgia' (Battaglia, 1995) – the symbolic recreation of the past to validate the present – was central to their quest. At the time of writing, with only one more year of *Buffy* to go, and several months before the new series is broadcast, the instability of this fan group is already rising to the surface. For now, fans will have to be content with re-runs, negotiating again for a particular night to party in their new space, and deciding how to construct their next shared identity.

Conclusion

In this chapter I have used the case of a regular media fan event, the *Buffy* night at The Seven Stars, to illustrate the ways in which contemporary groupings and appropriation of space cannot be understood adequately through subcultural theory. I would argue that it is simply too blunt a tool to unravel the complexity of local cultural practices within the current globalized cultural economy. Indeed, this account has been just one slice out of a much more detailed pie that attempts to track and analyse the nature of 'glocal' media fandom in today's global world. It is just one example of the significance and the, usually invisible, hard work that often underpins all (youth) groupings, belying the surface gloss of spontaneity and 'nowness' that characterises so much of contemporary culture. The ongoing quest for a 'temporary free enclave' (Bey, 1991) that experiential communities can call their own, reminds us again of the central role of locality without which cultural texts cannot emerge to become meaningful in everyday life. While youth 'subcultures' are seen as being active, fan communities still tend to be understood only as audiences, constituted by their relationships to the texts rather than by their active engagement in popular culture. Such frameworks tend to overlook what all individuals and groups *do* to turn global texts into local resources (Bennett, 2000; Miles, 2000). In a world that is ever-changing and uncertain, youth cultures do what they can to capture a moment and make it their own. Indeed, the fleeting moment is often preferable, for, as Zygmunt Bauman argues 'the hub of postmodern life strategy is not identity building but avoidance of fixation' (1996, p. 24). While the commercial global media networks provide the resource for shared 'self-making' (Battaglia, 1995), it is still the local appropriated space than enables the re-inscribing of the global identity into 'glocal' frameworks and meaning.

Notes

1 Rupert Giles, as Buffy's 'watcher', is also largely invisible to the outside world. In his usual guise, he is a very British school librarian, a font of wisdom and knowledge about the occult, the supernatural and the issues of 'growing up'.

2 Slayage.com, the online International Journal of Buffy Studies, lists (and links to) critical and scholarly essays about the television series, and BuffySearch.com lists most of the sites currently operating. My own qualitative work has been carried out face to face with fans from five countries – the USA, Australia, Great Britain, Israel, Spain – and through numberless communications via global website fan bases and email.

3 Haikim Bey, the self-declared 'ontological anarchist' proposes through his performed and written works that people should seek out and appropriate 'free enclaves' – spaces where a kind of revolution of self and community can re-emerge. His work has been used effectively by a number of scholars looking at youth music cultures and other ritualized phenomena (see, for example, Gibson, 1999 and Luckman, 2001).

4 The word's derivation from 'fanatic' of course suggests such excesses, as most commentators of fandom acknowledge.

5 Chaney argues that ordinary people have limited means to do this. They can only manipulate the surface because taste can only be exercised 'according to what is made available by industries of culture' (Chaney, 1996b, p. 100).

6 New residential developments in the area led to a re-zoning and the implementation of new licensing and noise restrictions. Complaints by new residents to the local government caused changes to be imposed on the hotels. The new restrictions meant that the hotels were required 'to operate between 50–70 dB, about the same noise level as a passing car or a television set'(Freeborn, 2001, np). The moves affected a number of hotels in the city, including The Seven Stars.

7   For a concize and extremely accessible overview of the development of the concept of play, see Turner, 1982, pp. 33–5.

8   'It's wrong to think of playing as the interruption of ordinary life. Consider instead playing as the underlying, always-there continuum of experience' (Schechner, 1993, p. 42).

9   Bourdieu describes such play as 'a feel for the game' (Bourdieu and Wacquant, 1992), meaning the ways in which individuals learn to negotiate the complexities of everyday life. His use of this same metaphor recognizes that play has a very serious function indeed. See Handelman, 1990 and Schechner, 1993 for some fascinating accounts of the political power of play in contemporary scenarios.

10 Ask the shop owner to put the item aside so that it can be purchased through small payments over time.

11 'Lurking' means reading others' comments but not writing a message oneself. 'Posting' means fully engaging in conversation in website discussion boards. 'Chatting', of course, could mean real-time, on-line conversations.

12 Angel is Buffy's ex-boyfriend, a vampire with a soul. This series began in 1999 and, until Buffy changed networks in 2001, the story arcs between the two programmes continually intertwined. This meant that there would be constant intertextal references between the two, and often characters and time lines would cross from one programme to another. If Buffy telephones Angel in her own series, the next episode of Angel might show his side of the conversation.

13 The transfer of Buffy to UPN while Angel remained on the WB network meant there was no longer a reason for the Australian networks to feel that they should broadcast the programmes on the same evening

14 The campaign to keep the live music at this hotel and several others in Adelaide has been an ongoing battle between the Hotel Association, the state government, local councils and private developers. The battle to save local live music venues is not restricted to Adelaide, but is being raged across Australia (for more information, see Freeborn, 2001; Homan, 2002).

15 Media fans are rarely enthusiasts for just one programme, but are usually fans of particular genres. Few of the Buffy fans were enthusiasts for *Sex in the City*. Most were keen on other science fiction programmes such as *Star Trek* or *Star Wars* films, and would organize some fan events for those. However, the fact that the bar was 'fan friendly' was a good start.

CHAPTER 11

Virtual Subculture? Youth, Identity and the Internet

ANDY BENNETT

Research on the Internet points to its having had a considerable impact on the nature of communication and social interaction. In particular, it is argued, the Internet has added a significant new dimension to the 'time – space compression' (Harvey, 1989) associated with developments in global communication systems, further displacing the boundedness of social interaction with the restrictions of time, and opening up new, relatively instantaneous, channels of trans-local and trans-temporal communication (Foster, 1997). At the same time, it is suggested, the 'virtual spaces' created by the Internet offer possibilities for the construction of new, 'online' identities (Bassett, 1991; Jones, 1997). In relation to youth, the possibilities presented by the Internet for new forms of communication, cultural exchange and identity formation are claimed to be particularly pertinent, 'the young [being] exposed more than others to the influence of new media' and appearing 'to take naturally to a life of MP3s, MTV and chatroom gossip' (Boëthius, 1995, p. 48; Miller and Slater, 2000, p. 13). Moreover, through offering young people new avenues for communication at a global level, the Internet has been conceptualized as providing a potentially significant new resource for the formation of counter-hegemonic and subversive strategies that were previously unachievable on such a scale. For example, as Diani (2000) notes, the Internet has proved a particularly valuable resource for anti-capitalist groups in planning global protest events (see also, Smith, 2001).

Against the backdrop of this new *virtual* frontier, 'subculture' is beginning to acquire a renewed resonance as a theoretical model for the sociological study of youth. For example, Healy argues that the Internet can 'accurately be described as a loose collection or "ecosystem" of subcultures', while Bassett refers to Internet chat rooms as 'subcultural spaces' (1991, pp. 65, 538). One explanation for this trend might be the flexibility of the term 'subculture'

162

itself. Paradoxically, the vagueness and intangibility that led certain theorists to question the application of subculture in face-to-face, real-time contexts (see, for example, Clarke, 1974; Fine and Kleinman, 1979) may seem to provide the very key to an understanding of how online relationships are formulated and perpetuated on the Internet. To put this another way, if conventional applications of 'subculture' were deemed to be unworkable because of their failure to engage with the continuity between 'subcultural' existence and a range of other social relationships and commitments, familial, peer group or otherwise, researchers appear to see the Internet as offering new levels of freedom from such relationships and commitments. This, in turn, may lead to new ways of conceptualizing subculture, based around the relative exclusivity offered by membership of an Internet-based fan site or chatline, where 'inclusion' is achieved, for example, through the demonstration of 'specialist' knowledge and expertise in relation to music, film, sport or a variety of other forms of youth leisure. The purpose of this chapter is to evaluate how far the concept of subculture might be given a new currency through its application to a social development that was unforeseen when the term 'subculture' was first applied to the study of style and leisure-based youth groups by the Birmingham CCCS during the early 1970s.

Subculture and the Internet

Subcultural theory and the subcultural critiques that followed are associated primarily with the pre-digital age. As such, these studies are each grounded in a common set of 'taken for granted' assumptions concerning the basic socio-cultural properties of youth cultural groups. Thus, youth cultures are portrayed as being closely-knit, stylistically distinct groups whose collective sensibilities are grounded in shared notions about, for example, the importance of community (Cohen, 1972; Clarke, 1976; Brake, 1985) and the symbolic defence of space (Jefferson, 1976). With the increasing eclecticism of youth style noted by Muggleton (2000), such accounts of youth are rapidly becoming obsolete. Indeed, the development of the Internet has further problematized such definitions of youth culture. Thus we can no longer take it for granted that membership of a youth culture involves issues of stylistic unity, collective knowledge of a particular club scene, or even face-to-face interaction. On the contrary, youth cultures may be seen increasingly as cultures of 'shared ideas', whose interactions take place not in physical spaces such as the street, club or festival field but in the virtual spaces facilitated by the Internet.

Such a recasting of youth also has implications for conventional subcultural critiques, a number of which have suggested that one of the key failings of subcultural theory is its inability to resolve the contradiction between the notion of tight, coherent subcultures and the continuities between 'subculture' and the parent culture (see, for example, McRobbie, 1980; Jenkins, 1983). As Healy (1997) notes, however, studies of the Internet frequently stress the freedom it gives individuals to transcend the limitations of physical place and the social relationships that exist there: 'No longer limited by geographical happenstance to the interactions that might develop in a town or neighbourhood... individuals can free themselves from the accidents of physical location to create their own virtual places' (p. 60). The potential offered by the Internet for such a virtual bringing together of individuals spread across different global and cultural sites is such, according to Hine (2000), that the Internet itself must be seen as a 'cultural context' – that is, as a new site for the formation of alliances grounded in common beliefs and shared practices. Viewed from this perspective, it becomes easy to see the attractiveness for some theorists in viewing the Internet as a 'subcultural' space – a space in which, freed from the socio-economic and cultural constraints of their daily lives, young people are at liberty to form new alliances, grounded in trans-locally communicated youth cultural discourses.

In many respects, this notion of the Internet as a subcultural space is analogous to the concept of 'virtual community' (Rheingold, 1994), an established trope and central point of debate in the growing academic literature on the Internet (see, for example, Healy, 1997; Lockard, 1997; Watson, 1997). Rheingold (1994) describes virtual communities as 'webs of personal relationships in cyberspace' (p. 5). Stated more broadly, 'virtual community' expresses the widely held view that, because of the possibilities it offers for transcending spatial and temporal boundaries, the Internet is giving rise to new expressions of 'community' based not on face-to-face interaction and shared local knowledges but rather around regular exchanges of information via online discussions facilitated, for example, by chatrooms, fansites or one-to-one email communications.

While few theorists deny the potential offered by the Internet for new forms of trans-temporal and trans-local communication, the argument that these are giving rise to virtual communities remains contentious. An early study of Internet communications suggested that the unequal distribution of both 'access' to and 'technical knowledge' of the Internet severely undermined the concept of the virtual community because of the limits it imposed on participation (Interrogate the Internet; 1996, p. 19). This view is supported by Lockard (1997), who draws attention to the often prohibitive cost of Internet access for would-be private users. Approaching the issue from a different angle, Wilbur (1997) argues that the question of individual commitment is a key problematic in the realization of virtual communities. Thus, he observes:

> Any study of the virtual community will involve us in the difficult job of picking a path across a shifting terrain, where issues of presence, reality, illusion, morality, power, feeling, trust, love, and much more, set up roadblocks at every turn. (Wilbur, 1997, p. 20)

Clearly, in their attempts to usurp the virtual community thesis, such critiques run the risk of essentializing, or at best over-simplifying, the definition of community in its more conventional 'offline' context. Through their implied notion of community as a fixed and 'stable' collective, reliant upon, for example, regular face-to-face interaction and shared local experience – as opposed to the allegedly fleeting and unstable nature of interactions on the Internet – these studies fail to acknowledge the increasingly romantic nature of such interpretations of community. Research in the related disciplines of sociology, and culture and media studies has highlighted repeatedly the increasing fluidity, instability and temporality of collective life in contemporary social settings (see, for example, Featherstone, 1991b; Beck, 1992; Chaney, 1996a; Maffesoli, 1996). Nevertheless, critical readings of the virtual community thesis do at least point to some of the problems inherent in straightforward applications of the term 'community' to instances of Internet communication and interaction, no matter how frequent and rule-bound these appear to be. Indeed, Wilbur (1997) suggests that, rather than viewing the Internet and face-to-face communication as being qualitatively different domains of social life, one might more productively see them as being related and overlapping forms of interaction. According to Wilbur, the relationship between online and offline communications is one that can be mapped in terms of a series of continuities, the realization of online communications and relationships being grounded in offline, everyday experience, and vice versa. Wilbur's observation has clear implications for our understanding of the Internet in relation to youth. Rather than viewing the Internet as a 'cultural', or 'subcultural' context, it is perhaps better conceptualized as a cultural resource appropriated within a pre-existing cultural context, and used as a means of engaging symbolically with and/or negotiating that context.

Online/Offline Continuities in Contemporary Youth Culture

The continuing relevance of local, everyday contexts in the appropriation and use of more 'traditional' media has been noted extensively (see, for example, Thompson, 1995; Lull, 2000). In a more specifically youth-related context, Liechty's (1995) study of Nepali youth in Kathmandu focuses on the way in which global media and consumer products are functioning to create 'a new cultural space [in which sections of Nepali] youth are debating what is means to be Nepali, young and modern – all categories that are themselves new and open' (pp. 170–1). The conflation noted here by Liechty between local and global influences in the construction of identity may similarly be relevant in the case of local appropriations of new media products such as the Internet. This view is supported by Miller and Slater in their work on the cultural signific-ance of the Internet in Trinidad. According to Miller and Slater (2000), while Trinidadians make very varied use of the Internet in daily life, grounded notions of identity and shared local knowledges are central to all relations entered into online:

> Trinidadians...seemed highly aware, whenever they were online, that they were meeting the rest of the world as Trinis. They might be aware of this in either a nationalistic, patriotic sense (they were Trinidadians encountering other countries) or through a broader sense of the cultural specificity of their tastes, ways of doing things and communicating things. (p. 86)

Such sensibilities also extended to Trinidadian youth who regarded 'the Inter-net as a place to perform their Trini-ness' (ibid., p. 7). Thus, Miller and Slater observe that youth in Trinidad:

> inhabits and enjoys a world of MTV, Entertainment Today, soaps and Nike, and the websites they commonly visited reflected this offline culture and were much the same as that [sic] visited by any 'global youth'. Nonetheless, they spoke of themselves as Trinidadians encountering these cultural forms, whether on- or off line: for example... music-oriented Trini youths talking about online cultural resources said that although they respected rap and hip hop, they were concerned to encounter all forms of music in terms of their long-term tradition, in which Trinidadian 'soca' music has been able to incorporate varied musical forms through soul, rap and techno. (ibid.)

These findings suggest clear continuities between the online and offline worlds of Trinidadian youth. It follows, then, that for young people situated in a variety of socio-cultural contexts, the discourses of identity used in online communi-cations are likely to be framed by offline, everyday local experience. Moreover, when such 'localized' narratives of identity are rehearsed on the Internet, effectively they enter a global domain where they are noted and responded to by users across a range of geographically diffuse sites. Thus, in a very real sense, rather than transcending notions of 'localness', the Internet can be seen as a medium through which such local identities are accentuated.

A further example of such online/offline continuity in contemporary youth culture is provided in Watson's (1997) study of Phish.Net, a website established by fans of US alternative rock band, Phish. As with other fan websites, Phish.Net serves as medium for discussion and debate between followers of the band. Significantly, however, much of what is said online derives directly from lived out, face-to-face experience. This is illustrated through the collective codes of acceptable 'fan conduct' communicated online by hardcore Phish fans, such codes being grounded in the experience of the more conventional feelings of togetherness engendered by the face-to-face experience of the concert venue. Thus, as Watson observes: 'Although Phish.Net is considered by its members to be a forum for debate (among other things), certain fan values regarding respect for the band and appropriate fan behavior both on the Net and at shows are not considered to be debatable' (p. 113).

Interestingly, this reciprocity between online and offline experience also functioned in the opposite direction – with aspects of fan-discourse that began as online exchanges being consolidated through their incorporation into the concert hall experience:

> During 1993, fan mail and debate on the Phish.Net newsgroup about the contents of a particular verse of unprinted lyrics elicited three Phish newsletters filled with the band's multiple joke answers to fan letters about the verse...During the ensuing tour, the band changed the lyrics of that verse in performance to alternate [sic] suggested answers from the publicly answered fan letters. (ibid., p. 106)

Online/offline continuities in contemporary youth cultural discourse such as those described above clearly problematize the notion of the Internet as a subcultural context or space. Just as earlier critiques of subcultural theory argued that issues of overlap and blurring between so-called 'dominant' and 'subcultural' sensibilities rendered the notion of subculture unworkable, so the groundedness of online communications between young people in local everyday life, characterized by the links between online debate and face-to-face experience, generates similar problems for the notion of the Internet as a 'subcultural space'. In terms of its conventional sociological meaning, then, it seems clear that the use of subculture as a model for understanding online interactions between young people is equally problematic, and for many of the same reasons, as applications of subculture in the study of youth in pre-digital, face-to-face contexts.

At this point, however, it is worth reiterating an argument I have made in earlier work concerning the increasingly apparent disjuncture between subculture's conventional sociological significance, as an abstract theoretical model, and its use in everyday, vernacular contexts (Bennett, 1999a). Detached from the meanings inscribed by sociologists, subculture has become an increasingly reflexive and arbitrary term, both in its use by the mass media and, as a direct consequence of this, by young people themselves. It seems to me that such everyday use and understanding of subculture offers scope for a rethinking of the concept, not as a top-down theoretical model, but as a creative strategy in the hands of young people themselves. The richness of the narrative imagery inherent in the term 'subculture', particularly its ready-made connection with a number of highly desirable self images – streetwise, 'in-the-know', cool, select and so on – make it a very attractive and culturally viable concept for young people. Such everyday use of subculture aligns with Peter Martin's notion of subculture as a form of reflexively enacted collective representation rather than an entity in itself (see Chapter 1). If we can accept this shift from 'analytical model' to 'folk model' (Jenkins, 1983) as a basis upon which to evaluate the socio-cultural significance of subculture, then the concept of 'virtual subculture' assumes a very different resonance.

Virtual Subculture as a Creative Strategy

In the previous section of this chapter I began to note how the Internet functions as a creative resource for young people in their symbolic negotiation of everyday life. Indeed, when viewed in this context, there are clear continuities between youth's ready appropriation and use of the Internet and other, more 'traditional', forms of media. Writing during the mid-1980s, Bausinger (1984) noted youth's 'feeling of power with regard to technology . . . practised by them in their skilled handling of hi-fi gear and video [and] which also becomes visible in 'channel-hopping' or zapping' (p. 347). Such displays of media and consumer 'competence' (Chaney, 1996a) have been centrally defining features of youth culture since the rise of the post-Second World War youth market (see, for example, Chambers, 1985). However, because of its more interactive qualities, the Internet opens up creative possibilities for young people that go significantly beyond those associated with more conventional forms of media. Hall and Newbury (1999) suggest that the creative potential of the Internet for youth is illustrated most clearly in the enhanced 'opportunities' that it offers 'for cultural participation', and for the management and promotion of their own 'concerns' (pp. 100–1). I want now to consider some of the ways in which youth's creative use of the Internet as means of cultural participation may engender self-constructed and reflexive forms of 'subcultural' identity.

A central feature of contemporary youth culture is the practice of fandom. As research on youth and music has variously illustrated (see, for example, Frith, 1987; Bennett, 2000), fandom is a central practice both in the construction of collective identities and in the rendering of such identities as 'authentic'. In recent years, the Internet has given rise to a range of new creative strategies for the articulation of fandom and the creation of fan discourses. For example, Kibby's (2000) work on music 'chat pages' notes how these orientate around a 'ritual sharing of information' and stories based on specialized fan knowledge (p. 95). According to Kibby, it is the exchange of such stories and information that forms the 'link [and thus] commonality between chatters' (ibid.). A similar example of such online sharing and exchange of information is provided in my own work on the 'Canterbury Sound' (Bennett, 2002). The term 'Canterbury Sound' was coined originally by journalists during the late-1960s to describe groups such as Soft Machine and Caravan, whose membership each contained one or more individuals from the defunct Canterbury-based jazz/rock band, the Wilde Flowers (see Frame, 1993). During the 1990s, interest in the Canterbury Sound was revived in the form of Calyx: the official Canterbury Sound website. As with Kibby's example of online fandom, Calyx became a forum for debate between fans concerning various aspects of the Canterbury Sound, and those groups who were deemed to define it centrally. The website also facilitated a series of discussions and debates about the role of Canterbury itself in the creation of the musical style, thus giving rise to a series of collective myths concerning how the experience of growing up in Canterbury had imbued Canterbury musicians with artistic influences and 'a certain Englishness' which, it was argued, they brought to their music.

As a cultural resource in the context of everyday life, then, the Internet takes its place alongside a range of other resources through which young people are able to fashion meaningful and 'authentic' identities, framed around issues of knowledge, power and exclusivity – all key elements of subcultural member-ships such as these are understood reflexively and enacted by young people. The aura of exclusivity attached to participation in online discussions of music and/or other youth-orientated popular cultural forms is intensified because of several factors. First, participation in such online exchanges is circumscribed both by the issue of access to and skill in using the Internet. Indeed, as Facer and Furlong (2001) observe, among young people in contemporary society, computer technology remains a far from commonly accessible resource. Second, in such online contexts, displays of knowledge and competence, referred to by Thornton (1995) as 'subcultural capital', can be technologically enhanced, through the design of personal wesbites featuring music, images and text, all of which function to enhance the individual's intended image as a committed and experienced clubber, record collector, DJ or musician and so on.

Indeed, the creative use of the Internet as a medium for displays of 'subcul-tural' capital in this way is by no means limited to the field of music. Individuals participating in a range of contemporary youth cultural activities regularly use the Internet as a means of communicating with 'like-minded' others, while at the same time asserting their insider knowledge and authority. This is illustrated by Borden's study of skateboarding, one aspect of which is an examination of the increasing use of the Internet by skaters as a means of illustrating their skill and expertize. As Borden (2001) observes, 'from these sites skaters represent skate moves through textual descriptions, choreographic codes using the ASCII character set, still photographs and movie clips' (pp. 118–19). Borden further notes how, in addition to information on such practical skills and knowledge, skater websites also provide a channel for 'incessant conversation on a myriad of topics from how to perform tricks, equipment, phrases, ramp design, drugs, the existence of God, general abuse, to (most popular of all) skate shoe design' (ibid., p. 118). Here, again, is a clear example of how, through technologically enhancing young people's ability to demonstrate their expertize in and specialist knowledge of specific youth cultural activity – and allowing the dissemination of such expertize and knowledge over a much wider area – the possibility is enriched for new forms of reflexively understood collective subcultural identity among contemporary youth.

The creative possibilities offered by the Internet for cultural participation have also resulted in other collective innovations which, through promoting notions of inclusivity and exclusivity, have similarly provided a basis for the construction of alternative/underground/subcultural identities. A notable example here is the contemporary US cult film *The Blair Witch Project*, produced on a budget of $6,000 (see Branston, 2001) and described by Tunbridge (2000) as 'the first Internet-driven theatrical release' (p. 18). The film adopts a quasi-documentary style in its depiction of three Film and Media students from the University of Maryland who travel to Burkittsville, a small rural town situated on the edge of the Blair Woods. According to local folklore, the Woods are haunted by Elly Kedwood (the Blair Witch), a former Burkittsville resident banished from the town in 1785 after having been found guilty of witchcraft. The purpose of the students' visit to Burkittsville is to make a documentary about the Blair Witch; this is to involve both interviews with Burkittsville residents and a trip into the Blair Woods to find evidence of the Witch. On entering the woods, the students quickly become lost and, following an increasingly desperate struggle to find the way back to their car, disappear without trace. The film purports to be based on actual footage shot by the students and discovered in the woods one year after their disappearance.

Prior to the official US release of *The Blair Witch Project* in the summer of 1999, its makers, Daniel Myrick and Eduardo Sanchez, devised a unique strategy to create awareness about the film. In June 1998, while *The Blair Witch Project* was still in production, they launched a website to provide basic information about the film. Web surfers who initially found the site were given no indication that the material presented there related to a fictional story. Moreover, as the website grew, additional material that would not appear in the final version of the film was added. As Tunbridge observes: 'This included interviews with the police conducting the initial searches for the students, extensive interviews with private investigator C. D. "Bucky" Buchanan...and a history of the Blair Witch dating back to the 1780s' (ibid., p. 19). In addition to creating an underground audience for *The Blair Witch Project*, assuring its cult status even before the film's official release, the Internet also provided a channel for correspondence between those interested in the film. Moreover, as it became clear that *The Blair Witch Project* was in fact a fictional account that cleverly manipulated fact and fiction, fans began to engage in creative use of the Internet as a means of participating in the 'production' of the Blair Witch story. Twenty dedicated fansites were formed and became the forum for a culture of storytelling and sub-text writing around the main plot of *The Blair Witch Project*.

The *Blair Witch* example is interesting, not only because of its illustration of the Internet as means of creative participation, both in the production of a film narrative and a 'cult' phenomenon, but also because of the way it demonstrates the reflexivity inherent in expressions of 'alternativeness' or 'undergroundness'. As awareness grew that *The Blair Witch Project* was a fictional narrative, interest in the film switched from morbid curiosity to a desire to engage in the creative overlapping of fiction and fact that greeted each new visitor to the *Blair Witch* website. Similarly, the fact that images and text from *The Blair Witch Project* were available online well before the film's official release in the cinema meant that those 'in the know' were able to use their access to and knowledge of the *Blair Witch* concept both as a talking point – at school, in bars, venues and other locations – and as a way of claiming 'insider status' in relation to a filmic phenomenon which, even as it was quickly gaining cult status, was still unknown and inaccessible to most people.

The culturally complex ways in which young people construct their own versions of alternative or underground culture – and how these are bound up with the locally grounded specificities of everyday life – has never been at the centre of academic interpretations of 'subculture'. As noted earlier, in sociology, cultural studies and related disciplines, 'subculture' has been treated exclusively as an abstract, analytical model in 'top down' categorizations of youth. However, if it is now acknowledged that social identities are constructed and enacted more reflexively (Featherstone, 1991b; Chaney, 1996a) then it seems clear that 'subculture', if is to retain relevance for our understanding of youth, must be regarded as a reflexively constructed lifestyle project (Chaney, 1996a) rather than an abstract analytical term.

The fact that this transference of the authority to name and define 'subculture' from social theorists to young 'subculturalists' themselves should occur at a time when the Internet, together with other new forms of media, is becoming

increasingly central to everyday life is significant in terms of the creative possibilities available to young people to articulate expressions of 'underground' or
'alternative' culture. As the online activity that emerged around the *Blair
Witch* story illustrates, the possibilities that the Internet offers young people
for cultural participation now extend far beyond the types of symbolic transformation of products and resources, noted, for example, by Hebdige (1979)
in relation to punk. Rather, such products and resources can themselves
become both the object and product of collective creativity. Through involving themselves in the production of the *Blair Witch* story, individuals were able
to take issues of fandom and 'membership' of the cult scene to a new level
orientated around collective ownership of the concept. It seems evident that,
as the Internet becomes more widely available and the types of computer
software available for domestic use more sophisticated, this democratisation of
the creative process will intensify, giving rise to increasing forms of collective
participation in audio-visual projects.

Conclusion

The purpose of this chapter has been to evaluate the significance of subculture
as a model for our understanding of young people's creative cultural involvement
with the Internet. In the first part of the chapter it was suggested that existing
interpretations of the Internet as a 'subcultural space' are unworkable, because
of their insistence on treating 'subculture' as an abstract theoretical concept
whose defining properties can only be identified and understood through
'top-down' analysis. In doing so, it was argued, such applications of subculture
render it an unworkable concept in much the same way as conventional subcultural theory in that, through their attempts to theorize subcultures as tight,
coherent groupings, they gloss over the lived-out, everyday contexts in which
young cultural activities take place. In particular, it was suggested, studies of
youth and the Internet often overlook the continuities between online and
offline interactions between young people. The second part of the chapter put
forward a new means of understanding subculture's significance in relation to
the Internet based around young people's reflexive understanding of subculture
and its everyday use in local contexts. Viewed from this perspective, it was
argued, subculture, and virtual subculture, acquire a new resonance as folk
models (Jenkins, 1983) – that is, as cultural resources actively defined by young
people themselves and used as a means of negotiating cultural spaces in local,
everyday contexts. In this respect, it was suggested, the Internet takes on a
particularly prominent role as an interactive medium through which youth is
able both to construct and to collectively display its reflexively understood
'subcultural' status.

Afterword

SIMON FRITH

I don't expect this was quite the editors' intention, but after reading this collection of essays on youth studies 'after subculture' I found myself thinking more about youth studies *before* subculture. The authors here reflect critically on what the CCCS brought to the analysis of youth culture; I wondered what had been lost, and whether it was still possible to think about youth lives and looks and styles without instinctively, as it were, reaching for the concept (however hedged about these days with reservations) of youth subculture.

In her instructive chapter on Russian youth culture (Chapter 8), Hilary Pilkington suggests that 'emergent strands of "post-subcultural" theorizing do not adequately engage with youth cultural practices outside the "global core"'. In Russia, she argues, the 'emotional communities' of youth are rooted 'neither in "subcultural style" nor in post-subculture lifestyle-constituting consuming practices, but in an embodied communicative practice'. Pilkington thus points to the difference between Russian and 'global core' youth cultures. But what struck me about her research findings was the remarkable similarity between her young people and the Yorkshire teenagers I observed in the mid-1970s.[1] Pilkington's key terms – alternative versus mainstream, progressive versus normal, individualist versus conformist – matched those I found. Is her account of how local and global orientations work in everyday youth practice no longer applicable to British youth culture? For them too, music is one of the 'cultural resources available to young people as they negotiate the present and envisage the future', and Pilkington shows how youth groups are constituted by communicative practices, by the everyday social activities that are the setting for their creation of shared symbols.

Pilkington's chapter exemplifies Peter Martin's observation in Chapter 1 that the sociology of culture is turning at present from attempts to 'decode' or 'decipher' texts or cultural objects towards a concern with the ways in which they are used by real people in real situations, and towards the description of the 'interactional' work done by people as they make – and make sense of – their social worlds. What is at issue here is not the empirical difference between Russian and British, or German, youth practice, but the methodological difference between subcultural and interactional youth theory. Martin argues that the use of the term 'subculture' to describe certain sets of youth practice means focusing attention 'on the modalities of the symbolic representation of the social world'. Subcultural analysis does not involve any systematic attempt to identify actual groups of people, or to describe actual social practice. This is not its point.

I am sure Martin is right about this, and many of the essays in this book criticise the subcultural approach to youth accordingly, but they also raise an implicit historical question about the sociology of sociology. Why did subcultural theory have such an impact on the British (and, then, the European) academy in the 1970s? Why, a quarter of a century on, is it still the youth theory against which new thinking (as exemplified in this book) has to be measured?

In the introduction to the book, Andy Bennett and Keith Kahn-Harris describe how British subcultural theory drew on 'the Chicago School's conceptualization of subculture as a means of understanding deviance in a socially situated context'. In doing so, in reworking 'this model of subcultural deviance as a means of interpreting the stylistic responses of working class youth in post-war Britain', the CCCS scholars were also suggesting an alternative approach to the two dominant traditions of youth study in Britain – social psychology and educational sociology. As it happens, both these traditions were concerned with the behavioural and institutional effects of social class, and both theorized the dynamics of group behaviour and the effects of class cultural norms. Where they differed from the CCCS approach was in their anxiety about the process of growing up and the problems of 'socialization', and in their research interest in unspectacular youth.

From this perspective, the way in which subcultural theory 'radicalized' British youth studies is more complex than it may at first seem. When I began researching youth and music in the 1970s I was reading Peter Willmott, Brian Jackson and Ray Gosling in *New Society*, on-the-ground studies of 'ordinary' youth growing up in specific families and schools, streets, clubs and pubs.[2] All these writers were political, writing to have an impact on educational and youth policy, and to improve the conditions of the working class. Subcultural theory, Bennett and Kahn-Harris suggest, abandoned this focus on locality not just as a matter of theory but also methodologically. I would add that it also abandoned the focus on youth policy and took little interest in debates about the youth services, young offenders or educational organization. Even with respect to the academic tradition from which the concept of subculture itself came – criminology – the subculturalists themselves seemed little interested in policy-driven research, in studies of the social worlds of drug abuse, youth violence or theft. The paradoxical effect was that this new theory *of* youth seemed in some way to be quite detached from the work of academics working *with* youth. As David Chaney suggests in Chapter 2 here, the importance of the CCCS's work lay elsewhere: it pioneered a theoretical approach to the 'fragmented culture' that marked out social change at the end of the twentieth century. Youth culture was a useful site for the first explorations of what was involved here; but subcultural theory was not simply (or even, perhaps, primarily) about youth.

In retrospect, certainly, it is easier to explain the impact of cultural studies in terms of the history of the academy than the history of teenagers. Cultural studies at Birmingham were rooted in literary studies. The initial CCCS approach to youth culture was influenced more by the literary critical concern with cultural values than by sociological or social policy issues. One reason why subcultural theory was particularly concerned with 'the modalities of symbolic representation' was that many of the early Centre students were trained in textual analysis, and were intrigued by the same structural and poststructural textual theories that were then becoming influential across the Humanities. In this respect, subcultural theory, however it presented itself rhetorically, can be related more easily to simultaneous developments in art history, film studies and literary theory than to what was happening at that time in sociology departments. This is most obvious, I think, in the work of Dick Hebdige. Hebdige's *Subculture: The Meaning of Style* (1979), the best selling of the Birmingham books, became a basic text in art schools rather than social science faculties.

Indeed, it could be argued that this was the moment (the late 1970s) when media studies, drawing its central inspiration from cultural studies, broke off from sociology and developed as a new kind of academic field. Certainly, in the 1980s it was given its own shape by a number of material factors. Its expansion was clearly tied into the evolution of the polytechnic sector (and the transformation of communications departments), but the very rapidity of the growth of departments of cultural and media studies had its own research consequences: textual analysis is very much cheaper than fieldwork; and subcultural readings lend themselves to textbook examples and classroom exercises rather more readily than does ethnography or survey research.

And the various critiques of subcultural theory here reminded me of something else: the uneasy tone of much of the work. These were studies in which scholarly authority was not adopted easily, in which the 'us' and 'them' of the researcher and the researched was clearly present but also often ambiguous. Are youth subcultures being explained from the inside out, or anatomised from the outside in? There are anxieties here of age and anxieties of class. Subcultural studies were developed by members of a particular academic generation, themselves socially mobile (the beneficiaries of the 1945 Education Act). These scholars certainly seemed to be outside the spectacular youth cultures that interested them – the Teds, mods and punks, but did not discuss them either from the perspective of educationalists or policy-makers, and did not draw on any sense of cultural superiority. At the same time, in political terms, subcultural theory was post-1960s, critical of Frankfurt cultural theory while retaining class as the dynamic of social and cultural relations. Class, to put it another way, was, like youth, abstracted from its construction in everyday social practice and given instead a discursive reading. Either way, subcultural writing is distanced from the phenomena it studied as an effect not of social superiority but of theoretical position.

I am not sure that such problems have all been solved by writing 'after subculture'. Sian Lincoln's essay (Chapter 6) on teenage girls' bedroom culture, for example, is a subtle and illuminating piece of everyday research, but on reading it I wondered whether Sian Lincoln herself had not had a bedroom when growing up, had never herself been part of such a teenage culture? The status of the researcher is particularly complex in youth studies. To put it simply: all researchers have been teenagers; and none of them are when they do their research. Where should their own experience come in? One aspect of the subcultural legacy, it seems to me, is the need to make youth somehow *different*. Like Keith Kahn-Harris in Chapter 7 and Paul Hodkinson in Chapter 9, Lincoln is concerned to explore the banality of everyday life – its unspectacularity, as Kahn-Harris puts it. But all three writers still want to celebrate the lives they examine as some kind of opposition to dominant ideology. They do not relate their valuable empirical studies to analogous sociological work on amateurs, on hobbies, on collectors, on the everyday performing activities of identity and sociability, but still hanker, despite themselves, for evidence of resistance and transgression. One of the effects of subcultural theory, in short, is the continuing assumption that a girl or boy with an ostentatiously pierced body is being more 'resistant' to dominant culture than if they were, say, to join a radical political organization or even, come to that, a choir.[3] This remains a major difference between youth studies after and before subculture.

In his essay on the Extreme Metal scene, Kahn-Harris suggests that 'youth cultural practice since the 1970s has shown an implicit awareness of the dangers of the exposure that spectacle brings'. The varying survival strategies of different 1980s and 1990s subcultures are 'a sign of the penetration of the concerns of the CCCS into non-academic discourse'. I am not altogether convinced by this argument. Such reflexive strategies are more likely to involve religious beliefs than musical tastes (and one interesting feature of the Extreme Metal scene is its religiosity), and the subcultural suspicion of exposure (as with Hodkinson's goths) is more likely to derive from the widely-held mainstream cultural suspicion of commerce and the media. The irony here, of course, is that subcultural theory, with its emphasis on style communities and the power of symbolic identities, fed much more clearly into commercial understandings of youth culture – as a matter of markets, brands, fashion, consumption and advertising – than it did into everyday social practices.

And here lies the most significant shift in youth studies before and after subculture. Then youth was an age category; now, it seems, it isn't, or isn't necessarily. To read this book to find out what is meant now by 'youth' and 'youth culture' is to get a paradoxical answer. On the one hand, as Chaney suggests, 'youth' as constructed in subcultural and postsubcultural discourse describes lifestyles and means of identity that are no longer age specific. Geoff Stahl writes here (Chapter 3) about the independent music scene in Montreal; Paul Sweetman interviews people with tattoos and body piercings (Chapter 5); Gerry Bloustien observes *Buffy* fans (Chapter 10); and Andy Bennett (Chapter 11) speculates on Internet communities. None of these essays is really about contemporary youth cultures, if youth is still taken to describe people of a certain age. The implication is that 'youth' has now become a different sort of category altogether.

On the other hand, if, as Peter Martin suggests, youth culture must be approached 'through the actual practices of individual groups in real social settings', then it becomes apparent that the social settings specific to young people have not changed very dramatically since the 1970s. The institutional contexts in which people grow up – families, schools, localities, markets, the workplace, state agencies – provide (to use Paul Hodkinson's useful term) the cultural *substance* with which the young are now said to play. This is the reason that Pilkington's work on Russian youth has so much resonance for youth studies generally, and why Ben Carrington and Brian Wilson are quite right to argue, in Chapter 4, that youth studies must continue to treat issues of power and inequality whatever the limits of the subcultural concept of resistance.

One of the working principles of the sociology of youth used to be that youth is an unusual social category because it describes a process of transition rather than a stable social role. In the most detailed youth studies here – Lincoln on teenage girls in Britain in Chapter 6, and Pilkington on young people in Russia in Chapter 8 – this sense of youth as involving the management of social change is still apparent. And, from this perspective, one of the problems of both subcultural and many post-subcultural concepts is that they seem to freeze youth into a particular moment of consumption and display. It is worth remembering, finally, that members of those 1960s and 1970s spectacular youth cultures did grow up, that today's youth are their children, and that the continuity of culture (and the study of culture) is just as interesting a sociological phenomenon as the more visible fashion parade of changing consumer styles and 'reflexive identities'.

Notes

1 See Frith (1978).
2 See, for example, Dale and Griffith (1965); Willmott (1966); Jackson (1968).
3 For a classic account of the sociological importance of such social activities as singing, see Finnegan (1989). For the pioneering sociological study of the amateur, see Stebbins (1979).

Bibliography

Abrams, M. (1959) *The Teenage Consumer* (London: London Press Exchange).

ABS Census Report 1996 (*www.abs.gov.au*).

Althusser, L. (1971) 'Ideology and the State', in *Lenin and Philosophy and Other Essays* (London: New Left Books).

Amersley, C. (1989) 'How to Watch Star Trek', *Cultural Studies*, 3(3): 323–39.

Amin, A. and Thrift, N. (1994) *Globalization, Institutions and Regional Development in Europe* (Oxford: Oxford University Press).

Anderson, B. (1983) *Imagined Communities* (London: Verso).

Angus, I. (1989) 'Circumscribing Postmodern Culture', in I. Angus and S. Jhally (eds), *Cultural Politics in Contemporary America* (London: Routledge).

Arnason, J. (1993) *The Future that Failed. Origins and Destinies of the Soviet Model* (London and New York: Routledge).

Atkinson, P. and Housley, W. (2003) *Interactionism: An Essay in Sociological Amnesia* (London: Sage).

Back, L. (1996) *New Ethnicities and Urban Culture: Racisms and Multiculture in Young Lives* (London: UCL Press).

Back, L. (2002) 'The Fact of Hybridity: Youth, Ethnicity and Racism', in D. Goldberg and J. Solomos (eds), *A Companion to Racial and Ethnic Studies* (London: Basil Blackwell).

Bakare-Yusuf, B. (1997) 'Raregrooves and Raregroovers: A Matter of Taste, Difference and Identity', in H. Mirza (ed.), *Black British Feminism: A Reader* (London: Routledge).

Bakari, I. (1999) 'Exploding Silence: African-Caribbean and African-American Music in British Culture Towards 2000', in A. Blake (ed.), *Living Through Pop* (London: Routledge).

Bakhtin, M. (1984) *Rabelais and his World* (trans. H. Iswolsky) (Bloomington, Ind.: Indiana University Press).

Banerjea, K. (2000) 'Sounds of Whose Underground? The Fine Tuning of Diaspora in an Age of Mechanical Reproduction', *Theory, Culture and Society*, 17(3): 64–79.

Barclay, M., Jack, I. A. D. and Schneider, J. (2001) *Have Not Been the Same: The CanRock Renaissance* (Toronto: ECW Press).

Bassett, C. (1991) 'Virtually Gendered: Life in an On-line World', in K. Gelder and S. Thornton (eds), (1997) *The Subcultures Reader* (London: Routledge).

Bataille, G. (1993) *The Accursed Share: An Essay on General Economy* (trans. R. Hurley) Vols 2 and 3 (New York: Zone Books).

Battaglia, D. (1995) *The Rhetorics of Self-Making* (Berkeley, Calif.: University of California Press).

Bauman, Z. (1987) *Legislators and Interpreters: On Modernity, Post-modernity and the Intellectuals* (Cambridge: Polity Press).

Bauman, Z. (1992a) *Intimations of Postmodernity* (London: Routledge).

Bauman, Z. (1992b) 'Survival as a Social Construct', *Theory, Culture and Society*, 9(1): 1–36.

Bauman, Z. (1996) 'From Pilgrim to Tourist – or a Short History of Identity', in S. Hall and P. du Gay (eds), *Questions of Cultural Identity* (London: Sage).

Bauman, Z. (1998) *Globalization. The Human Consequences* (New York: Columbia University Press).

Bausinger, H. (1984) 'Media, Technology and Daily Life', *Media, Culture and Society*, 6: 343–51.

Beck, U. (1992) *Risk Society: Towards a New Modernity* (London: Sage).

Beck, U. (1994) 'The Reinvention of Politics: Towards a Theory of Reflexive Modernization', in U. Beck, A. Giddens and S. Lash (eds), *Reflexive Modernization: Politics, Tradition and Aesthetics in the Modern Social Order* (Cambridge: Polity).

Beck, U. (2000) *What is Globalization?* (Cambridge: Polity).

Beck, U., Giddens, A. and Lash, S. (1994) *Reflexive Modernization: Politics, Tradition and Aesthetics in the Modern Social Order* (Cambridge: Polity Press).

Becker, H. S. (1957) 'The Professional Jazz Musician and his Audience', in R. S. Denisoff and R. A. Peterson (eds), (1972) *The Sounds of Social Change* (Chicago: Rand McNally).

Becker, H. S. (1963) *Outsiders: Studies in the Sociology of Deviance* (New York: Free Press).

Becker, H. S. (1989) 'Ethnomusicology and Sociology: A Letter to Charles Seeger', *Ethnomusicology*, 33: 275–85.

Bell, D. and Kennedy, B. (eds) (2000) *The Cybercultures Reader* (London: Routledge).

Bennett, A. (1997a) ' "Village Greens and Terraced Streets": Britpop and Representations of "Britishness" ', *Young: Nordic Journal of Youth Research*, 5(4): 20–33.

Bennett, A. (1997b) 'Going Down the Pub': The Pub Rock Scene as Resource for the Consumption of Popular Music', *Popular Music*, 16(1): 97–108.

Bennett, A. (1999a) 'Subcultures or Neo-Tribes?: Rethinking the Relationship Between Youth, Style and Musical Taste', *Sociology*, 33(3): 599–617.

Bennett, A. (1999b) 'Hip Hop am Main: The Localisation of Rap Music and Hip Hop Culture', *Media, Culture and Society*, 21(1): 77–91.

Bennett, A. (2000) *Popular Music and Youth Culture: Music, Identity and Place* (London: Macmillan).

Bennett, A. (2001) *Cultures of Popular Music* (Buckingham: Open University Press).

Bennett, A. (2002) 'Music, Media and Urban Mythscapes: A Study of the Canterbury Sound', *Media, Culture and Society*, 24(1): 107–20.

Bennett, A. and Peterson, R.A. (eds) (forthcoming 2004) *Music Scenes: Local, Trans-Local and Virtual* (Nashville, Tenn.: Vanderbilt University Press).

Bennett, T., Emmison, M. and Frow, J. (1999) *Accounting for Tastes: Australian Everyday Cultures* (Cambridge: Cambridge University Press).

Berger, H. M. (1999a) 'Death Metal Tonality and the Act of Listening', *Popular Music*, 18(2): 161–78.

Berger, H. M. (1999b) *Metal, Rock and Jazz: Perception and the Phenomenology of Musical Experience* (Hanover, NH: Wesleyan University Press).

Berger, P. and Luckmann T. (1966) *The Social Construction of Reality* (Harmondsworth: Penguin).

Berry, C. J. (1997) *Social Theory of the Scottish Enlightenment* (Edinburgh: Edinburgh University Press).

Bey, H. (1991) *T.A.Z.: The Temporary Autonomous Zone, Ontological Anarchy, Poetic Terrorism* (Brooklyn, NY: Autonomedia).

Bittner, E. (1974) 'The Concept of Organisation', in R. Turner (ed.), *Ethnomethodology: Selected Readings*. (Harmondsworth: Pengiun)

Blackman, S. J. (1998) 'The School: "Poxy Cupid!" An Ethnographical and Feminist Account of a Resistant Female Youth Culture: The New Wave Girls', in T. Skelton and G. Valentine (eds), *Cool Places: Geographies of Youth Cultures* (London: Routledge).

Bloustien, G. (2000) 'Teddy Bear Chains and Violent Femmes: Play Video and the Negotiation of (Gendered) Space', in J. McLeod and K. Malone (eds), *Researching Youth* (Hobart: ACYS).

Bloustien, G. (2001) 'Far from Sugar and Spice', in B. Baron and H. Kotthoff (eds), *Gender in Interaction* (The Hague: Benjamins Press).

Bloustien, G. (2002) 'Fans With a Lot at Stake: Serious Play and Mimetic Excess in *Buffy the Vampire Slayer*', *European Journal of Cultural Studies*, 5(4): 427–50.

Bloustien, G. (2003) *Girl Making: A Cross-Cultural Ethnography on the Processes of Growing Up Female* (New York: Berghahn Press).

Blum, A. (2001) 'Scenes', *Public: Cities/Scenes*, 22–3: 7–36.

Blumer, H. (1969) 'Sociological Implications of the Thought of George Herbert Mead', in H. Blumer (ed.), *Symbolic Interactionism: Perspective and Method* (Berkeley: University of California Press).

Bocock, R. (1993) *Consumption* (London: Routledge).

Böethius, U. (1995) 'Youth, the Media and Moral Panics', in J. Fornäs and G. Bolin (eds), *Youth Culture in Late Modernity* (London: Sage).

Borden, I. (2001) *Skateboarding, Space and the City: Architecture and the Body* (Oxford: Berg).

Bourdieu, P. (1997) *Outline for a Theory of Practice* (London: Cambridge University Press).

Bourdieu, P. (1984) *Distinction: A Social Critique of the Judgement of Taste* (trans. Richard Nice) (London: Routledge & Kegan Paul).

Bourdieu, P. (1990) *In Other Words: Essays Towards a Reflexive Sociology* (trans. M. Adamson) (Stanford, Calif.: Stanford University Press).

Bourdieu, P. (1991) *Language and Symbolic Power* (Cambridge: Polity Press).

Bourdieu, P. (1993) *The Field of Cultural Production: Essays on Art and Literature* (New York: Columbia University Press).

Bourdieu, P. (1998) *Practical Reason: on the Theory of Action* (Cambridge: Polity Press).

Bourdieu, P. and Wacquant, L. J. D. (1992) *An Invitation to Reflexive Sociology* (Chicago, Ill.: University of Chicago Press).

Brake, M. (1985) *Comparative Youth Culture: The Sociology of Youth Cultures and Youth Subcultures in America, Britain and Canada* (London: Routledge & Kegan Paul).

Branston, G. (2001) *Cinema and Cultural Modernity* (Buckingham: Open University Press).

Buraway, M., Blum, J., George, S., Gille, Z., Gowan, T., Haney, L., Klawiter, M., Lopez, S., Ó Rian, S. and Thayer, M. (2000) *Global Ethnography: Forces, Connections, and Imaginations in a Postmodern World* (Berkeley, Calif.: University of California Press).

Butler, J. (1997) *Excitable Speech: A Politics of the Performative* (New York: Routledge).

Calcutt, A. (1998) *Arrested Development: Popular Culture and the Erosion of Adulthood* (London: Cassell).

Carrington, B. (2001) 'Decentering the Centre: Cultural Studies in Britain and its Legacy', in T. Miller (ed.), *A Companion to Cultural Studies* (Oxford: Basil Blackwell).

Castells, M. (1998) *End of Millennium: The Information Age: Economy, Society and Culture*, Vol. 3, (Oxford: Basil Blackwell).

Chambers, I. (1985) *Urban Rhythms: Pop Music and Popular Culture* (London: Macmillan).

Chaney, D. (1993) *Fictions of Collective Life: Public Drama in Late Modern Culture* (London: Routledge).

Chaney, D. (1994) *The Cultural Turn: Scene-Setting Essays in Contemporary Cultural History* (London: Routledge).

Chaney, D. (1996a) *Lifestyles* (London: Routledge).

Chaney, D. (1996b) '"Ways of Seeing" Reconsidered: Representation and Construction in Mass Culture', *History of the Human Sciences*, 9(2): 39–51.

Chaney, D. (1998) 'The New Materialism? The Challenge of Consumption' (Review article), *Work, Employment and Society*, 12(3): 533–44.

Chaney, D. (2001a) 'From Ways of Life to Lifestyles: Rethinking Culture as Ideology and Sensibility', in J. Lull (ed.), *Culture in the Communication Age* (London: Routledge).

Chaney, D. (2001b) 'Lifestyle and Cultural Citizenship', Paper presented to ESRC Research Seminar Series 'Citizenship and its Futures', University College, Northampton, 23 February.

Chaney, D. (2002a) *Cultural Change and Everyday Life* (Basingstoke: Palgrave).

Chaney, D. (2002b) 'Cosmopolitan Art and Cultural Citizenship', *Theory Culture and Society*, 19(1–2): 157–74.

Cheeseman, P. (1993) 'The History of House Supplement', *DJ Magazine*, no. 87, April.

Clark, T. J. (1999) *Farewell to an Idea: Episodes from a History of Modernism* (London: Yale University Press).

Clarke, G. (1981) 'Defending Ski-Jumpers: A Critique of Theories of Youth Subcultures', in S. Frith and A. Goodwin (eds) (1990) *On Record: Rock, Pop and the Written Word* (London: Routledge).

Clarke, J. (1976) 'The Skinheads and the Magical Recovery of Community', in S. Hall and T. Jefferson (eds), *Resistance Through Rituals: Youth Subcultures in Post-War Britain* (London: Hutchinson).

Clarke, J., Hall, S., Jefferson, T. and Roberts, B. (1976) 'Subcultures, Cultures and Class: A Theoretical Overview', in S. Hall and T. Jefferson (eds), *Resistance Through Rituals: Youth Subcultures in Post-War Britain* (London: Hutchinson).

Clarke, M. (1974) 'On the Concept of Sub-Culture', *British Journal of Sociology*, 15(4): 428–41.

Cohen, A. (1955) *Delinquent Boys: The Culture of the Gang* (London: Collier-Macmillan).

Cohen, P. (1972) 'Subcultural Conflict and Working Class Community', *Working Papers in Cultural Studies*, 2: 5–70.

Cohen, P. (1997) Cohen, P. (1972) 'Subculture Conflict and Working Class Community', in K. Gelder, K. and S. Thornton (eds) *The Subcultures Reader* (London: Routledge).

Cohen, Sara (1991) *Rock Culture in Liverpool: Popular Music in the Making* (Oxford: Clarendon Press).

Cohen, Sara (1994) 'Identity, Place and the "Liverpool Sound"', in M. Stokes (ed.), *Ethnicity, Identity and Music: The Musical Construction of Place* (Oxford: Berg).

Cohen, Sara (1998) 'Sounding Out the City: Music and the Sensuous Production of Place', in A. Leyshon, D. Matless and G. Revill (eds), *The Place of Music* (New York: Guilford Press).

Cohen, Stanley (1987) *Folk Devils and Moral Panics: The Creation of the Mods and Rockers*, 3rd edn (Oxford: Basil Blackwell).

Collin, M. (1997) *Altered State: The Story of Ecstasy Culture and Acid House* (London: Serpent's Tail).

Collins, R. (1981) 'On the Microfoundations of Macrosociology', *American Journal of Sociology*, **86**: 984–1014.

Condry, I. (2000) 'The Social Production of Difference: Imitation and Authenticity in Japanese Rap Music', in H. Fehrenbach and U. Poiger (eds), *Transactions, Transgressions, Transformations. American Culture in Western Europe and Japan* (Oxford: Berghahn Books).

Dale, R. R. and Griffith, S. (1965) *Down Stream: Failure in the Grammar School* (London: Routledge & Kegan Paul).

Dant, T. (1999) *Material Culture in the Social World: Values, Activities, Lifestyles* (Buckingham: Open University Press).

Davydov, Iu. (1977) 'Kontrkul'tura I Krizis Sotsializatsii Molodezhi V Usloviiakh "Obshchestva Potrebleniia"', *Sotsiologicheskie Issledovaniia* 3: 78–87.

DeMello, M. (1995a) ' "Not Just for Bikers Anymore": Popular Representations of American Tattooing', *Journal of Popular Culture*, **19**(3): 37–52.

DeMello, M. (1995b) 'The Carnivalesque Body: Women and Tattoos', in The Drawing Center, *Pierced Hearts and True Love: A Century of Drawings for Tattoos* (New York and Horolulu: The Drawing Center/Hardy Marks Publications).

DeNora, T. (1997) 'Music and Erotic Agency – Sonic Resources and Social–Sexual Action', *Body and Society*, **3**(2): 43–65.

Diani, M. (2000) 'Social Movement Networks Virtual and Real', *Information, Communication and Society*, **3**(3): 386–401.

du Gay, P. and Pryke, M. (eds) (2001) *Cultural Economy: Cultural Analysis and Commercial Life* (London: Sage).

Duncan, N. (ed.) (1996) *Body Space: Destabilizing Geographies of Gender and Sexualities* (London: Routledge).

Durkheim, E. (1982 [1895]) *The Rules of Sociological Method* (London: Macmillan).

Epstein, J. S. (ed.) (1998) *Youth Culture: Identity in a Postmodern World* (Malden, Mass.: Blackwell).

Evans, C. (1997) 'Dreams That Only Money Can Buy... Or, the Shy Tribe in Flight From Discourse', *Fashion Theory*, **1**(2): 169–88.

Evans, D. (1997) 'Michel Maffesoli's Sociology of Modernity and Postmodernity: An Introduction and Critical Assessment', *The Sociological Review*, **45**(2): 221–43.

Eyerman, R. (1994) *Between Culture and Politics: Intellectuals in Modern Society* (Cambridge: Polity Press).

Facer, K. and Furlong, R. (2001) 'Beyond the Myth of the "Cyberkid": Young People at the Margins of the Information Revolution', *Journal of Youth Studies*, **4**(4): 451–69.

Falk, P. (1995) 'Written in the Flesh', *Body & Society*, **1**(1): 95–105.

Featherstone, M. (1991a) *Consumer Culture and Postmodernism* (London: Sage).

Featherstone, M. (1991b) 'The Body in Consumer Culture', in M. Featherstone, M. Hepworth and B. Turner (eds), *The Body: Social Process and Cultural Theory* (London: Sage).

Featherstone, M. (1995) *Undoing Culture: Globalization, Postmodernism and Identity* (London: Sage).

Featherstone, M., Lash, S. and Robertson, R. (eds) (1995) *Global Modernities* (London: Sage).

Fel'dshtein, D. and Radzhikhovskii, L. (eds) (1988) *Psikhologicheskie Problemy Izucheniia Neformal'nikh Molodezhnikh Ob"edinenii* (Moscow: APN SSSR).

Fenster, M. (1995) 'Two Stories: Where Exactly Is the Local', in W. Straw, S. Johnson, R. Sullivan and P. Friedlander (eds), *Popular Music: Style and Identity* (Montreal: The Centre for Research on Canadian Cultural Industries and Institutions).

Fine, G. A. (1993) 'The Sad Demise, Mysterious Disappearance, and Glorious Triumph of Symbolic Interactionism', *Annual Review of Sociology* (19): 61–87.

Fine, G. A. and Kleinman, S. (1979) 'Rethinking Subculture: An Interactionist Analysis', *American Journal of Sociology*, **85**(1): 1–20.

Finnegan, R. (1989) *The Hidden Musicians: Music-Making in an English Town* (Cambridge: Cambridge University Press).

Fiske, J. (1989) *Understanding Popular Culture* (London: Routledge).

Fiske, J. (1992) 'The Cultural Economy of Fandom', in L. A. Lewis (ed.), *The Adoring Audience: Fan Culture and Popular Media* (London: Routledge).

Fornäs, J. (1995) 'Youth Culture in Modernity', in J. Fornäs and G. Bolin (eds), *Youth Culture in Late Modernity* (London: Sage).

Fornäs J., Lindberg, U. and Sernhede, O. (1995) *In Garageland: Rock, Youth and Modernity* (London: Routledge).

Foster, D. (1997) 'Community and Identity in the Electronic Village', in D. Porter (ed.), *Internet Culture* (London: Routledge).

Fox, K. J. (1987) 'Real Punks and Pretenders: The Social Organization of a Counterculture', *Journal of Contemporary Ethnography*, 16(3): 344–70.

Frame, P. (1993) *Rock Family Trees* (London: Omnibus Press).

Freeborn, A. (2001) 'Save our State: Keep Music Alive' (http://www.altarnative.com/2001/september/localnative/thelocals/australia.htm).

Frith, S. (1978) *The Sociology of Rock* (London: Constable).

Frith, S. (1983) *Sound Effects: Youth, Leisure and the Politics of Rock* (London: Constable).

Frith, S. (1984) *The Sociology of Youth* (Ormskirk: Causeway Press).

Frith, S. (1987) 'Towards an Aesthetic of Popular Music', in R. Leppert and S. McClary (eds), *Music and Society: The Politics of Composition, Performance and Reception* (Cambridge: Cambridge University Press).

Frith, S. (1996) *Performing Rites: On the Value of Popular Music* (Oxford: Oxford University Press).

Gaines, D. (1990) *Teenage Wasteland: Suburbia's Dead End Kids* (New York: HarperCollins).

Gay, L. C. (1995) 'Rockin' the Imagined Local: New York Rock in a Reterritorialized World', in W. Straw, S. Johnson, R. Sullivan and P. Friedlander (eds), *Popular Music: Style and Identity* (Montreal: The Centre for Research on Canadian Cultural Industries and Institutions).

Geertz, C. (1973) 'Thick Description: Toward an Interpretative Theory of Culture', in *The Interpretation of Cultures* (New York: Basic Books).

Gelder, K. and Thornton, S. (eds), (1997) *The Subcultures Reader* (London: Routledge).

Gibson, C. (1999) 'Subversive Sites: Rave Culture, Spatial Politics and the Internet in Sydney, Australia', *Area*, 31(1): 19–33.

Giddens, A. (1981) *The Class Structure of the Advanced Societies* (London: Hutchinson).

Giddens, A. (1991) *Modernity and Self-Identity: Self and Society in the Late Modern Age* (Cambridge: Polity Press).

Giddens, A. (1994) 'Living in a Post-Traditional Society', in U. Beck, A. Giddens and S. Lash, *Reflexive Modernization: Politics, Tradition and Aesthetics in the Modern Social Order* (Cambridge: Polity Press).

Gilroy, P. (1993) *Small Acts: Thoughts on the Politics of Black Culture* (London: Serpent's Tail).

Gilroy, P. (2002) *There Ain't No Black in the Union Jack: The Cultural Politics of Race and Nation*, 2nd edn, (London: Routledge).

Gladwell, M. (1997) 'The Coolhunt', accessed July 1st, 2002 (http://www.gladwell.com/1997/1997_03_17_a_cool.htm)

Godina, A. (1999) 'Vzaimodeistvie subkul'tury i kul'tury (na primere dvizheniia indeanistov)', in V. Kostiusheva (ed.), *Molodezhnie Dvizheniia i Subkul'tury Sankt-Peterburga (Sotsiologicheskii i antropologicheskii analiz)* (St. Petersburg Izdatel'stvo Norma).

Goffman, E. (1971) *The Presentation of Self in Everyday Life* (London: Pelican Books).

Gonzalez, J. A. (2001) 'Cultural Fronts: Towards a Dialogical Understanding of Contemporary Cultures', in J. Lull (ed.), *Culture in the Communication Age* (London: Routledge).

Gottschalk, S. (1993) 'Uncomfortably Numb: Countercultural Impulses in the Postmodern Era', *Symbolic Interaction*, 16(4): 351–78.

Gramsci, A. (1971) *Selections from the Prison Notebooks* (London: Lawrence & Wishart).

Grassmuck, V. (1999) 'Eine Lebensform der Zukunft? Der Otaku', in D. Matejovski (ed.), *Neue, schöne Welt? Lenbensformen der Informationsgesellschaft* (Herne: Heitkamp Edition, S.157–77 (accessed electronically at http://waste.informatik.hu-berlin.de/Grassmuck/Texts/otaku99.html).

Grassmuck, V. (2000) 'Man, Nation and Machine. The Otaku Answer to Pressing Problems of the Media Society' (accessed electronically at http://waste.informatik.hu-berlin.de/Grassmuck/Texts/otaku00_e.html).

Greenfeld, K. (1993) 'The Incredibly Strange Mutant Creatures Who Rule the Universe of Alienated Japanese Zombie Computer Nerds', *Wired*, 1(1), March/April.

Gregson, N., Brooks, K. and Crewe, L. (2001) 'Bjorn Again? Rethinking 70s Revivalism through the Reappropriation of 70s Clothing', *Fashion Theory*, 5(1): 3–28.

Griffin, C. (1993) *Representations of Youth* (Cambridge: Polity Press).

Gronow, J. (1997) *The Sociology of Taste* (London: Routledge).

Grossberg, L. (1984) ' "I'd Rather Feel Bad Than Not Feel Anything At All": Rock and Roll, Pleasure and Power', *Enclitic*, **8**, 94–110.

Hall, R. and Newbury, D. (1999) ' "What Makes You Switch On?" Young People, the Internet and Cultural Participation', in J. Sefton-Green (ed.), *Young People, Creativity and New Technologies: The Challenge of Digital Arts* (London: Routledge).

Hall, S. (2002) 'Windrush Songs: How Calypso Changed Britain', *The Guardian Review*, 28 June, pp. 2–4.

Hall, S. and Jefferson, T. (eds) (1976) *Resistance Through Rituals: Youth Subcultures in Post-War Britain* (London: Hutchinson).

Hall, S., Critcher, C., Jefferson, T., Clarke J. and Roberts, B. (1978) *Policing the Crisis: Mugging, the State and Law and Order* (London: Macmillan).

Handelman, D. (1990) *Models and Mirrors: Towards an Anthology of Public Events* (Cambridge: Cambridge University Press).

Hannerz, U. (1996) *Transnational Connections* (London: Routledge).

Hargreaves, J. (1986) *Sport, Power and Culture* (Cambridge: Polity Press).

Harrell, J. (1994) 'The Poetics of Deconstruction: Death Metal Rock', *Popular Music and Society*, **18**(1): 91–107.

Harris, D. (1992) *From Class Struggle to the Politics of Pleasure: The Effects of Gramscianism on Cultural Studies* (London: Routledge).

Harvey, D. (1989) *The Condition of Postmodernity* (London: Basil Blackwell).

Harvey, D. (1996) *Justice, Nature and the Geography of Difference* (Oxford: Basil Blackwell).

Healy, D. (1997) 'Cyberspace and Place: The Internet as Middle Landscape on the Electronic Frontier', in D. Porter (ed.), *Internet Culture* (London: Routledge).

Hebdige, D. (1976) 'The Meaning of Mod', in S. Hall and T. Jefferson (eds), *Resistance Through Rituals: Youth Subcultures in Post-War Britain* (London: Hutchinson).

Hebdige, D. (1979) *Subculture: The Meaning of Style* (London: Routledge).

Hebdige, D. (1987) *Cut 'n' Mix. Culture, Identity and Caribbean Music* (Old Woking: Comedia/Methuen).

Hebdige, D. (1988) *Hiding in the Light* (London: Comedia/Routledge).

Hesmondhalgh, D. (1998) 'Essay Review: Club Culture Goes Mental', *Popular Music*, **17**(2): 247–53.

Hesmondhalgh, D. (1999) 'Indie: The Aesthetics and Institutional Politics of a Popular Music Genre', *Cultural Studies*, **13**(1): 34–61.

Hesmondhalgh, D. (2001) 'British Popular Music and National Identity', in D. Morley and K. Robbins (eds), *British Cultural Studies: Geography, Nationality and Identity* (Oxford: Oxford University Press).

Hetherington, K. (1998a) 'Vanloads of Uproarious Humanity: New Age Travellers and the Utopics of the Countryside', in T. Skelton and G. Valentine (eds), *Cool Places: Geographies of Youth Cultures* (London: Routledge).

Hetherington, K. (1998b) *Expressions of Identity: Space, Performance, Politics* (London: Sage).

Hine, C. (2000) *Virtual Ethnography* (London: Sage).

Hodkinson, P. (2001) *Subculture as Substance: The Identities, Values, Practices and Infrastructure of the Goth Scene*, Ph.D. thesis, University of Birmingham, UK.

Hodkinson, P. (2002) *Goth: Identity, Style and Subculture* (Oxford: Berg).

Hoggart, R. (1957) *The Uses of Literacy* (London: Chatto & Windus).

Hollands, R. (1995) 'Friday Night, Saturday Night: Youth Cultural Identification in the Post-Industrial City', University of Newcastle, Department of Social Policy Working Paper No. 2.

Hollands, R. (2002) 'Divisions in the Dark: Youth Cultures, Transitions and Segmented Consumption Spaces in the Night-Time Economy', *Journal of Youth Studies*, **5**(2): 153–71.

Homan, S. (2002) 'Cultural Industry or Social Problem? The Case of Australian Live Music', *MIA: Culture: Development, Industry*, no. 102, February.

Hughes, J. A., Sharrock, W. W. and Martin, P. J. (2003) *Understanding Classical Sociology*, 2nd edn (London: Sage).

Humphrey, C. (1995) 'Creating a Culture of Disillusionment: Consumption in Moscow, a Chronicle of Changing Times', in D. Miller (ed.), *Worlds Apart. Modernity Through the Prism of the Local* (London: Routledge).

Huq, R. (1999) 'Living in France: The Parallel Universe of Hexagonal Pop', in A. Blake (ed.), *Living Through Pop* (London: Routledge).

Hutnyk, J. and Sharma, S. (2000) 'Music and Politics: An Introduction', *Theory, Culture and Society*, **17**(3): 55–63.

Ikonnikova, S. (1974) *Molodezh': Sotsiologicheskii i sotsial'no-psikhologicheskii Analiz* (Leningrad: Leningradskii Gosudarstvenii Universitet).

Ikonnikova, S (1976) *Kritika Burzhuaznikh Kontseptsii "Molodezhnoi Kul'tury"* (Moscow: Obshchestvo 'Znanie' RSFSR).

Interrograte the Internet (1996) 'Contradictions in Cyber Space: Collective Response', in R. Shields (ed.), *Cultures of Internet: Virtual Spaces, Real Histories, Living Bodies* (London: Sage).

Irwin, J. (1997) 'Notes on the Status of the Concept Subculture', in K. Gelder and S. Thornton (eds), *The Subcultures Reader* (London: Routledge).

Islamshina, T. G., Tseitlin, R. S., Salagaev, A. L., Sergeev, S. A., Maksimova, O. A. and Khamzina, G. R. (1997) *Molodezhnie Subkul'tury* (Kazan: Kazanskii Gosudarstvennii Tekhnologicheskii Universitet).

Jackson, B. (1968) *Working Class Community* (London: Routledge & Kegan Paul).

Jackson, P. (1989) *Maps of Meaning: An Introduction to Cultural Geography* (London: Unwin Hyman).

Jameson, F. (1982) 'Postmodernism and Consumer Society', in H. Foster (ed.), (1985), *Postmodern Culture* (London: Pluto Press).

Jameson, F. (1991) *Postmodernism or the Cultural Logic of Late Capitalism* (London: Verso).

Jefferson, T. (1976) 'Cultural Responses of the Teds: The Defence of Space and Status', in S. Hall and T. Jefferson (eds), *Resistance Through Rituals: Youth Subcultures in Post-War Britain* (London: Hutchinson).

Jenkins, H. (1992) *Textual Poachers: Television, Fans and Participatory Culture* (New York: Routledge).

Jenkins, R. (1983) *Lads, Citizens and Ordinary Kids: Working Class Youth Lifestyles in Belfast* (London: Routledge & Kegan Paul).

Jenkins, R. (2002) *Foundations of Sociology: Towards a Better Understanding of the Human World* (Basingstoke: Palgrave).

Jenson, J. (1992) 'Fandom as Pathology: The Consequences of Characterization', in L. A. Lewis (ed.), *The Adoring Audience: Fan Culture and Popular Media* (London: Routledge).

Jervis, J. (1999) *Transgressing the Modern* (London: Basil Blackwell).

Jhally, S. and Lewis, J. (1992) *Enlightened Racism: The Cosby Show, Audiences, and the Myth of the American Dream* (Boulder, Col.: Westview Press).

Jones, S. (1988) *Black Culture, White Youth: The Reggae Tradition from JA to UK* (Basingstoke: Macmillan).

Jones, S. (ed.) (1997) *Virtual Culture: Identity and Communication in Cybersociety* (London: Sage).

Kahn-Harris, K. (2000) ' "Roots"? The Relationship Between the Global and The Local Within the Extreme Metal Scene', *Popular Music* **19**(1): 13–30.

Kahn-Harris, K. (2001) *Transgression and Mundanity: The Global Extreme Metal Music Scene*, Ph.D. thesis, Goldsmiths College, London.

Kahn-Harris, K. (2002) 'Death Metal and the Limits of Musical Expression', in M. Cloonan and R. Garofalo (eds), *Policing Popular Music* (Philadelphia': Temple University Press).

Kellner, D. (1992) 'Popular Culture and the Construction of Postmodern Identities', in S. Lash and J. Friedman (eds), *Modernity and Identity* (Oxford: Basil Blackwell).

Kharkhordin, O. (1999) *The Collective and the Individual in Russia. A Study of Practices* (Berkeley, Calif.: University of California Press).

Khudaverdian, V. (1977) 'O nekotorikh novikh tendentsiiakh v sovremennoi burzhuaznoi sotsiologii molodezhi (kriticheskii analiz)', *Sotsiologicheskie Issledovaniia*, **3**: 71–7.

Khudaverdian, V. (1986) *Sovremennie Al'ternativnie Dvizheniia (Molodezh' Zapada i 'Novii Irratsionalizm')* (Moscow: Mysl).

Kibby, M. D. (2000) 'Home on the Page: A Virtual Place of Music Community', *Popular Music*, **19**(1): 91–100.

Kostiusheva, V. (ed.) (1999) *Molodezhnie Dvizheniia i Subkul'tury Sankt-Peterburga (Sotsiologicheskii i antropologicheskii analiz)* (St. Petersburg: Izdatel'stvo Norma).

Kristeva, J. (1982) *The Powers of Horror: An Essay on Abjection* (trans. L. S. Roudiez) (New York: Columbia University Press).

Kruse, H. (1993) 'Subcultural Identity in Alternative Music Culture', *Popular Music*, **12**(1): 31–43.

Kuchmaeva, I. (1987) 'Molodezhnie sub-kul'turnie ob"edineniia kak faktor dinamiki kul'tury', in I. Kuchmaeva (ed.), *Subkul'turnie Ob"edineniia Molodezhi: Kriticheskii Analiz* (Moscow).

Kurbanova, A. (1985) 'Fenomen "subkul'tur" i ideologicheskaia bor'ba', in *Problemy*

Kul'tury v Sovremennom Kapitalisticheskom Obshchestve (Tsennostnie Aspekty) (Moscow).

Kurbanova, A. (1986) 'Protsess samorealizatsii lichnosti v molodezhnikh subkul'turakh', in *Kul'tura i Lichnost' v Kapitalisticheskom Obshchestve* (Moscow).

Laing, D. (1985) *One Chord Wonders: Power and Meaning in Punk Rock* (Milton Keynes: Open University Press).

Landry, C. (2000) *The Creative City: A Toolkit for Urban Innovators* (London: Earthscan).

Lash, S. (1993) 'Reflexive Modernization: The Aesthetic Dimension', *Theory, Culture and Society*, 10(1): 1–23.

Lash, S. (1994) 'Reflexivity and Its Doubles: Structure, Aesthetics, Community', in U. Beck, A. Giddens and S. Lash (eds), *Reflexive Modernization. Politics, Tradition and Aesthetics in the Modern Social Order* (Cambridge: Polity).

Lash, S. (1999) *Another Modernity: A Different Rationality* (Oxford: Basil Blackwell).

Lash, S. and Urry, J. (1994) *Economies of Signs and Space* (London: Sage).

Lefebvre, H. (1971) *Everyday Life in the Modern World* (trans. S. Rabinovitch) (London: Allen Lane).

Lefebvre, H. (1991) *The Production of Space* (Oxford: Basil Blackwell).

Lemert, E. M. (1972) *Human Deviance, Social Problems and Social Control* (Englewood Cliffs, NJ: Prentice-Hall).

Leonard, M. (1998) 'Paper Planes: Travelling the New Grrrl Geographies', in T. Skelton and G. Valentine (eds), *Cool Places: Geographies of Youth Cultures* (London: Routledge).

Lewis, G. H. (1992) 'Who Do You Love?: The Dimensions of Musical Taste', in J. Lull (ed.), *Popular Music and Communication*, 2nd edn (London: Sage).

Leys, C. (1983) *Politics in Britain: An Introduction* (London: Verso).

Liechty, M. (1995) 'Media, Markets and Modernization: Youth Identities and the Experience of Modernity in Kathmandu, Nepal' in V. Amit-Talai and H. Wulff (eds), *Youth Cultures: A Cross-Cultural Perspective* (London: Routledge).

Lipsitz, G. (1994) *Dangerous Crossroads: Popular Music, Postmodernism and the Poetics of Place* (New York: Verso).

Lockard, J. (1997) 'Progressive Politics, Electronic Individualism and the Myth of Virtual Community', in D. Porter (ed.), *Internet Culture* (London: Routledge).

Luckman, S. (2001) 'What Are They Raving on About? Temporary Autonomous Zones and "Reclaim the Streets"', *Perfect Beat*, 5(2), January: 49–68.

Lull, J. (2000) *Media, Communication and Culture: A Global Approach*, 2nd edn (Cambridge: Polity Press).

Lull, J. (ed.) (2001a) *Culture in the Communication Age* (London: Routledge).

Lull, J. (2001b) 'Superculture for the Communication Age', in J. Lull (ed.), *Culture in the Communication Age* (London: Routledge).

Maffesoli, M. (1988) 'Jeux De Masques: Postmodern Tribalism' (trans. C. R. Foulkes), *Design Issues*, 4(1–2): 141–51.

Maffesoli, M. (1991) 'The Ethics of Aesthetics', *Theory, Culture and Society*, 8(1): 7–20.

Maffesoli, M. (1996) *The Time of the Tribes: The Decline of Individualism in Mass Society* (trans. D. Smith) (London: Sage).

Maines, D. R. (2001) *The Faultline of Consciousness: A View of Interactionism in Sociology* (Hawthorne, NY: Aldine de Gruyter).

Malbon, B. (1998) 'Clubbing: Consumption, Identity and the Spatial Practices of Every-Night Life', in T. Skelton and G. Valentine (eds), *Cool Places: Geographies of Youth Cultures* (London: Routledge), pp. 266–88.

Malbon, B. (1999) *Clubbing: Dancing, Ecstasy and Vitality* (London: Routledge).

Marchessault, J. and Straw, W. (eds) (2001) 'Scenes and Sensibilities', *Public: Cities/Scenes*, 22–3.

Martin, B. (1981) *A Sociology of Contemporary Cultural Change* (Oxford: Basil Blackwell).

Martin, P. J. (1987) 'The Concept of Class', in R. J. Anderson, J. A. Hughes and W. W. Sharrock (eds), *Classic Disputes in Sociology* (London: Allen & Unwin).

Martin, P. J. (1995) *Sounds and Society: Themes in the Sociology of Music* (Manchester: Manchester University Press).

Martin, P. J. (2000) 'Music and the Sociological Gaze', *Svensk Tidskrift for Musikforskning* (Swedish Journal of Musicology), 82: 41–56.

Massey, D. (1994) *Space, Place and Gender* (Cambridge: Polity Press).

Matveeva, S. (1987) 'Subkul'tura v dinamike kul'tury', in I. Kuchmaeva (ed.) *Subkul'turnie Ob"edineniia Molodezhi: Kriticheskii Analiz* (Moscow).

Matza, D. and Sykes, G. M. (1961) 'Juvenile Delinquency and Subterranean Values', *American Sociological Review*, 26(5): 712–19.

Mays, J. B. (1954) *Growing Up in the City* (Liverpool: Liverpool University Press).

McNamee, S. (1998) 'The Home: Youth, Gender and Video Games: Power and Control in the Home', in T. Skelton and G. Valentine (eds) *Cool Places: Geographies of Youth Cultures* (London: Routledge).

McNay, L. (1999) 'Gender, Habitus and the Field: Pierre Bourdieu and the Limits of Reflexivity', *Theory, Culture and Society*, 16(1): 95–117.

McRobbie, A. (1980) 'Settling Accounts with Subcultures: A Feminist Critique', in S. Frith and A. Goodwin (eds), (1990) *On Record: Rock Pop and the Written Word* (London: Routledge).

McRobbie, A. (1981) *Feminism for Girls: An Adventure Story* (London: Routledge & Kegan Paul).

McRobbie, A. (1989) 'Second Hand Dresses and the Role of the Rag Market', in A. McRobbie (ed.), *Zoot Suits and Second Hand Dresses: An Anthology of Fashion and Music* (London: Macmillan).

McRobbie, A. (1991) *Feminism and Youth Culture from Jackie to Just Seventeen* (London: Macmillan).

McRobbie, A. (1993) 'Shut Up and Dance: Youth Culture and Changing Modes of Femininity', *Cultural Studies*, 7(3): 406–26.

McRobbie, A. (1994) *Postmodernism and Popular Culture* (London: Routledge).

McRobbie, A. and Garber, J. (1976) 'Girls and Subcultures: An Exploration', in S. Hall and T. Jefferson (eds), *Resistance Through Rituals: Youth Subcultures in Post-War Britain* (London: Hutchinson).

McRobbie, A. and Garber, J. (1997) 'Girls and Subcultures', in K. Gelder and S. Thornton (eds), *The Subcultures Reader* (London: Routledge).

McRobbie, A. and Thornton, S. (1995) 'Rethinking "Moral Panic" for Multi-Mediated Social Worlds', *British Journal of Sociology*, 46(4): 559–74.

Mellor, P. A. and Shilling, C. (1997) *Re-Forming the Body: Religion, Community and Modernity* (London: Sage).

Melly, G. (1972) *Revolt into style: The Pop Arts in Britain.* (Harmondsworth: Penguin).

Melville, C. (2000) 'Mapping the Meanings of Dance Music', *The UNESCO Courier*, July/August: 40–1.

Merton, R. K. (1938) 'Social Structure and Anomie', *American Sociological Review*, 3: 672–82.

Merton, R. K. (1957) *Social Theory and Social Structure* (London: Collier-Macmillan).

Messaris, P. (1997) *Visual Persuasion: The Role of Images in Advertising* (London: Sage).

Middleton, R. (1990) *Studying Popular Music* (Buckingham: Open University Press).

Miles, S. (1995) 'Towards an Understanding of the Relationship Between Youth Identities and Consumer Culture', *Youth and Policy*, 51: 35–45.

Miles, S. (2000) *Youth Lifestyles in a Changing World* (Buckingham: Open University Press).

Miller, D. (ed.) (1995) *Acknowledging Consumption: A Review of New Studies* (London: Routledge).

Miller, D. and Slater, D. (2000) *The Internet: An Ethnographic Approach* (Oxford: Berg).

Miller, D. S. (1988) 'Youth, Popular Music and Cultural Controversy: The Case of Heavy Metal', Ph.D. thesis, University of Texas, Austin.

Mitchell, T. (1996) *Popular Music and Local Identity: Rock, Pop and Rap in Europe and Oceania* (New York: Leicester University Press).

Montesquieu, C. (1748) *L'Esprit des Lois* (The Spirit of Laws).

Morgan, D. H. J. (1996) *Family Connections: An Introduction to Family Studies* (Cambridge: Polity Press).

Morley, D. (1980) *The Nationwide Audience: Structure and Decoding* (London: BFI).

Moynihan, M. and Søderlind, D. (1998) *Lords of Chaos: The Bloody Rise of the Satanic Metal Underground* (Venice, Calif.: Feral House).

Muggleton, D. (1997) 'The Post-subculturalist', in S. Redhead, D. Wynne and J. O'Connor (eds), *The Clubcultures Reader: Readings in Popular Cultural Studies* (Oxford: Basil Blackwell).

Muggleton, D. (2000) *Inside Subculture: The Postmodern Meaning of Style* (Oxford: Berg).

Mungham, G. and Pearson, G. (eds) (1976) *Working-Class Youth Culture* (London: Routledge & Kegan Paul).

Murdock, G. and McCron, R. (1976) 'Youth and Class: The Career of a Confusion', in G. Mungham and G. Pearson (eds), *Working-Class Youth Culture* (London: Routledge & Kegan Paul).

Nederveen Pieterse, J. (1997) 'Multiculturalism and Museums: Discourse About Others in the Age of Globalization', *Theory, Culture and Society*, 14(4): 123–44.

Negus, K. (1996) *Popular Music in Theory: An Introduction* (Hanover, NH: Wesleyan University Press).

Negus, K. (1998) 'Cultural Production and the Corporation: Musical Genres and the Strategic Management of Creativity in the US Recording Industry', *Media, Culture and Society*, **20**(3): 359–79.

Negus, K. (1999) *Music Genres and Corporate Cultures* (London: Routledge).

Newitz, A. (1994) 'Anime Otaku: Japanese Animation Fans Outside Japan', *Bad Subjects*, (13), April.

Newton, F. (1961) *The Jazz Scene* (Harmondsworth: Penguin).

Noble, D. (2000) 'Ragga Music: Dis/Respecting Black Women and Dis/reputable Sexualities', in B. Hesse (ed.), *Un/settled Multiculturalisms: Diasporas, Entanglements, Transruptions* (London: Zed Books).

Noys, B. (1995) 'Into the "Jungle"', *Popular Music*, **14**(3): 321–32.

O'Conner, A. (2000) 'An Anarcho-Punk Gathering in the Context of Globalisation', Paper presented at the 2000 Third International Crossroads in Cultural Studies' Conference, University of Birmingham.

Olson, M. J. V. (1998) '"Everybody Loves Our Town": Scenes, Spatiality, Migrancy', in T. Swiss, J. Sloop and A. Herman (eds), *Mapping the Beat: Popular Music and Contemporary Theory* (Oxford: Basil Blackwell).

Omel'chenko, E. (2000) *Molodezhnie Kul'tury i Subkul'tury* (Moscow: Institut Sotsiologii RAN).

Orlova, E. (1987) 'Subkul'tury v strukture sovremennogo obshchestva', in I. Kuchmaeva (ed.), *Subkul'turnie Ob"edineniia Molodezhi: Kriticheskii Analiz* (Moscow).

Osgerby, B. (1998) *Youth in Britain Since 1945* (Oxford: Basil Blackwell).

Oushakine, S. (2000) 'The Quantity of Style. Imaginary Consumption in the New Russia', *Theory, Culture and Society*, **17**(5): 97–120.

Parker, D. (1998) 'Rethinking British Chinese Identities', in T. Skelton and G. Valentine (eds), *Cool Places: Geographies of Youth Cultures* (London: Routledge).

Patrick, J. (1973) *The Glasgow Gang Observed* (London: Eyre Methuen).

Pearson, G. (1983) *Hooligan: A History of Respectable Fears* (London: Macmillan).

Pearson, G. (1994) 'Youth Crime and Society', in M. Maguire, R. Morgan and R. Reiser (eds), *The Oxford Handbook of Criminology* (Oxford: Clarendon Press).

Pearson, G. and Twohig, J. (1976) 'Ethnography Through the Looking Glass: The Case of Howard Becker', in S. Hall and T. Jefferson (eds), *Resistance Through Rituals: Youth Sub-Cultures in Post-War Britain* (London: Hutchinson).

Perkins, W. (1996) 'The Rap Attack: An Introduction', in W. Perkins (ed.), *Droppin' Science: Critical Essays on Rap Music and Hip Hop Culture* (Philadelphia, PA: Temple University Press).

Petrov, A. (1995) 'The Sound of Suburbia (Death Metal)', *American Book Review*, **16**(6): 5.

Petterson, J. (2000) 'No More Song and Dance: French Radio Broadcast Quotas, Chansons, and Cultural Exceptions', in H. Fehrenbach and U. Poiger (eds), *Transactions, Transgressions, Transformations: American Culture in Western Europe and Japan* (Oxford: Berghahn Books).

Peukert, D. (1983) 'Die "Wilden Cliquen" in den zwanziger Jahren', in W. Breyvogel (ed.), *Autonomie und Widerstand: Zur Theorie und Geschichte des Jugendprotestes* (Essen: Rigidon).

Pilkington, H. (1994) *Russia's Youth and Its Culture: A Nation's Constructors and Constructed* (London: Routledge).

Pilkington, H. (ed.) (1996a) *Gender, Generation and Identity in Contemporary Russia* (London: Routledge).

Pilkington, H. (1996b) 'Farewell to the Tusovka: Masculinities and Femininities on the Moscow Youth Scene', in H. Pilkington (ed.), *Gender, Generation and Identity in Contemporary Russia* (London: Routledge).

Pilkington, H. (1996c) 'Young Women and Subcultural Lifestyles: A Case of "Irrational Needs"?', in R. Marsh (ed.), *Women in Russia and Ukraine* (Cambridge: Cambridge University Press).

Pilkington, H. (1998) '"The Future is Ours": Youth Culture in Russia, 1953 to the Present', in C. Kelly and D. Shepherd (eds), *Russian Cultural Studies: An Introduction* (Oxford: Oxford University Press).

Pilkington, H., Omel'chenko, E., Flynn, M., Bliudina, U. and Starkova, E. (2002) *Looking West? Cultural Globalization and Russian Youth Cultures* (University Park, PA: Penn State University Press).

Pini, M. (1997) 'Women and the Early British Rave Scene', in A. McRobbie (ed.), *Back to Reality: Social Experience and Cultural Studies* (Manchester: Manchester University Press).

Pini, M. (2001) *Clubcultures and Female Subjectivity: The Move from Home to House* (New York: Palgrave).

Pitts, V. (1998) ' "Reclaiming" the Female Body: Embodied Identity Work, Resistance and the Grotesque', *Body and Society*, 4(3): 67–84.

Poiger, U. (2000) *Jazz, Rock and Rebels: Cold War Politics and American Culture in a Divided Germany* (Berkeley, Calif.: University of California Press).

Polhemus, T. (1995) *Streetstyle: From Sidewalk to Catwalk* (London: Thames & Hudson).

Polhemus, T. (1997) 'In the Supermarket of Style', in S. Redhead, D. Wynne and J. O'Connor (eds), *The Clubcultures Reader: Readings in Popular Cultural Studies* (Oxford: Basil Blackwell).

Raboy, M. (1990) *Missed Opportunities: The Story of Canada's Broadcasting Policy* (Montreal: McGill-Queen's University Press).

Raboy, M. (1996) 'The Hybridization of Public Broadcasting', in M. Raboy (ed.), *Public Broadcasting for the 21st Century* (London: John Libbey Media).

Radway, J. (1984) *Reading the Romance: Women, Patriarchy, and Popular Literature* (Chapel Hill, NC: University of North Carolina Press).

Rayport Rabodzeenko, J. (1998) 'Creating Elsewhere, Being Other: The Imagined Spaces and Selves of St. Petersburg Young People, 1990–95', Ph.D. thesis, University of Chicago.

Redhead, S. (1990) *The End-of-the-Century Party: Youth and Pop Towards 2000* (Manchester: Manchester University Press).

Redhead, S. (1993a) 'The End of the End-of-the-Century Party', in S. Redhead (ed.), *Rave Off: Politics and Deviance in Contemporary Youth Culture* (Aldershot: Avebury).

Redhead, S. (ed.) (1993b) *Rave Off: Politics and Deviance in Contemporary Youth Culture* (Aldershot: Avebury).

Redhead, S., Wynne, D. and O'Connor, J. (eds) (1997) *The Clubcultures Reader: Readings in Popular Cultural Studies* (Oxford: Basil Blackwell).

Reimer, B. (1995) 'Youth and Modern Lifestyles', in J. Fornäs and G. Bolin (eds), *Youth Culture in Late Modernity* (London: Sage).

Reitveld, H. (1993) 'Living the Dream', in S. Redhead (ed.), *Rave Off: Politics and Deviance in Contemporary Youth Culture* (Aldershot: Avebury).

Reynolds, S. (1990) *Blissed Out: The Raptures of Rock* (London: Serpent's Tail).

Reynolds, S. (1997) 'Rave Culture: Living Dream or Living Death?', in S. Redhead, D. Wynne and J. O'Connor (eds), *The Clubcultures Reader: Readings in Popular Cultural Studies* (Oxford: Basil Blackwell).

Reynolds, S. (1998) *Generation Ecstasy: Into the World of Techno and Rave Culture* (Toronto: Little, Brown).

Reynolds, S. and Press, J. (1995) *The Sex Revolts: Gender, Rebellion and Rock'n'Roll* (London: Serpent's Tail).

Rheingold, H. (1994) *The Virtual Community: Finding Connection in a Computerized World* (London: Secker & Warburg).

Richard, B. and Krüger, H. (1998) 'Ravers' Paradise?: German Youth Cultures in the 1990s', in T. Skelton and G. Valentine (eds), *Cool Places: Geographies of Youth Cultures* (London: Routledge).

Richardson, J. T. (1991) 'Satanism in the Courts: From Murder to Heavy Metal', in J. T. Richardson, J. Best and D. Bromley (eds), *The Satanism Scare* (New York: Aldine de Gruyter).

Rietveld, H. (1997) 'The House Sound of Chicago', in S. Redhead, D. Wynne and J. O'Connor (eds), *The Clubcultures Reader: Readings in Popular Cultural Studies* (Oxford: Basil Blackwell).

Ritzer, G. (1993) *The McDonaldization Thesis: An Investigation into the Changing Character of Contemporary Social Life* (London: Sage).

Ritzer, G. (1998) *The MacDonaldization Thesis: Explorations and Extensions* (London: Sage).

Roberts, R. (1971) *The Classic Slum* (Manchester: Manchester University Press).

Robertson, R. (1995) 'Glocalisation: Time – Space and Homogeneity – Heterogeneity', in M. Featherstone, S. Lash and R. Roberstson (eds), *Global Modernities* (London: Sage).

Robinson, D., Buck, E. and Cuthbert, M. (1991) *Music at the Margins: Popular Music and Global Cultural Diversity* (London: Sage).

Rose, T. (1994a) 'A Style Nobody Can Deal With: Politics, Style and the Postindustrial City in Hip Hop', in A. Ross and T. Rose (eds), *Microphone Fiends: Youth Music and Youth Culture* (London: Routledge).

Rose, T. (1994b) *Black Noise: Rap Music and Black Culture in Contemporary America* (London: Wesleyan University Press).

Ross, A. (1994) 'Introduction', in A. Ross and T. Rose (eds), *Microphone Fiends: Youth Music and Youth Culture* (London: Routledge).

Rowe, D. (1995) *Popular Cultures: Rock Music, Sport and the Politics of Pleasure* (London: Sage).

Russell, K. (1993) 'Lysergia Suburbia', in S. Redhead (ed.), *Rave Off: Politics and Deviance in Contemporary Youth Culture* (Aldershot: Avebury).

Sakwa, R. (1996) *Russian Politics and Society* (London: Routledge).

Sapsford, R. J. (1981) 'Individual Deviance: The Search for the Criminal Personality' in M. Fitzgerald, G. McLennan and J. Pawson (eds), *Crime and Society: Readings in History and Theory* (London: Routledge & Kegan Paul).

Schechner, R. (1993) *The Future of Ritual* (London: Routledge).

Schickle, R. (1985) 'Coherent Strangers', in *Intimate Strangers: The Culture of Celebrity* (Garden City, NY: Doubleday), pp. 255–85.

Selwood, S. (ed.) (2001) *The UK Culture Sector: Profile and Policy Issues* (London: Policy Studies Institute Report No. 877).

Shank, B. (1994) *Dissonant Identities: The Rock 'n' Roll Scene in Austin, Texas* (Hanover NH: University Press of New England).

Sharma, S., Hutnyk, J. and Sharma, A. (eds) (1996) *Dis-orienting Rhythms: The Politics of the New Asian Dance Music* (London: Zed Books).

Sharrock, W. W., Hughes, J. A. and Martin, P. J. (2003) *Understanding Modern Sociology* (London: Sage).

Shchepanskaia, T. (1991) 'The Symbols of the Youth Subculture', *Soviet Education*, 33(10): 3–16.

Shields, R. (1991a) 'Introduction to 'The Ethics of Aesthetics'', *Theory, Culture and Society*, 8(1): 1–5.

Shields, R. (1991b) *Places on the Margin: Alternative Geographies of Modernity* (London: Routledge).

Shields, R. (1992) 'Spaces for the Subject of Consumption', in R. Shields (ed.), *Lifestyle Shopping: The Subject of Consumption* (London: Routledge).

Shields, R. (1996) 'Foreword: Masses or Tribes?', in M. Maffesoli, *The Time of the Tribes: The Decline of Individualism in Mass Society* (London: Sage).

Shilling, C. (1993) *The Body and Social Theory* (London: Sage).

Silverman, D. (1993) *Interpreting Qualitative Data: Methods of Analysing Talk, Text and Interaction* (London: Sage).

Skelton, T. and Valentine, G. (eds) (1998) *Cool Places: Geographies of Youth Cultures* (New York: Routledge).

Smith, J. (2001) 'Globalizing Resistance: The Battle of Seattle and the Future of Social Movements', *Mobilization*, 6(1): 1–19.

Smith, R. and Maughan, T. (1998) 'Youth Culture and the Making of the Post-Fordist Economy: Dance Music in Contemporary Britain', *Journal of Youth Studies*, 1(2): 211–28.

Sokolov, M. (1999) 'Subkul'turnoe izmerenie sotsial'nikh dvizhenii: kognitivnii podkhod', in V. Kostiusheva (ed.), *Molodezhnie Dvizheniia i Subkul'tury Sankt-Peterburga (Sotsiologicheskii i antropologicheskii analiz)* (St. Peterburg: Izdatel'stvo Norma).

Stahl, G. (1999) ' "Still Winning Space?": Updating Subcultural Theory', *Invisible Culture: An Electronic Journal for Visual Studies* http://www.rochester.edu/in_visible_culture/issue2/stahl.htm

Stahl, G. (2001) 'Tracing Out an Anglo-Bohemia: Musicmaking and Myth in Montreal', in *Public: Cities/Scenes*, 22/23: 99–122.

Stallybrass, P. and White, A. (1986) *The Politics and Poetics of Transgression* (London: Methuen).

Stanley, C. (1997) 'Not Drowning but Waving: Urban Narratives of Dissent in the Wild Zone', in S. Redhead, D. Wynne and J. O'Connor (eds), *The Clubcultures Reader: Readings in Popular Cultural Studies* (Oxford: Basil Blackwell).

Stebbins, R. (1979) *Amateurs: On the Margin Between Work and Leisure* (Beverly Hills, Calif.: Sage).

Stevenson, N. (ed.) (2001) *Culture and Citizenship* (London: Sage).

Stratton, J. (1985) 'On the Importance of Subcultural Origins', in K. Gelder and S. Thornton (eds), (1997) *The Subcultures Reader* (London: Routledge).

Strauss, A. L. (1978) *Negotiations: Varieties, Contexts, Processes, and Social Order* (San Francisco: Jossey Bass).

Straw, W. (1991) 'Systems of Articulation, Logics of Change: Communities and Scenes in Popular Music', *Cultural Studies*, 5(3): 368–88.

Straw, W. (1997) 'Sizing up Record Collections: Gender and Connoisseurship in Rock Music Culture', in S. Whiteley (ed.), *Sexing the Groove* (London: Routledge).

Straw, W. (1999) [1998] 'The Thingishness of Things', Keynote address for the 'Interrogating Subcultures' conference, University of Rochester, 27 March 1998; published on-line 1999 in *Invisible Culture: An Electronic Journal for Visual Studies* (http://www.rochester.edu/in_visible_culture/issue2/straw.htm).

Straw, W. (2001a) 'Scenes and Sensibilities', *Public: Cities/Scenes*, 22–3: 245–57.

Straw, W. (2001b) 'Dance Music', in S. Frith, W. Straw and J. Street (eds), *The Cambridge Companion to Pop and Rock* (Cambridge: Cambridge University Press).

Street, J. (1995) '(Dis)Located? Rhetoric, Politics, Meaning and the Locality', in W. Straw, S. Johnson, R. Sullivan and P. Friedlander (eds), *Popular Music: Style and Identity* (Montreal: The Centre for Research on Canadian Cultural Industries and Institutions).

Sweetman, P. (1999a) 'Anchoring the (Postmodern) Self? Body Modification, Fashion and Identity', *Body & Society*, 5(2–3): 51–76.

Sweetman, P. (1999b) 'Marked Bodies, Oppositional Identities? Tattooing, Piercing and the Ambiguity of Resistance', in S. Roseneil and J. Seymour (eds), *Practising Identities: Power and Resistance* (London: Macmillan).

Sweetman, P. (1999c) 'Only Skin Deep? Tattooing, Piercing and the Transgressive Body', in M. Aaron (ed.), *The Body's Perilous Pleasures* (Edinburgh: Edinburgh University Press).

Sweetman, P. (2001a) 'Stop Making Sense? The Problem of the Body in Youth/Sub/Counter-Culture', in S. Cunningham-Burley and K. Backett-Milburn (eds), *Exploring the Body* (Basingstoke: Palgrave).

Sweetman, P. (2001b) 'Reflexivity and Habitus: Bourdieu, Body Projects, and the Flexible or "Professional" Self', Paper presented at '2001: A Sociological Odyssey', BSA Annual Conference, Manchester Metropolitan University.

Sweetman, P. (2001c) 'Shop-Window Dummies? Fashion, the Body, and Emergent Socialities', in J. Entwistle and E. Wilson (eds), *Body Dressing* (Oxford: Berg).

Tait G. (1993) 'Reassessing Street Kids: A Critique of Subcultural Theory', in R. White (ed.), *Youth Subcultures* (Hobart: NCYS), reprinted from *Youth Studies Australia* 11(2) 1992; 'Youth, Personhood and 'Practices' of the Self': Some New Directions for Youth Research'.

Taylor, T. (1997) *Global Pop: World Music, World Markets* (London: Routledge).

Thompson, J. B. (1995) *The Media and Modernity: A Social Theory of Modernity* (Cambridge: Polity Press).

Thompson, K. (1998) *Moral Panics* (London: Routledge).

Thornton, S. (1994) 'Moral Panic, the Media and British Rave Culture', in A. Ross and

T. Rose (eds), *Microphone Fiends: Youth Music, Youth Culture* (New York: Routledge).

Thornton, S. (1995) *Club Cultures: Music, Media and Subcultural Capital* (Cambridge: Polity Press).

Thornton, S. (1997) 'The Social Logic of Subcultural Capital', in K. Gelder and S. Thornton (eds), *The Subcultures Reader* (London: Routledge).

Thrasher, F. (1927) *The Gang* (Chicago, Ill.: University of Chicago Press).

Tolson, A. (1997) 'Social Surveillance and Subjectification: The Emergence of "Subculture" in the Work of Henry Mayhew', in K. Gelder and S. Thornton (eds), *The Subcultures Reader* (London: Routledge).

Tomlinson, A. (1990) 'Introduction: Consumer Culture and the Aura of the Commodity', in A. Tomlinson (ed.), *Consumption, Identity and Style: Marketing, Meanings, and the Packaging of Style* (London: Routledge).

Tseëlon, E. (1995) *The Masque of Femininity: The Representation of Woman in Everyday Life* (London: Sage).

Tunbridge, N. (2000) 'Guerrilla Tactics: How the Blair Witch Team Spun a Web to Capture the Public's Interest', *Inside Film*, no. 15: 18–19.

Turner, B. (1992) *Regulating Bodies: Essays in Medical Sociology* (London: Routledge).

Turner, B. (1999) 'The Possibility of Primitiveness: Towards a Sociology of Body Marks in Cool Societies', *Body and Society*, 5(2–3): 39–50.

Turner, V. (1974) *Dramas, Fields and Metaphors: Symbolic Action in Human Society* (London: Cornell University Press).

Turner, V. (1982) *From Ritual to Theatre: The Human Seriousness of Play* (New York: Performing Arts Journal Publications).

Wagner, P. (1994) *A Sociology of Modernity: Liberty and Discipline* (London: Routledge).

Wallace, C. and Kovatcheva, S. (1998) *Youth in Society: The Construction and Deconstruction of Youth in East and West Europe* (London: Macmillan).

Walser, R. (1993) *Running With The Devil: Power, Gender and Madness in Heavy Metal Music* (Hanover NH: Wesleyan University Press).

Warde, A. (1994) 'Consumption, Identity-Formation and Uncertainty', *Sociology*, 28(4): 877–98.

Warde, A. (1997) *Consumption, Food and Taste: Culinary Antinomies and Commodity Culture* (London: Sage).

Warde, A. and Martens, L. (2000) *Eating Out: Social Differentiation, Consumption and Pleasure* (Cambridge: Cambridge University Press).

Waters, C. (1981) 'Badges of Half-Formed, Inarticulate Radicalism: A Critique of Recent Trends in the Study of Working Class Youth Culture', *International Labor and Working Class History*, 19: 23–37.

Watson, N. (1997) 'Why We Argue About Virtual Community: A Case Study of the Phish.Net Fan Community', in S. Jones (ed.), *Virtual Culture: Identity and Communication in Cybersociety* (London: Sage).

Weber, M. (1978 [1919]) 'The Distribution of Power Within the Political Community: Class, Status, Party' in *Economy and Society: An Outline of Interpretive Sociology* (Berkeley, Calif.: University of California Press).

Weber, M. (1978 [1919]) *Economy and Society*, Vol. 1 (Berkeley, Calif.: University of California Press).

Webster, F. (2002) *Theories of the Information Society*, 2nd edn (London: Routledge).

Weinstein, D. (2000) *Heavy Metal: The Music and its Culture*, 2nd edn (New York: Da Capo Press).

Whiteley, S. (1998) 'Repressive Representations: Patriarchy in Rock Music of the Counterculture', in T. Swiss, J. Sloop and A. Herman (eds), *Mapping the Beat: Popular Music and Contemporary Theory* (Oxford: Basil Blackwell).

Whyte, W. F. (1993) *Street Corner Society: The Social Structure of an Italian Slum*, 4th edn (Chicago, Ill.: University of Chicago Press).

Widdicombe, S. and Wooffitt, R. (1995) *The Language of Youth Subcultures: Social Identity in Action* (London: Harvester Wheatsheaf).

Wieners, B. (ed.) (1997) *Burning Man* (San Francisco: HardWired).

Wilbur, S.P. (1997) 'An Archaeology of Cyberspaces: Virtuality, Community, Identity', in D. Porter (ed.), *Internet Culture* (London: Routledge).

Williams, R. (1958) *Culture and Society 1780–1950* (London: Chatto & Windus).

Williams, R. (1961) *The Long Revolution* (London: Chatto & Windus).

Williams, R. (1977) *Marxism and Literature* (Oxford: Oxford University Press).

Williams, S. (1998) 'Modernity and the Emotions: Corporeal Reflections on the (Ir)rational', *Sociology*, 32(4): 747–69.

Willis, P. (1977) *Learning to Labour: How Working Class Kids Get Working Class Jobs* (Farnborough: Saxon House).

Willis, P. (1978) *Profane Culture* (London: Routledge & Kegan Paul).

Willis, P. (1990) *Common Culture: Symbolic Work at Play in the Everyday Cultures of the Young* (Milton Keynes: Open University Press).

Willmott, P. (1966) *Adolescent Boys of East London* (London: Routledge & Kegan Paul).

Wilson, B. (2002a) 'The "Anti-Jock" Movement: Reconsidering Youth Resistance, Masculinity and Sport Culture in the Age of the Internet', *Sociology of Sport Journal*, 19(2): 207–34.

Wilson, B. (2002b) 'The Canadian Rave Scene and Five Theses on Youth Resistance', *Canadian Journal of Sociology*, 27(3): 373–412.

Wilson, E. (1990) 'These New Components of the Spectacle: Fashion and Postmodernism', in R. Boyne and A. Rattansi (eds), *Postmodernism and Society* (London: Macmillan).

Wulff, H. (1995) 'Introduction: Introducing Youth Culture in its Own Right: The State of the Art and New Possibilities', in V. Amit-Talai and H. Wulff (eds), *Youth Cultures: A Cross-Cultural Perspective* (London: Routledge).

Zweig, F. (1961) *The Worker in an Affluent Society: Family Life and Industry* (London: Heinemann).

Websites accessed

http://hotwired.com/packet/silberman/archive
www.slayage.tv
http://xeon.mine.nu:2070/migitis/episodes.htm
www.buffy.com
www.buffysearch.com

Index

193